THE BROKEN CONTRACT

THE
BROKEN
CONTRACT

MAKING OUR DEMOCRACIES ACCOUNTABLE,
REPRESENTATIVE, AND LESS WASTEFUL

SAQIB IQBAL QURESHI

LIONCREST
PUBLISHING

THE BROKEN CONTRACT
Making Our Democracies Accountable, Representative, and Less Wasteful

ISBN   978-1-5445-0962-4 *Hardcover*
       978-1-5445-0961-7 *Paperback*
       978-1-5445-0960-0 *Ebook*
       978-1-5445-1491-8 *Audiobook*

IN MEMORY

Dad would have said, "It is quite interesting what you have written in the book, bayta. I understand it better than the last one. I'm going to read it again soon, to really study it, but let me get something from Waitrose right now. We need some eggs."

Patrick would have said, "Mabruuk man. I like it. I do wanna chat with you about some of it though, get your take. But I like it. What do you plan to do with it? What are you thinking?"

Adeeba Aunty would have said, "Saqib, I'm so proud of you bayta. I haven't got time to read it and I'm not really that interested in the topic; but I know that whatever you've written, it's wonderful."

CONTENTS

INTRODUCTION

My family and I live in the Box Grove neighborhood of Markham, a town that styles itself a city. Over three hundred thousand people live in Markham, which is located nineteen miles (thirty kilometers) northeast of downtown Toronto. In 2013, after several years of discussions, the municipal government of Markham made a written promise that Box Grove would get a park by 2016. The project was repeatedly delayed, although the municipal government gave no explanations or apologies. They didn't even bother to communicate that there would be delays. The citizens of Box Grove had to figure that out themselves.

During a 2019 meeting between the city government and residents, the discussion turned to the park. The designated site was still as much an eyesore as it had been before the project was announced so long before. During the meeting, I stood up and asked the city officials, "Given that you've repeatedly failed on your commitments so far, why should we trust you?"

The deputy mayor replied, "Well, don't. What choice do you have?"

At that point, I turned and left the meeting. What more was there to say? Why listen to an organization that breaks commitments and then dismisses concerned residents so high-handedly?

DECLINING DEMOCRACY

My family, like our neighbors, bought our house back in 2010, paying extra because of the park to be built across the street. In 2012, we moved into our new home, looking forward to enjoying the park. Maybe we'd take walks there after dinner or teach our kids how to cycle or enjoy meals with friends. Our neighbor's son, Samir, relished the prospect of playing sports there with his friends. Maybe the park would have a basketball court, a tennis court, or a baseball field.

While a Toronto suburb's failure to start and finish a park promised years ago may seem inconsequential in the great scheme of things, it's not trivial to us Box Grove residents. A few of the original families who moved into brand new homes purchased at a premium have since left. Samir has grown up and moved on to university. My children still have no park where they can play outdoors.

The deputy mayor, unlike us, apparently does find the matter trivial. What's most significant about my exchange with him is the attitude behind his response. It's symptomatic of fundamental problems facing liberal Western democracies—including the United States, Canada, the United Kingdom, Australia, and New Zealand. These issues have now begun to tear our social fabric apart.

The basic problem is that our Western democracies aren't really democracies if we define democracy as a government that represents us, its citizens; is accountable to us; and does not waste the resources we are required to pay in taxes. There's a shortfall in all three factors—representation, accountability, and efficiency—each of which is each essential to what we mean by and have a right to demand of democracy.

Democracy is one of those words, like terrorism or human rights, that can seem to mean anything, yet oddly, also often means nothing. It's thrown around so much that its meaning has, frankly, been lost. If both Sweden and North Korea can insist that they are democracies, the word has lost its meaning.

I see democracy as more of an emotional and cultural rather than an electoral or legalistic phenomenon. At its heart, our democracy is not just about a vote every four or five years. Voting might be democracy's modern badge of honor, but our democracy is so much more than that. Meaningful democracy, at least as it has evolved in the West, refers to the *relationship* between those who manage the country's government and us, its citizens. And, like any successful relationship, it requires give-and-take on both sides. Without that relationship, we get anemic, unresponsive, and wasteful "democracies," even if there are regular, honest elections.

In this sense, our version of democracy is really a social contract, to use a term employed by the eighteenth-century philosopher Jean-Jacques Rousseau, among many others. At the heart of any social contract is the concept of individuals surrendering part of their freedom and resources to the state in return for security and the collective good. Citizens own the government in a democracy, not vice versa. That's an essential characteristic of Western liberal democracies.

Our system of government professes to protect and nurture its citizens, but our governments have been and are violating our democratic social contract. That same contract is now broken. A contract lawyer would say that our governments are in material breach of their obligations. This is bad news both for the quality of government service and, even worse, our ability to hold on to our democratic ideals. Let's stress again that this contract and set of expectations are so much more important to our democracy than voting regularly in elections.

Still, our so-called democratic governments may well have never or rarely been as accountable, representative, and efficient as they are today. Nobody can sensibly argue that current Western democracies are less representative than those of two centuries ago. For a start, women now sit in every major Western legislature, and most Western democracies have seen at least one woman become the government's chief executive officer. The US is the obvious exception, and that won't change for a while. Also, some representatives who are not financially wealthy now sit in most legislatures.

However, today's advances in communication technology have made us much more aware of the gap between what our democracy is and what we should expect and demand of it. We citizens now know a lot more than our predecessors did. We can bring a level of scrutiny that governments have never had to deal with before. Though we still don't have visibility into huge parts of government workings, the visibility we do have still lets us examine the results of government in some detail.

We have become far more conscious of how self-protective our elected politicians and governments are. It may well be human nature to do a job with half an eye focused on personal benefit.

But the fact remains that our government officials act in their own, rather than citizens' interests more often than our social contract intends or should permit. It's not just the frequency of this behavior that's troubling. It's the scale of the cost, which sometimes runs into billions of tax dollars.

This "self before citizens" prioritization ought to worry us deeply. Trouble usually follows when public policy becomes disconnected from the expectations, wants, and aspirations, as well as the fears, pains, and concerns of the people it's meant to serve. Though our expectations as citizens may not have changed drastically in recent decades, our awareness and access to information and opinion have. We're not quite there yet, but we have a gut sense that our democracies, to paraphrase Lincoln, are a step too close to being "of the government, by the government, and for the government" rather than the people.

Government is a massive player in our everyday lives. It consumes our wealth through taxation, employs vast numbers of people, and exercises phenomenal powers. It's almost impossible to avoid being touched by government and its workings every single day. Even if we sat alone at home, windows shaded and doors locked, our defense and police forces are still working for us. Government also maintains, operates, and regulates much of the infrastructure we rely on, such as water access. Government is something like gravity. You don't really notice it because it's practically everywhere, all the time.

Unfortunately, as we realize that our government is less of a democratic system than we expect it to be, many of us have become frustrated by or inured to the social contract's corrosion. Discontent with government's detachment has been bubbling beneath the surface for some time now, again, in large part, because of the speed with which technology now makes us aware of government shortfalls.

In the case of the Box Grove park, residents were so fed up with the lack of progress that we petitioned the mayor to intervene. The entire campaign was electronic, conducted instantaneously with a keyboard and mouse. That was in 2017. The mayor's office confirmed receipt of the petition but otherwise never responded, another example of democratic governments' frustrating lack of responsiveness to citizens. It's now 2020, and we still have nothing more than a plan of the proposed park.

We want an efficient and effective government—one that doesn't take our hard-earned money in taxes only to turn around and squander it through inefficient and ineffective action. There is, for instance, a cost involved in delay and procrastination that government seems oblivious to. When there are delays, not only is work not delivered, but we, the taxpayers, continue to pay for ongoing fixed costs and salaries. Cost overruns and the absence of a performance-based culture only add to the problem.

We also want a government comprised of people from our communities, however diverse they may or may not be. One that doesn't govern while segregating and protecting itself inside an ivory tower. One that doesn't see the world through the lens of a narrow, often privileged identity. One that embraces the problems of ordinary citizens, including those most in need, whose issues are too often dismissed as marginal. In short, we want government officials of influence to live and experience the same life everyone else does. How can they truly represent us otherwise?

Finally, we want an accountable government, not one immune

from scrutiny or public oversight. We pay our governments and officials to work for us, but how often do we evaluate the trust we place in them? How often do we hold our officials, both elected and unelected, responsible and call them to account? Let's get this straight and let's get it out early—we don't do that during elections. We might think our votes are part of a process of "accountability," but we don't have to dig too far to see that what happens during the election season doesn't constitute accountability. We'll cover this in more detail later.

LESS WASTEFUL

Our governments are remarkably wasteful compared to private-sector organizations and companies. A municipal government like Toronto's can spend several years deliberating about constructing a bike shed, never mind building it, as overhead such as salaries and fixed costs continue to accrue.[1] The shed ends up costing more than the initial estimate—C$2.5 million more, in fact—and that surprises no one.

Let's underscore that. If a government project runs over its original budget, none of us would be surprised. Nor will anyone fall off their chair if we learn that not a single government official was penalized for the delay and cost overrun. It's what we have unfortunately learned to expect of the public sector.

In the private sector, a CEO confronting such waste would make heads roll, since they're under pressure to deliver results under time constraints. You don't succeed in the corporate world if you repeatedly go over budget—or spend years figuring out what kind of bike shed you need. Most CEOs also own their own businesses. For them, the office building, salaries, and benefits—all costs to be paid for every day of delay—are top of mind.

That sense of urgency and consequence is missing in government, where meetings…on meetings…on meetings take place far too often, and often include people who should never have been invited. Jeff Bezos's "Two Pizza Rule"—never have a meeting where two pizzas can't feed the entire group, which limits the number of invitees to eight—is alien in the public sector. And in those public-sector meetings, nothing needs to happen because there's little emphasis on being efficient with resources.

I don't mean to portray every government meeting as a waste of time. Or that government wastes every tax dollar it extracts. Or that every government project is a mess. Of course, there are pockets of value and performance and even outstanding work in the public sector. However, far too often, the public sector's use of resources is slower and less efficient than the private sector's, and the services delivered are comparatively subpar.

Any honest government worker, especially one with contrasting private-sector experience, will tell you this is so. By and large, there's a higher level of apathy to getting things done in the public sector, coupled with too much attention to protecting your backside. You don't see nearly as much of this in the private sector, where the emphasis tends to be on getting the job done on budget and on time.

In fact, the concept of time as a resource has little resonance in the public sector, which contrasts sharply with the private sector's recognition that "time is money." Government under-appreciates time and seems not to recognize that it might, in fact, be our most valuable resource. After all, we can never get it back once it's gone. While in the US the phrase "time is money" is attributed to Benjamin Franklin, it originated from far earlier sources. Yet, no matter how enduring and apt the adage, the public sector still hasn't learned it. It does not give time its due value, and this shields public-sector projects from deadline pressure.

If you're told that you have a strict limit of thirty minutes or an hour to perform a task, you find a way to focus your efforts on doing what is required in the time allotted. The private sector consistently puts this kind of time pressure on everybody from the most junior staffers to the CEO. This appreciation of time then migrates to suppliers, partners, and other business stakeholders. It's contagious.

In contrast, and with reference to Parkinson's Law, the longer the timeframe, the more the work expands to fill it. If you tell a civil servant they've got three weeks to put something into practice, they'll do it in three weeks or maybe four. If you tell them three months, they'll take three months—or maybe four or five. In the public sector, deadlines are more readily pushed back, while in the private sector, somebody is always there to remind you that the meter is ticking. Even if no cash is handed over, costs are being incurred and it will be tough to explain delays and overruns.

NOT REPRESENTATIVE

Today, government in Western democracies is not *of* the people. Ordinary citizens simply aren't represented in the government's upper echelons, where it really counts. This isn't new, but we are now far more aware of it than we have ever been. The evidence is out there, just a few clicks away.

Let's ground the big word—what exactly do we mean by government? Government has two components: elected officials—a small minority with disproportionate influence—and the unelected civil service, which is far larger and tends to be more permanent. For our purposes, we exclude contract talent who are officially in the private sector but effectively work as public-sector appendages.

We begin by focusing on elected officials: senators, members of Parliament (MPs), mayors, governors, presidents, and so on. These officials are, by and large, wealthier than the average citizen—often much wealthier. The median net worth of US senators in 2015 was US$3.2 million, while for members of Congress it was US$900,000.[2] Most US federal elected politicians are millionaires.

In contrast, the median net worth of their constituents' households, which on average consist of three people, was not even US$80,000.[3] You don't need a doctorate in psychology to appreciate that elected officials' wealth makes it harder for them to share a typical person's perspective on life and the universe, let alone empathize with constituents whose economic worth is not even 5 percent of their own.

Our elected officials also tend to come from specific ethnic and gender backgrounds. A far greater percentage of Caucasians are found in the elected end of government than exist in the general populations, except perhaps in New Zealand. In the West, only one government CEO, Barack Obama, has ever been non-Caucasian, and he too had a Caucasian mother.

Meanwhile, though women outnumber men in the overall population of every single Western liberal democracy, men typically outnumber women in Western legislatures by a ratio of two to one. A telling illustration of men's outsized influence in government comes from the United States and Canada. The US, despite its vocal crusade of gender equality in the far reaches of the globe, has never had a female head of state. Canada is hardly better. In 1993, more than a century after Canada's creation, Kim Campbell got the top job, but only when Brian Mulroney retired. She served as prime minister for a grand total of 132 days.

This means that our elected officials' experience, life lessons, and perception of society's most urgent problems do not and cannot arise from a reality shared with their constituents. These officials aren't representative of the lives and experiences of those they're meant to serve, especially those most in need. It's one thing to understand an experience intellectually and quite another to live it.

The same applies in the upper reaches of the civil service. Low- and mid-level unelected officials may be more representative of the general population, but this isn't true of those who wield power, have influence, and make decisions. Top-tier public employees have an ethnic and gender profile similar to elected officials and are, more often than not, male graduates of a small group of top-tier schools and universities (including my own, alas).

Only 7 percent of the UK's general population attended private school, in contrast to 71 percent of senior judges and 62 percent of senior officers in the armed forces.[4] It's troubling that the people who run the many branches of government are cut from the same cloth as elected officials and not the broader body of citizens. This is simply not representative government. And it's unhealthy for everyone.

You might push back that the top private-sector firms are equally unrepresentative, that in the West their upper echelons are dominated by older, extremely wealthy white men. However, private-sector firms don't exist to *represent* us. Government does. There's a fundamentally different *raison d'être* to their purpose, one which has no bearing on their obligations to perform efficiently and be accountable to their stakeholders.

NOT ACCOUNTABLE

Let's simplify another important concept: Western liberal democracy. Accountability means being held to what you've promised or made a commitment to do. You say what you're going to do, you then do or don't follow through, and you're evaluated accordingly. In other words, you are accountable. The idea is surprisingly simple. We should be held to account for the job, task, or responsibility that we've signed up for. We, the general public, should have the means to make sure that the people who represent us, and whom we support with our taxes, have done what they said they would.

In reality, our governments tend not to work that way, despite us wanting to believe that our electoral system has some sort of accountability mechanism. The problem is structural to some extent. In parliamentary systems such as in the UK, Australia, New Zealand, and Canada, the party with the most MPs, not the country's citizens, chooses the prime minister. In these countries, the citizens have never chosen their head of state, which sounds a wee bit disturbing when you pause and think about it.

British citizens, for instance, have never been asked to vote for their prime minister. The PM has never been on the ballot except as a candidate for a local MP. And, in the instances of Harold Macmillan and the first terms of both John Major and Boris Johnson, citizens didn't even have an immediate say in choosing the MPs who would vote in the new prime minister.

The prime minister, in turn, assumes the helm of government, deciding on key goals, priorities, policies, and the selection of ministers. The person we elect as our representative has almost no say in this big picture. Unless our local MP happens to be the one of 650 who is chosen by the party with a majority of MPs as prime minister. Now that I make mention of it, the British prime minister doesn't even have to be an elected MP. We need to make sure we understand and are honest with ourselves about the core mechanics here.

Citizens, however, aren't privy to much of the prime minister's performance or calendar. If we don't really know what they've been up to, how do we hold them to account? Did a smart civil servant clean up a mess the prime minister made? Did the prime minister contain what could have been a major economic recession caused by a foreign crisis, shrinking a big problem to something smaller? How would we know? We, as citizens, have little insight on what work a prime minister did today or will do tomorrow. Except, of course, the information their office chooses to release.

And further, the legislature, which one hopes would hold the prime minister accountable, is usually controlled by the prime minister's party. Ambition inevitably interferes with accountability. Appeasing the prime minister gets MPs promoted. Part of the game is to raise questions in Parliament that allow the prime minister to say what he or she wants to say, while keeping difficult questions off the record. In the all-too-obvious conclusion of one Canadian analyst, "MPs are not allowed in to be an effective advocate for the communities they represent or hold the government to account."[5]

Accountability, or its lack, is also a challenge in American government. Yes, presidents face voters' judgment at election time, but that judgment is compromised given the electoral college system, incarcerated citizens' inability to vote, and the huge number of citizens who can't be bothered to vote. That in itself tells us something about the estrangement of the state from society.

Voting as a means of ensuring accountability is further weakened by knowledge gaps. What presidents have or have not done, and the promises they have made and more often have not delivered on, have been largely forgotten or obscured when it's time to enter the voting booth, especially given the quantum of information and disinformation foisted on the public during election campaigns. We don't meaningfully track their commitments and struggle to keep track of their performance.

What specifically was the president's role in or contribution to the achievements that occurred during his tenure? We don't know. But it's doubtful these were as significant as he would like to claim. Or as damning as his opponents might argue. As in the parliamentary system, there is virtually no way to know what American elected officials are really doing. How can we then possibly hold them accountable?

Even if we did know what the president did or didn't do, the people's elected representatives may not want to hold other officials to account. Recall Senate Majority Leader Mitch McConnell telling reporters in 2019 that he would be coordinating closely with Donald Trump on his impeachment. It's not the legislature's job to defend the executive branch. That's the whole premise of the separation of powers. The Senate is meant to judge, independently and rigorously, if a president has committed impeachable offenses.

There's nevertheless usually at least a pretense that elected representatives will try to follow through on promises if only to get reelected. But in the civil service, there's even less accountability. Civil servants are something of a law unto themselves. Citizens can't fire them, and dismissing them is even a challenge for the senior civil servants they report to. As a result, the civil service is denied an important incentive for ensuring good work. As we'll see, without exaggeration, getting fired in the public sector can be statistically harder than being hired as a NASA astronaut.

You, as a citizen, have a tenuous connection to and virtually no leverage over the vast majority of civil servants. If they tell you they'll do something and don't follow through, there's typically little or nothing you can do about it. The official who emailed me that the City of Markham would complete our park by 2016 is a good example. She's now comfortably retired on one of the most generous pension plans in the world, which I have no choice but to help fund. And yet there's no way that park will be built less than five years from that promised date.

Civil servants make up more than 99 percent of Western governments. If you can't influence or touch 99 percent of a government, how can you possibly describe the government as democratic or accountable? Not recognizing this operational reality is self-deceptive. But we shouldn't have to accept this simply because it's always been this way or because it's how the system is set up. We're not brain-dead. We shouldn't ignore the reality that 99 percent of our government is not elected, and citizens have no real means to police their actions.

SOME MODEST PROPOSALS

We must resist the impulse to despair. I really mean that. The ancient Greek philosopher Archimedes, referring to the technology of the time, famously said, "Give me a lever long enough and a fulcrum on which to place it, and I will move the world." Communications technology can become a lever to move our social contract in several different directions. The trick is first to recognize the problem and then to find the right fulcrum to place the lever on.

A few relatively small-scale, tactical solutions that would be easy to implement have the potential to shift government in a more democratic direction. We can bring citizens several steps further toward the core of our political system, which, in theory, is our domain and where we belong. Deep-rooted, large-scale structural changes are not required. We don't need to reinvent government to fix it. We don't need to subscribe to Aleksandr Dugin's *The Fourth Political Theory* that we must destroy everything before we can start over.[6] That's a bit much to swallow and, as with anything that drastic, hard to control once unleashed.

What are some examples of what we might do? One solution for the inefficiency and waste of resources would be to create an independent government agency whose job it is to police the rest of government, much as an independent internal affairs unit monitors police departments. This agency would have to be empowered to push, shove, investigate, and ask meaningful questions without restraint. It would require a strong mandate.

You might think we already have such agencies. Yes and no. Government audit agencies prepare reports that largely gather dust. This agency wouldn't do that. Instead of thousand-page documents dense with legalese and accounting jargon, this agency will communicate findings so that ordinary people get it. Using top-tier mass-communication and advertising methods and techniques, its findings would have an impact. It would tell those who pay taxes what is really happening.

If a team of government employees mismanages a project that wastes a billion dollars, this will be clearly pointed out so that necks are on the line. If that team saves a billion dollars, I'd expect our agency to make them heroes. The agency's reports will not be communicated in annual reports but on YouTube, Twitter, and the full portfolio of media so that the entire fabric of the citizen population, not just people in ivory towers, is engaged.

Another idea, and one to make government more representative of the population at large, is to limit the terms of both elected and unelected officials. Instead of forty-year government-service terms, there should be caps of, say, twelve years for elected officials and twenty years for the civil service. Greater churn will make it easier to get a more representative government that reflects demographic shifts.

Without churn, we produce officials like the forty-year-old conservative Andrew Scheer, who lost his bid for prime minister in Canada's 2019 elections. Except for a few weeks as a waiter and a few weeks doing something incredibly opaque in the insurance industry, Scheer has worked in politics his entire career. He's been an MP since the age of 25. That's it—the sum of his professional experience.

I hate to use a cliché, but he needs to get a real, regular job like the rest of us. If Scheer had applied to immigrate to Canada as a "skilled worker," he would have been denied. Why? Because the state doesn't see evidence that he's capable of making a meaningful contribution to society. Yet there he was, a candidate for prime minister with a track record of having delivered nothing. Ever. I hope he doesn't take this personally—he may be a very genuine and nice chap. It's just plain ridiculous that he should be given the job of the country's CEO.

I'm not suggesting that if churn transitioned Scheer into a regular job, he wouldn't be replaced by a quasi-clone. But churning officials does increase the possibility of a more representative set of elected officials—a woman to lead the Conservative Party, perhaps, or a Sikh, a member of a community that Conservatives went after in the 1990s.[7] Term caps open the door to a wider spectrum of people and a more representative government. It's simply healthier for democracy. Elected politicians can argue all they want, but term limits *are good* for our democracy.

As for accountability, promises and commitments are an essential part of the social contract and, at long last, need to be taken seriously. We should not shrug them off as mere campaign marketing ploys. Commitments must be delivered on, in much the same way that we citizens pledge to pay our taxes and suffer consequences if we don't. After all, if we can't trust campaign pledges, what's the point in having elections? Integrity matters, a point Warren Buffett put rather neatly: "Look for three things in a person. Intelligence, energy, and integrity. If they don't have the last one, don't even bother with the first two."[8]

One way to ensure action on campaign pledges is to record

the promises that candidates make and periodically review their follow-through. Our councilors here in Markham made promises to get elected. No such campaign promise has been independently audited or assessed. Ever. It's not hard to imagine how such an ongoing assessment would affect a councilor's mindset and actions when looking to get reelected. They wouldn't spend half their day presenting awards and taking selfies. Do I need to mention the park again?

A parallel tactic would be to open officials' calendars or diaries to public scrutiny. In fact, at least in Markham, a councilor can maintain a full-time job for a private-sector employer, which may have extensive commercial relationships with the town's municipal authority. And that councilor can choose to spend much of his or her working time for that same employer, while we wouldn't be any the wiser.

If notated calendars publicly explained the purpose and outcome of meetings and appointments, as well as what officials achieved each day, we'd get answers to questions like, "What are you working on? What have you done or achieved today, this week, and this month? Did you do anything except have your photo taken?" You'd think that officials would embrace such a productivity tool. The lack of appetite for something like this in the corridors of powers is a bit disconcerting. But not surprising.

Open calendars would apply to both elected *and* unelected government officials. There's no across-the-board reason why civil servants should be excused from explaining to citizens what they achieved on any given day or week or what they worked on. We pay their salaries. They are working for us. We should, therefore, know what they did. It's that simple. Unless, of course, their primary focus isn't working for us.

CITIZEN QURESHI

I was born and raised in London by British Pakistani parents. I attended The Haberdashers' Aske's Boys School, one of England's top private schools, and got both an undergraduate degree and a doctorate at the London School of Economics. I worked as a banker at HSBC Investment Bank and as a consultant for McKinsey & Company. My wife is Canadian, and, after relocating to her native country, I founded and still run a real estate development firm specializing in student housing.

What does this have to do with expertise in government affairs? Nothing, or very little, and that's precisely the point.

What I really am is a concerned citizen, and it's around the citizen that, in theory, our Western democracy is based. What we've lost sight of is that it's not the government or legislature—nor spin doctors and political pundits—but the citizens who own the state. Our democracy is meant to be run for its citizens. At least that's how we define democracy in the Western liberal tradition. Thus, being a citizen is the best vantage point from which to speak about the nature of our democracy and how it can improve.

I have no vested interests beyond finding leverage points from which to improve our democracy. I don't carry the burden of being paid by a special interest group, think tank, or consulting business. I'm neither a political wannabe nor a has-been. My livelihood doesn't depend on book sales, subscriptions to my blog, or a university salary. As a result, I don't carry the baggage that most others who seek to make a difference in politics or government seem to. I'm just gonna speak my mind.

So, what's my beef? I think we're at a momentous stage in

Western democracy. And it's not just the impact of coronavirus on our society, politics, and economics, though it's worth flagging the virus as a catalyst for a deeper, underlying trend. The largest global epidemic since the Spanish Flu of 1918 has turned our world upside down. Unemployment has rocketed as sharply as economic production has fallen, this in a mere instant. Travel has come to a near halt. And significant inadequacies in our governments have been widely exposed. We all see the world through a different lens.

And as we emerge from this tragedy, we will inevitably reflect on the world that we transitioned from. One aspect will surely be around epidemiology, and the role of the World Health Organization, international travel, and domestic preparedness. Another subject we will look at differently is global warming, with greater trust in the scientific evidence and an awareness of our interconnected world.

A final focus will be our relationship with the state. It is then that we need more people to surface, "I don't know how we accepted what we did—but, let's get back to basics. I'm a citizen, and this government needs to revolve around its citizens. I pay taxes consistently and on time, and I need to know what my government is doing. Are they spending the money I give them wisely? Are elected and unelected government officials accountable? Do they represent the full spectrum of society? Are they really working for us?"

Most of us, I'm afraid, have allowed our government to drift, having lost sight of our position as the bedrock of the democratic system. The citizen body struggles to get beyond the demands of work, home, and family to adopt a broader, more engaged perspective. That's understandable considering work commute times, the eight-hour shift, the time and attention that must go to dependents, especially children, and everything else in our daily lives. Modernity, with all its choices, may as well be a synonym for "busy." I'm not parking the blame for our relationship with government entirely on the public sector.

The pennies began to drop for me years before COVID-19 hijacked our airwaves, during a series of government interactions that inspired me to write this book. Some of them occurred in the UK, where I'm from, and some in the US and Canada. Some were relatively innocuous. Others had me wasting a lot of time running around. After migrating to Canada, my reactions to these interactions got stronger and bolder.

I came to realize that government in Canada, with its multiple tiers, sees itself as being quite detached and immune from the citizen population. Too often, both elected and unelected government officials look on citizens as little more than something to manage. Too many in government are in it to protect and further the system, the power hierarchy, and their careers. Unfortunately, we, the citizens, let this happen. We allow our democracy to drift from its *raison d'être*.

This is not to say things are much better in the US, UK, Australia, or New Zealand. It's just that the distance between citizens and government, it seems to me, is somewhat more blatant in Canada. Public-sector officials who consider themselves "masters" rather than servants got me thinking, "Hang on a minute. How is it that the private sector seems to waste less, is more accountable, and is even more representative than the public sector? Ethically, shouldn't it be the other way around?"

If I voluntarily give money to a business for a product or service,

I expect a certain level of performance. That should be even truer when I have no choice but to pay for a service, as government requires. Perhaps more so if some of my co-funders are homeless or living in poverty. That is not how the story unfolds; the government doesn't face the private sector's competitive pressures. Still, morally, because government forces us to pay taxes, it has a greater moral responsibility to deliver.

I remember one particularly miserable experience I had in the office of a Toronto government agency, followed by a perfectly pleasant one when I then went to a Tim Hortons café. In the agency, I lined up for forty minutes to get a license, finally got to the service window, and presented my papers. With jaw resting on one hand, the silent attendant glanced at the documents and stuck out four fingers. I didn't understand at first but eventually realized that I had to go to service window four with its own separate line. I asked her to help out, given I'd already waited forty minutes in a line that it wasn't obvious, at least to me, was the wrong one. She just shut her service window and walked into the back, possibly for her coffee break.

My contrasting experience minutes later at Tim Hortons is typical of what we expect of the private sector. Receiving cheerful, efficient service as I got my coffee, I couldn't help but think, "That's interesting. The person whose salary I have to pay gave me shoddy service. She didn't smile, make me feel good, and was completely unhelpful. I chose to help pay for the wages of the guy at the café, and he was nice and pleasant and got things done very fast. Why is that?"

WHAT YOU'LL FIND

This book is written by an ordinary citizen—someone like you, notwithstanding my fascination with dunking Rich Tea biscuits into tea, eating peanut butter straight from a jar, or, for that matter, all things *Downton Abbey*. It's also written by somebody surfacing many of the issues you probably ponder and reflect on occasionally, but don't get around to stringing together into a coherent whole, let alone talk about. Much of the data will not surprise you. The narrative, however, hopefully will strike some chords.

The voice of citizens is missing from the heart of the government in modern Western democracies. Now more than ever, we are aware of the gulf between the state and us. More citizens in the West feel less connected to their governments than at any point in recent history. An astonishing 61 percent of Britons were dissatisfied with their democracy in 2019. We're in "political landslide" territory, which is especially ironic since we live in an era of unprecedented technology, which should enable us to connect more easily with other people. But this technology seems to have had the opposite effect.

I hope this book initiates a dialogue to help shake us from our slumber and make us think more deeply about the democracies in which we live. The book's first part deals with the big picture: How did our democracies get into the circumstances we now find them and ourselves in? Why is this happening here and now? What is the influence of our contemporary, highly technological society on government, and can those same technologies and trends be part of the solution as well as the problem?

The book's second, third, and fourth parts each deal with the three major issues troubling our pseudo-democracies: government waste, representation, and accountability. The first chapter of each of these three parts looks at the problem, while the second chapter explores potential solutions.

The purpose here is to provoke thinking that can then lead to the discussion and debate required for action. The solutions I propose are not a settled policy program. Rather, they are thoughts about practical interventions. I'd like nothing better than for what I propose here to inspire a much wider set of better suggestions.

We need to rouse ourselves from the apathy and hopelessness under which we all struggle and reassert ourselves as owners of the governments that are meant to serve us and our needs. Hence this book.

PART I

EXAMINING THE BROKEN SOCIAL CONTRACT

CHAPTER 1

THE BROADER LANDSCAPE

A government that's a democracy, in the way the word is understood in the Western liberal tradition, should be representative of and accountable to its citizens and mustn't waste the taxes those citizens are obligated to pay. That, in a sentence, is what our democracy is all about. And it is precisely those same democracies that are deeply deficient in these essentials, which we'll examine in depth.

First, however, let's widen the lens and our perspective. Let's take a step back. We live in a time of increasing political stress and volatility, even or especially in such countries as the US and the UK, which had been quite stable in the recent past. Every era is new and different. Ours, socially and politically, feels quite a bit more so than what we're used to, even if we put coronavirus's impact to one side.

In the United States, the turnover of high-level officials in the Trump government is just one among many signals of instability. In his first three years, Trump had already employed more secretaries of defense than any other US president. In his second year of office, he lied an astonishing average of 8.6 times per day, while becoming one of the most divisive presidents in the modern era.[1] He has been publicly rebuked by the leaders of some of the US's closest allies, such as the UK, Canada, and Germany, as well as by the leaders of some of America's largest companies, including Disney and Apple.

There's more chaos across the Atlantic, as evidenced by Britain's Conservative Party. In September 2019, Prime Minister Boris Johnson, not even two months into his job, fired twenty-one MPs from the Tory Party, including the longest-serving parliamentary member and two former finance ministers. It made Harold Macmillan's sacking of seven cabinet ministers in 1962 look benign. Johnson's actions led to the resignations of two cabinet ministers, including his own brother. He also lost his party's majority in the House of Commons.

Johnson's sister went so far as to accuse her big brother of making "tasteless" and "reprehensible" remarks about Brexit.[2] David Cameron, the Conservative prime minister from 2010 to 2016, accused Johnson of both lying and placing his own personal career above the country's interests.[3] Britain's Supreme Court unanimously decided that Johnson had acted unlawfully in asking the Queen to suspend Parliament in September 2019. Some suggest that Johnson might have been the first modern prime minister to have lied to the monarch.

What's happening to our political landscape, and why is it happening now? Why do our political leaders seem at sixes and sevens? A wider perspective will give us a better vantage point from which to focus more sharply on specifics.

TECHNOLOGICAL CHANGE

One critical factor in today's political landscape is the information-technology revolution, which has been twenty to thirty years in the making. The internet has led to instant news-sharing. We have unprecedented and immediate access to data and news. We don't know everything, but we have more information faster than ever, often confirming our preexisting biases. The internet has been a great support for conspiracy theorists and those with a penchant for thinking well outside the box. Sightings of Elvis, Tupac Shakur, and Steve Jobs continue to satisfy all-too-willing devotees.

Not only do we have access to information, we can instantly assemble with other people and communities. Social media brings all sorts of groups together—good, bad, and in-between. We can join thousands of Lego, Malcolm X, or licorice fans within seconds. We can join broad or narrow communities and draw strength from that membership, as well as learn from and educate others. Of course, not every group is to everyone's liking. I confess I'm not the biggest fan of the plethora of white supremacist hate groups that Facebook has enabled to come together.

The technology revolution has also enabled us to instantaneously spread that mass of information and misinformation within our online communities and beyond. Opinions are shared with thousands, if not millions of people, who may be influenced to act. I have a certain sympathy for the criticism of Umberto Eco, the philosopher, literary critic, and semiotician: "Social media gives legions of idiots the right to speak when they once only spoke at a bar after a glass of wine, without harming the community…but now they have the same right to speak as a Nobel Prize winner. It's the invasion of the idiots."[4]

It's not just that we can share what we want, but the media isn't what it was. John Kennedy had many mistresses, as did many other previous US presidents, yet those stories never hit the national press. The press was far more compliant, and there was no social media. There was no extramarital scandal during his lifetime, even if his affair with Marilyn Monroe came close. Nor did Congress make any attempt to impeach him. The Camelot myth of the best and brightest persists in some quarters more than half a century after Kennedy was assassinated.

In contrast, Bill Clinton's one affair while president with Monica Lewinsky, happening in the midst of the information revolution, almost knocked him out of office. He had others, but they were before his presidency, so let's not dwell on those. The information was distributed instantly by an increasingly energetic media, years before the social media explosion beginning in 2006. CNN, the *New York Times*, and the rest of the liberal media establishment didn't hesitate to focus on the transgression.

Our context of independent and social media has made Trump the most mocked national leader in the history of mankind, a superlative he may not be inclined to brag about. And that same social media is the reason why a tweet from Katy Perry will go out to more than a hundred million people at speeds faster than Han Solo's Millennium Falcon. In the history of our species, we have never been able to reach that many people that quickly. Not Moses, Caesar, Jesus, Mohammed, Gandhi, Michelangelo, Newton, Einstein…none of them.

A century ago, we rarely heard about large amounts of money wasted by government mismanagement. Today, we can find a news article every week that makes mention of a few hundred million dollars or so that were squandered in the public sector or had to be paid out for cost overruns. Even if we have become fairly jaded to this kind of news, we still take note. We are still aware.

All this means that both the public and private sectors face an era of unprecedented volatility, where major events can suddenly emerge or old systems disintegrate just as quickly, bringing about fundamental change. A bad marketing campaign in Japan can easily impact sales in northwest London's Watford—in real time. A celebrity tweet encouraging a charitable contribution can raise millions of dollars in an hour.

The private sector, in its drive for survival, has responded to the pressures of the information technology revolution. Websites have become eye-catching. Production processes have been restructured to take advantage of real-time manufacturing technology. Through Siri and Alexa, many customers have basic artificial intelligence in their homes that facilitates product purchases and delivery. Music and video are delivered instantaneously.

In contrast, government, being a monopoly, simply hasn't had to change with the same speed and gusto. Given the lack of competition and accountability, the systems, processes, and people in the public sector haven't felt the same pressure to keep pace. For now, let's be mindful of the contrasting cultural ecosystems in which the private and public sectors operate, as we move on to explore the socioeconomic factors that characterize the present day.

INCOME STAGNATION AND INEQUALITY

The rise in economic inequality in Western democracies since the 1980s is an important part of both the foreground and background of current social and political change. Between the 1940s and 1970s, incomes across the West increased at about the same rate for both the wealthy and the rest of the population. According to The Economic Policy Institute, the income gap between the top and bottom quartiles in the US did not significantly change during this period.[5]

Following the embrace of the neoliberal economic agenda associated with Ronald Reagan in the US and Margaret Thatcher in the UK, wealth concentration became as sharply skewered as it was in the nineteenth and early twentieth centuries. In the US, the wealthiest 1 percent of the population now controls 40 percent of national wealth, twice the share that they controlled thirty years ago.[6] According to a recent study—even accounting for slavery, which then consisted of more than 10 percent of the population—income inequality in the US is higher today than it was in 1774.[7]

Between 1979 and 2013, again according to The Economic Policy Institute, real incomes in the US rose by only 15 percent for the bottom 90 percent of those employed, but by 138 percent for the top 1 percent.[8] In 1979, CEOs at the top 350 firms earned thirty times the typical worker's salary. By 2013, they earned 296 times as much.[9] Between 1989 and 2019, the top 1 percent of Americans became US$21 trillion wealthier, while the bottom half lost US$900 billion.[10]

On a compound basis, the vast majority of Americans experienced a real income growth of less than 0.5 percent per year for a third of a century. In fact, Thomas Piketty calculated that average real incomes in the US for the lower half of income earners have stagnated for 40 years at US$15,000.[11] During that time, depending on the index we use, the US stock market increased by about 12 percent per year. For those at the bottom tenth percentile, real hourly wages actually fell by 5 percent. The net worth of that bottom half-dipped so sharply that their liabilities now exceed their assets.

It's not just in the US that the rich have become so much richer, while everybody else has seen, at most, modest gains. In the UK, income inequality increased after 1979, having consistently fallen since the beginning of the twentieth century.[12] The top 1 percent, which owned some 13 percent of the national wealth when Thatcher assumed office, now controls 18 percent.[13] British average wages in 2020 are still nominally below the levels of 2007.[14] The real income reduction tells a harsher story still. The poorest half of the country now owns only 9 percent of the national wealth, and one in three children live below or near the poverty line.[15] COVID-19 and Brexit will both increase that tragic ratio.

In 1979, most of us would have had no way of finding any of this out. Or if we wanted to, it would have taken us several days. Today, it takes us mere minutes to dig up this information. While sitting at home. Dunking biscuits into a cup of tea.

Naomi Klein's best-seller *The Shock Doctrine*, presciently published just prior to 2008's Great Recession, is one of the most thorough analyses of the effects of the economic "liberalization" that the Reagan and Thatcher eras ushered in.[16] It contends that neoliberalism, as advocated by influential economist Milton Friedman, whose policies were put into motion under the auspices of the International Monetary Fund (IMF), basically stripped out or eliminated the middle class, widening the gap between the haves and have-nots.

While the IMF was not as completely supportive of the neoliberal agenda, as Klein argues, she convincingly demonstrates that neoliberal economics have significantly hurt the middle classes to the advantage of the wealthy. Globalization remains a cornerstone of neoliberal economics. The sharp increase in income disparity and the sociopolitical consequences we are now experiencing would not have come about if the wealthy hadn't almost unilaterally defined the path to globalization.

Privatization transferred wealth to the already wealthy, whose de facto marginal tax rates were slashed to the lowest they had been in almost half a century. This, in turn, compromised the availability and delivery of public services, especially for poorer people. Privatization not only hurt the middle and lower economic classes but ethnic minorities, communities which were and continue to be underrepresented in the upper echelons of Western democracies.[17]

Our particular globalization encouraged big corporations to outsource more of their production to cheap labor markets, further enriching the already privileged with greater profits. Western governments just didn't focus on how their middle and lower classes would fare when cheaper, foreign-based labor started producing what had been previously produced in their countries, which now import foreign-made products in ever-greater numbers. In 2003, about 40 percent of American and Western European manufacturing contracts involved foreign or international outsourcing. Today, the figure is about 70 percent.[18]

Joseph Stiglitz's acclaimed book *Globalization and Its Discon-*

tents, published in 2002, also strongly criticized the IMF and World Bank for an abusive globalization, geared towards protecting and enhancing the wealthiest at the cost of the poorest.[19] In minimizing government, he argued, the liberalization agenda not only led to "shock therapy" for entire societies but also brought about the financial crises in East Asia in 1997 and in Argentina and Russia in 1998.

Stiglitz's focus, however, was globalization's injurious impact on developing countries. The once chairman of the US Council of Economic Advisors and then the World Bank's Chief Economist underplayed globalization's damaging impact *inside* developed countries, especially on low- and middle-income earners. He also failed to give due attention to how the disconnection between ordinary citizens and their governments enabled the neoliberal globalization agenda. It's because the wealthy dominate Western "democratic" governments that we have had the type of globalization we have and why we and our economies are now reeling under a miscarriage of economic justice.

We need to remind ourselves that the people running Western democracies are usually wealthy. Their positions instinctively center on wealth generation, not wealth redistribution. Note, for instance, how in January 2020, instead of jumping up and down to forewarn the country of the pending catastrophe, four American senators on the Intelligence Committee sold several million dollars of shares after they had been briefed about the potential impact of COVID-19, and well before the stock market melted.[20] In fact, one of those senators, Richard Burr, had the audacity to actually publicly project confidence in February: "The United States is better prepared than ever before to face emerging public health threats, like the coronavirus."[21] Is that why he sold his shares?

The people who run the government, as well as the powers that they're beholden to and lobbied by, typically know how to make and save a lot of money. They have the means to hire people who work in a foreign country for a small fraction of their own country's minimum wage. They hire advisors familiar with all the tax breaks and know the lobbyists who can grease discussions with policymakers.

This reality—this economic and political environment—has enabled a handful of people to become very rich. And they've been able to fend off pressure from the have-nots. In *Winners Take All*, Anand Giridharadas shows how those at the peaks of the political economy have been and remain very able to tinker with the system cosmetically, providing enough cover to keep the rest of us placated while advancing a path for their own interests.[22]

Meanwhile, the vast majority of citizens haven't benefited much or at all. Since the 1990s, and especially following the 2008 recession, average incomes haven't risen. New Zealand's household income per capita increased from the equivalent of US$21,483 in late 2008 to US$23,020 in 2016—a rise of only 7 percent in eight years.[23] Nominal wage growth in Australia has nothing to brag about either—only slightly above 2 percent per year from 2012 to 2017, barely enough to offset inflation.[24] In Canada, median real incomes rose less than a single percent per year from 2005 to 2015.[25]

POLITICAL UNDERPINNINGS

It's understandable, then, that an increasing proportion of citizens find it much more difficult to make ends meet. There is the outsourcing of work to cheaper talent pools, which deflates incomes. There has also been a shift to temporary and part-time work, with all the associated insecurities and lack of benefits. And the threat of automation, for instance, in trucking, provides no comfort at all.

Given these circumstances, we can easily blame economics for much of the social and political turmoil we're now seeing in Western countries, a mistake Robert Reich made in his otherwise engaging book, *Aftershock*, which details the concentration of wealth in the US.[26] That's quite understandable given that politicians don't want us to examine the political structure that upholds their entire livelihood. Because economic issues dominate our conversations in terms of economic growth or personal cash flow, we're not digging deeper and directing our attention to the culture and infrastructure of our governance.

Our economic system, which is shrinking the middle class with ever-greater consumer debt, doesn't operate in a political vacuum. Our economies are both the cause and effect of our politics. The current economic situation exacerbates ordinary people's political frustrations, and in considerable measure, these economic issues stem from politics, specifically the separation of citizens and their "democracy."

A root cause of our economic pain is that we don't really live under the sort of democracy we think we do. In fact, I feel awkward calling what we have a "democracy." Our governments are not meaningfully representative. If they were, more people in the top tier of government would be asking, "How will privatization or off-shoring impact the poorer people in society? What are we doing about our society's bottom economic quartile? How will the proposed measure impact those at or below the poverty line?"

These issues are not a priority because the people running government don't think like those who are or have ever lived in the bottom quartile. They tend not to see the world through the lens of people who really do live paycheck to paycheck. They haven't lived on the streets. Or had to deplete their life savings to fund a medical emergency. The most influential folk in government, while having an intellectual awareness of these issues, also suffer from a dearth of the empathy that only comes from lived experience.

At some point, fueled by the economic drivers of continuing wage stagnation and economic disparity, citizens will start realizing that their politics isn't right and that their democratic government isn't actually "theirs." In fact, we're already at that point. It's just that many of us aren't yet fully conscious of the pain we're feeling. We haven't yet linked the dots between the turmoil we're experiencing and the role our current political system plays in causing it. Or maybe the coronavirus catastrophe will shake things up—as the editorial board at the *Financial Times* advised should happen in their piece, "Virus Lays Bare Frailty of the Social Contract."[27]

This isn't a failure of economic growth so much as a failure to ensure that a broad spectrum of citizens benefit from that growth. The frustrations that led to the rise of the UK's Independence Party, Donald Trump and the Alt Right in the US, and France's National Front are not entirely economic, even if they are often believed to be. Did economics play a part? Of course. But the mechanics of our "democratic" government—its modus operandi—have not only accentuated this broader frustration, but actually triggered much of today's economic challenges.

If Western democracies had been genuinely accountable to and representative of ordinary people, globalization would have accommodated and benefited a much wider swath of society. We would have had a very different globalization, and a much different political landscape than what we have now. Citizens would not feel so disenfranchised and disconnected from their governments. Unfortunately, the fruits of wealth creation ended in the laps of the haves, while the rest of us have had to continue to make do with the same income we had a couple of decades ago.

IMMIGRATION AND SOCIAL CHANGE

The rapid rate at which many of our communities are changing is just as deeply intertwined with the current political upheaval as the economic system. Things are moving much faster than ever before. We communicate faster. We source information faster. We execute tasks faster. We unfortunately seem to transmit global epidemics faster too. Of course, this increasing rate of change is due to technology, which we'll look at more fully later. But the causes of our current disorientation aren't limited to technological advances.

I was born in Edgware, a town in Greater London about nine miles (fifteen kilometers) northwest of the city center. I grew up there and in the adjacent town of Stanmore, where my family moved just as I became a teenager—tall, chubby, and a bit pompous. Stanmore's claims to fame are that Billy Idol was born there and Roger Moore once lived there. It's also where some British codebreakers, such as Alan Turing, were based during the Second World War.

A good friend of mine migrated from Edgware to northern England and didn't come back for some years. When he later returned, we took a walk down the main street, which is half a mile long. I still remember his profound alienation and diminished sense of belonging. This wasn't the place where he grew up. "What the heck happened here? So much has changed!" He pointed to several stores he'd never seen before while recalling the long-gone shops of his childhood.

What had changed was that many of the stores with English-language posters and English signs had become Eastern European. Instead of the small fried chicken take-away across from Woolworths, there was a Polish zapiekanka sandwich bar, packed with men who looked Eastern European. The traditional pub, a stone's throw from the police station, had been transformed to Clubul Romanesc Masons Arms. The cozy Indian restaurant next to the pub was now Casa Bucovineana.

My friend isn't particularly xenophobic. His own parents are from two ethnic backgrounds, and he never struck me as afraid of other ethnicities or religions. But, walking down Edgware High Street, I remember him feeling unsettled by Eastern European culture, which had arrived in part because of the European Union's (EU) migration policies, in his childhood hometown. He wanted things to be as they were. Or at least to have changed less.

I was slightly taken aback. After all, the Indian place that was my friend's go-to restaurant wasn't there a century back. Despite Britain's love of Indian food, you couldn't get good biryani in Edgeware until the 1990s. At some point, someone had probably asked a similar question, "How did that Indian restaurant get there? What's wrong with bangers and mash?"

Debates about immigration and racism are often misplaced.

When a lot of people express anger at immigration or at brown or black people, they're often—though not always—actually saying, "I don't want my local community to change so fast. I want a bit of nostalgia. I want things to be like when I was a teenager. I want the people around me to speak my language. I don't want to feel like a stranger in my own backyard."

It may well be that we as a species are not well prepared for the rate of social and cultural change we're now witnessing in our communities. While many uneasy citizens have begun blaming ethnic minorities, homosexuals, and women for their woes, our governments generally have only recently begun to wake up to the underlying emotions. The wider government is so used to neither listening nor being part of an accountable, representative process that its response has wavered between the deaf and inadequate.

Inadvertently, this has allowed more than a handful of disagreeable, hot-headed politicians to rise to the fore precisely because they've understood and perfectly tapped into this discomfort. These politicians realize that the citizen body doesn't want things to change so quickly. And they are exploiting that. They've benefited from imposing tariffs on imports and restricting immigration to soothe populist anxieties, even if these measures lower the real incomes of citizens and the stability of the social infrastructure they depend on.

DISENCHANTED CITIZENS

The breaches in our social contract have persisted partly because we don't want to call attention to them or even call them breaches. We live in a land of political make-believe where we willingly mislead and even lie to ourselves because it's easier and more convenient to do so than to point out and address what's wrong. Because if we did that, we'd either be reminded of our helplessness, or we'd cut into time already eroded by our busyness.

Let's stop fooling ourselves, as it doesn't help us in the long run. When we say that the American people elected Trump president, we do so knowing that, in fact, 80.5 percent of Americans didn't vote for him in the presidential elections. Only a fifth of the population did. Hillary Clinton won almost three million more votes than Trump. The ascension of Trump, despite the vote, was not an anomaly. Recall that Al Gore won over half a million votes more than George W. Bush did, yet the latter became president.

Likewise, when we say we hold our government to account, we know we can't touch 99.5 percent of it—the unelected civil service. Even the remaining 0.5 percent, the elected officials whom we think we hold accountable, are subject to a process that makes a mockery of accountability. The 0.5 percent serve their terms, then come back for reelection, while we have no idea what they actually did or didn't do for us in the meantime. Except what they choose to share. And even this fails to recognize that most of our representatives have almost no resources to follow through on their commitments once elected.

Living as Alices in Political Wonderland does little for us except save the energy we'd otherwise expend in confronting the disparity between our current perceptions and what we could see if we really tried. We have less faith in our political systems now than we've had in generations, and popular dissatisfaction with government continues to grow. The least we can do is stop pretending that it's business as usual and start devoting the time and energy to achieving a democracy that actually works for us.

There's a danger when citizens rightly feel that they lack any meaningful control of their political destiny or connection to government. It allows characters like Trump and Nigel Farage to give their audiences the perception that ordinary people are back in control—a remarkably energizing and addictive feeling. This helps explain why both leaders can lie incessantly without losing their core support. They're delivering a longed-for message that addresses a sense of alienation and fear of change: "We hear what you're saying, and we're following through. You don't want immigrants. You don't want jobs going to China. You don't want EU bureaucrats deciding what a banana looks like. We hear you. We don't want that either."

Populist leaders clearly have plenty of fodder at their disposal. They didn't assemble the fodder, though. We can thank generations of deaf political leaders for that. Now, we might, in fact, be in the midst of a slow-motion political revolution, one that has been unfolding for many years, which is ironic given that our technological progress seems to have fast-tracked almost everything else.

We can even see signs of the revolution in happy Canada, the land of athletes who apologize for winning, led by "nice guy and statement socks" Prime Minister Justin Trudeau. Research by Edelman, a communications firm, revealed in 2017 that 80 percent of Canadians believe that those running the country's institutions are out of touch with the people.[28] Sixty-three percent agreed or strongly agreed that politicians can't be trusted.[29] Canadians are more likely to trust an academic expert, employee, or financial analyst than a government official. In other words, Canadians don't like their politicians.

The number of young adults in Canada who believe democracy

is preferable to other political systems has dropped from 52 percent in 2012 to 36 percent in a few short years.[30] An Environics study in 2012 showed that only 10 percent of Canadians had "a lot of trust" in political parties and only 19 percent in Parliament.[31] Corroborating those findings, the government's own data revealed that only 38 percent of Canadians had "confidence" in their Parliament.[32] These are shocking results that should have hit the panic button in Ottawa but haven't. Minion after minion has been appointed to oversee "democratic reform," a job which has nothing to show for it.

In the US, there more signs of the slow-rolling revolution. In 2019, only 17 percent of people felt that they could trust their federal government to do the right thing always or most of the time.[33] This compares to 77 percent in 1964.[34] In 1974, during the Watergate crisis that removed Nixon from office and had tens of millions of people reeling in their political armchairs, that number stood at 36 percent. We are today at below half the levels of trust in the federal government we had during the Watergate scandal. More than half of Americans feel they can do a better job resolving the country's problems than their government can.[35] Most believe their elected officials are intelligent but dishonest and selfish.[36]

Yet, Americans still pay their taxes on time—for now. Not because they believe in the system, but because the system bullies their money from them. Since 2016, excluding sales taxes, working Americans on average have paid more than ten thousand dollars per year in tax.[37] That's a lot of money to pay for a system run by folks you think are dishonest. It might even feel like extortion.

Trust in government impacts policy effectiveness. The underlying difference between those countries that handled the outbreak of coronavirus well and those that made a mess of it isn't about democracy versus authoritarian. Or Western versus others. It's about the trust we have in our public institutions and especially the executive.[38] South Korea, Germany, Sweden, and Singapore are just some of those countries where citizens trust their government. Citizens accepted government advice, which enabled government to, in turn, manage the coronavirus outbreak reasonably well.

The UK, Italy, and US are countries with lower levels of trust in government, and oddly enough, also ended up making a mess of managing the coronavirus initial outbreak. It's hard to get people to do what you want them to do when they don't trust you. Thirty-nine percent of Italians had trust in Prime Minister Conte in February 2020.[39] Fewer still Brits felt the following month that they could trust Boris Johnson to handle the crisis.[40]

Mind you, that's a step up from the US. Excluding partisan pro or against Trump voters, 28 percent of Americans trust Donald Trump. He spent much of February 2020 trying to convince Americans that the entire coronavirus problem was both a Democrat conspiracy and under full control. Having fully reversed his tune a month later, he then watched tens of thousands of Americans walk to their graves and the entire citizen body plunge to the country's worst economic quarter in its history. No ifs or buts. Who, besides a die-hard Trump fan, can trust him?

Distrust not only hurts governance but damages our democracy by discouraging voting. What's the point of voting if you have no confidence in the system? In 2016, only 58 percent of eligible American voters bothered to cast a ballot in the most important election in the world. More than 40 percent didn't think it was worth the effort, much more than voted for Clinton, let alone Trump. I'm not talking about electing the official who conducts the local town meeting. I'm talking about a four-year term for the CEO of the most powerful military, political, and economic regime in the world.

The 42 percent of the electorate who decided voting wasn't worth the effort did so despite the media blitz surrounding American presidential elections. During the year-long campaign, voters were bombarded with messaging on television, in newspapers, and online. During 2016, it seemed the only place immune from political advertising was on boxes of baby cereal. Or possibly a solitary, remote cave. The political pollution was pretty intense.

If voters hadn't been subjected to this media frenzy, how many less would have shown up at the polls? Far fewer than 58 percent. That's a serious problem, given that those who don't vote still pay government coffers about a third of their income in taxes of various kinds. It's amazing that the political classes don't feel this needs to be fixed. Or maybe it's not so amazing, since any serious fixing would inevitably reduce their maneuverability. Let's not kid ourselves—every recent federal government initiative for democratic reform in the US has been cosmetic and led by political lightweights.[41]

People increasingly see government as a leviathan that exists disproportionately for its own purposes and agenda, greatly influenced by lobbyists, typically for big corporations, unions, and special interests such as the National Rifle Association—which oddly enough San Francisco lawmakers declared a "terrorist" organization in 2019. The lobbyists' and government's agendas rarely align with the ordinary citizen's.

Across the pond, there's an equally dim view of government as self-serving. In 2019, 50 percent of Britons believed that the main political parties and politicians didn't care about them.[42] At the same time, 63 percent thought the system was rigged to the advantage of the rich and powerful, while 72 percent agreed that the system needed "quite a lot" or "a great deal" of improvement.[43] Current British opinions of their system of government are, in fact, some of the lowest on record.[44]

Britons who felt that politicians put the country's needs over and above those of their political party decreased from 38 to 19 percent between 1986 and 2013.[45] They may be onto something, since 63 percent of Conservative Party MPs said in 2019 they would continue with Brexit, even if it meant Scottish secession, ending the four hundred years of the United Kingdom.[46] Even in the midst of coronavirus's devastating impact on life, society, and the economy, parts of the Conservative government were pushing full steam for Brexit.[47]

Living through the breakdown in our social contract, near-stagnant income growth, and the realization that we don't really matter in our democracy, disenchantment has us citizens increasingly rejecting one set of political norms after another. Instead of examining and tackling specific failures in the social contract, more of us—angry, frustrated, and disillusioned—are lashing out wildly, even when it's contrary to what's best for us.

Can there be more a more pronounced crystallization of the failure of the British political system than the rejection by 27 percent of Britons of their membership in the EU, as opposed to the 25 percent who voted to remain? All three main political parties fought to keep the UK in the EU, as did all living former prime ministers from both sides of the political divide.

The heads of state of Britain's leading trade partners also lent their support to "stay."

Let's not forget that the contrarian Leave campaign was led by Boris Johnson, who was fired from his first job for lying—twice (quite an achievement) and Nigel Farage, who peddled the idea that seventy-five-million Turks were about to join the EU, pack their bags, and migrate into the UK. How ironic that in April 2020, the *Daily Mail*, which helped sell Farage's lies as truths, confirmed that Turkey, which had already donated supplies to Italy and Spain, had sent planes of medical supplies to help the UK tackle the coronavirus epidemic.[48] Despite such untrustworthy advocates, Brexit was still voted in. Let's not forget that this doesn't take into account the 48 percent who didn't vote at all.

Brexit has already proved a gigantic shot in the foot for the UK. After Brexit won the day, but long before actual withdrawal from the EU, foreign investment in the UK dropped sharply, with the loss of a quarter million jobs and a slowdown in the economy.[49] Economists estimated that the economy lost 3 percent of its GDP between June 2016 and April 2019 because of the Brexit vote alone.[50] In other words, the vote cost every single Briton more than £1,000 in that brief period. That means it cost the country more than £600 million—every single week.[51] That's a serious shot in the foot.

And all that was before the devastation from the coronavirus, which the latest forecasts suggest will lead to an unemployment rate of 21 percent and economic contraction of 15 percent in the second quarter of 2020, both representing the highest in the country's long history.[52] This is the same crisis in which Germany donated (that's right, not invoiced) several million dollars of medical supplies to the UK.[53] Lest you're wondering, it's the same crisis in which London first rejected, and then sharply U-turned to get help for more medical supplies from the EU itself.[54] Karma is a boomerang.

Because governments aren't hearing their citizens, we're seeing deep antiestablishment sentiment from the population across the political spectrum.[55] This is not, as some believe, a niche pushback.

Nor is this reaction confined to the US, the UK, and other Anglo-Saxon democracies. In 2019, Germany saw the election of Stefan Jagsch, mayor of Waldsiedlung, its first neo-Nazi official since the days of the Third Reich. In Italy, the antiestablishment Five Star Movement, which a comedian founded in 2009, became the largest party in Parliament just nine years later, with 227 out of 630 seats in the Chamber and 112 out of 315 seats in the Senate. In France in 2017, the political novice Emmanuel Macron became the country's youngest-ever president at age thirty-nine, having formed a new political party only the year before. Something is in the air.

The societal vogue is now antiestablishment. What these upstarts have done so well is to articulate the wants of a lot of people whom the established political classes have repeatedly ignored. Millions of ordinary citizens very understandably want to have a say in their democracy. Irrespective of the underlying reality, the upstarts have met that emotional thirst. They've got the "political optics" right.

If we don't start taking a good, long, hard look at our democracies, we should expect harsher and increasingly sudden political agitation. We should expect more frustration and anger. And frankly, we should expect a society and political reality that are harsher than what we're comfortable with. We can either do some serious and honest thinking now or continue the drift onto even more dangerous ground. Our democracies are in crisis.

AWAKENING PERSPECTIVES ON "WORSE"

The problems we currently face are not because our democracies are more wasteful or less representative or accountable than they have been in the past. The democracy we had a hundred years ago wasn't more "democratic" than the one we have now. Oddly enough, what we have now is an obvious improvement. To reiterate, women, who comprise more than half the population in every Western democracy, now have a standing in government they didn't have a century ago.

What's different now is a more general distrust of government than in the past. Given the social and media fragmentation of the present late- or post-modern era, as societies, we're taking a far more critical view of institutions and authority. Increasingly obtrusive and ever-expanding media outlets have stripped away much of the myth and mystery surrounding our presidents and prime ministers.

For the most part, government processes and systems are oblivious to all this. This isn't entirely surprising since governments aren't known to be dynamic change agents. The core processes of appointing and holding both the elected government and the unelected civil service accountable have not changed in a century. We still vote for a candidate who is typically part of a national party. That person, who has almost no resources, does their thing, subject to the party line, for four or five years, nearly all of which is hidden from citizens. Failures are assigned to others far more lavishly than successes. And then we have another vote.

Interestingly, people in the public sector realize a lot has changed and that they're now under a microscope, with information and news delivered instantaneously. They have adapted, even if the processes that brought them into government predate their great-grandparents. Increasingly, controversial communications are spoken, not typed. Public comments are finely tailored, not shot from the hip. Let's just be honest that our systems and processes haven't adapted to the times, though politicians have. And that's left our democracy vulnerable, unstable, and frustrating.

It's as if the world, despite its communications revolution, is pretty much what it was when the Spanish Flu hit. Besides a few cosmetic changes, our democracies have not grown to meet our world's extraordinary rate of change. Many understand how the revolution in communication technology and social media has, in turn, revolutionized citizens' ability to source select news about government, unite among themselves, and accelerate the deterioration of the relationship between citizens and the state. But those wise to the danger have few solutions and are rarely in positions of political authority.

Whatever improvements we've seen in representation, accountability, and resource management haven't kept pace with our growing scrutiny of government or our ability to coalesce with others. As we citizens band together, the social media echo chamber cements our certainties and stokes our anger about the increasingly evident gap between the democracy we thought we had and the one we are actually experiencing. This can be seen either as a crisis or an opportunity to address long-standing fissures in the social contract. Most likely, it is both and something we need to confront.

CHAPTER 2

THE SOCIAL CONTRACT'S TERMS AND CONDITIONS

What is the social contract? Where is it codified? Who signed it? Can you visit it in a museum? Can you order a copy online?

No. It's not so simple.

A lot could and has been said about the history and philosophy of democracy, but I'll keep this brief. This form of government originated in and has become identified with ancient Athens. The word democracy comes from classical Greek and means rule or power (*kratos*) by the people or population (*demos*). Liberal, conservative, whatever your persuasion—it's worth keeping this big picture in the back of our minds. Democracy began with and means rule by the people. "People power," a term that originated in the US during the Vietnam War, is actually a terrific synonym for democracy.

Ancient Athens practiced what's called "direct democracy."

Athenian citizens—actually a relatively small percentage of the city's total population, since women, slaves, and minors weren't considered citizens—frequently gathered together to debate and vote on proposed laws. They didn't delegate or outsource the right to make laws. All citizens legislated. We often lose sight of this very important point.

This differs from the indirect, representative democracy practiced today in which citizens elect MPs, senators, and other representatives to write, debate, and vote on laws on their behalf. It's more than likely that ancient Athenians would have sneered at our arm's-length democracy—except Plato, who saw Athenian democracy as nothing more than the rule of the ignorant. And maybe Socrates too. "Democratically elected" carries an internal contradiction, since the whole point of a democracy is for citizens to run their state. Outsourcing this to a few politicians elected every four years or so and an unaccountable crew of civil servants misses the point altogether.

The Enlightenment, a European philosophical movement identified with seventeenth- and eighteenth-century England and France, had tremendous influence in laying out our modern concepts of democratic government. Two concepts are especially important in this context. The first, which the title of this book echoes, is the social contract. Though the concept predates Jean-Jacques Rousseau, it was given a new lease on life in that philosopher's work *The Social Contract*, written in 1762.

The second significant concept is that of the rights of the individual in society. While codified individual rights might be traced as far back as ancient Persia, the English philosopher John Locke linked them to the rights to "life, liberty, and estate."[1] That is why the men responsible for drafting the US constitution were intent on protecting individual rights from the collective—that is, the government—as were those who wrote the constitutions of Australia, New Zealand, and, most recently, Canada.

The average person doesn't philosophize about democracy at this level. Rousseau and Locke may well have impacted democracy's transformation from its origins in ancient Athens to the present day, but most of us haven't read a single page of their works. They're not light reading. To be honest, it's more like walking through a thick swamp. But their work does provide context for our examination of the social contract and how it's been violated.

Another crucial context is how we operate as citizens. We have certain inherent, gut expectations of and beliefs about our social and political life. When we look at democracy and, implicitly, at our social contract—even though we rarely use that term—we first think, "I have the right to vote for and elect the people who will govern my country." That is, we think in terms of the individual, not the tribe, clan, or extended family. Our particular, nuanced slant on democracy is that it's built around millions of such individuals.

But democracy actually means much more than voting, which is the icing on the cake. A democracy is a type of government where people power prevails. That means a government representative of *and* accountable to individual citizens, which conducts itself with a minimum of waste, efficiently deploying the limited tax resources. Representative, accountable, and efficient are the three absolute if implicit terms of the democratic social contract. We may not bother to vote. But those are our implicit demands.

These characteristics are fundamental to Western liberal democracy and how we perceive democratic government. They are nonnegotiable. Even if we don't articulate it, we citizens feel strongly that our government should be representative, accountable, and efficient. This, not voting every four years for 0.5 percent of the public sector, is the soul of our people power. This, not the electoral ballot, is what we mean when we talk about democracy.

It is these same expectations that are often absent in non-Western democracies. Those countries may still hold elections, but their citizens, for the most part, don't expect government accountability, representation, or efficiency. Elected officials are seen as the masters of the citizen population, as are those in the upper echelons of state institutions such as the civil service and armed forces. There is little or no expectation of government working for the people.

In contrast, in Western democracies we still have that expectation. Or at least enough of us have enough of that expectation. We seriously hope or entertain the notion that elected public officials work for us; that civil servants will perform public service; that our money won't be wasted; and that there will be elections guaranteeing accountability, notwithstanding so much evidence to the contrary.

In order to understand what's going wrong and how it can be fixed, let's look more closely at each of our democratic social contract's three fundamental terms and conditions.

REPRESENTATION

Representative government really means that, whatever your

identity, you can see yourself in the government. If you identify as a Sikh, you want to see a Sikh in government. When that happens, you'll be comforted that someone in government understands your cultural framework and how you see the world. In 2018, Sikhs constituted 12 percent of Trudeau's federal cabinet, despite accounting for only about one percent of the Canadian population. In our heterogeneous communities, the symbolic message this sent was far from trivial.

In 2015, I tried explaining to a confused Conservative MP from northern Ontario that South Asian people are reluctant to send their elderly parents to homes for seniors. It's culturally taboo. Instead, they prefer aging parents to live with them. Parents took care of their young ones, and in time, as parents age, that compliment is returned. I was surprised that the MP was surprised at this. But then it occurred to me that his party not only struggles to see the world from the perspective of South Asian Canadians, but has also periodically isolated and bullied them.

The rationale for and benefits of a representative government are that it helps, or should help, those in government understand who they're working for—the full spectrum of people—and what that diverse spectrum wants and needs. Understanding the needs, wants, fears, and hopes of citizens is as important in the public sector as understanding customer needs is in the private sector. It enables those designated to deliver goods and services to understand what needs to be delivered, in what priority, how, when, and to whom.

Our representative governments are meant to be composed of elected and unelected officials who reflect the composition of the population or electorate as a whole. For good reason, since a government comprised only of the wealthy will, despite the best of intentions, have a bias towards—the wealthy. Not only will such a government rarely make tackling poverty a priority, but even when it does, it won't have the lived knowledge to do a good job. It might be up there on the theory but will be lacking in grounded experience.

Similarly, a government primarily comprised of men tends not to prioritize women's issues. It really wouldn't know how to begin doing so. Any branch of government with few or no women can't understand women's social, economic, and political needs and problems. I can't help but recall the "Women in Society" conference at the University of Qassam in Saudi Arabia in 2012, attended by a couple hundred men and not a single woman. Not even a token one. That's an extreme, but it illustrates the point.

Many men can intellectually understand issues from sexual violence and workplace discrimination to pregnancy and abortion. It's hard to live in a Western city and be wholly oblivious to them. But intellectual understanding doesn't translate into lived, visceral awareness. I understand sexual harassment but don't know what it feels like to be subject to it. Women are far more likely than men to be victims of such harassment and are also more likely to report it.[2] While there are exceptions, men will consistently give it less importance than women do.[3]

Similarly, a government composed of Caucasians in a Caucasian-dominant yet multiethnic country won't likely prioritize tackling racial issues. It would struggle to understand the multiple manifestations of racism and how they feed and build off each other, let alone know how to resolve those issues even if it decided to try. If racism is to be tackled, those who suffer from the problem every day of their lives must be involved in defining the issues, as well as in coming up with and implementing solutions.

Another dimension of representation connects with government authority. In a pluralistic citizen population, minorities want to see officials like themselves in government. They need to feel their officials are capable of seeing the world from and can empathize with their perspective. Chinese-Canadians living in Markham appreciate that many of their elected officials are also Chinese-Canadians, some with a better grasp of Mandarin than English. It gives comfort to these citizens, which helps connect them to government, which in turn, fosters communication and sustains government authority.

Minorities who don't see people like themselves adequately represented feel alienated and think that the state belongs to other dominant communities. They sense their needs won't be understood, considered, or even consulted on issues that especially pertain to them. They might also have concerns about government officials discriminating against them. Citizens naturally feel disconnected from any state from which their community or identity is excluded.

Some positive movement has occurred. For instance, half of Trudeau's first cabinet were women. This gave women comfort that their perspectives and voices were now present at the highest levels of government. Women felt more ownership of the state. They didn't expect those female cabinet members to advocate for their interests above those of their country and party. Or at least I don't think they did. But their appointment gave the impression that government was more inclusive and, therefore, aware of a broader spectrum of experience.

WASTE

What's worse than wasting your own money? Somebody else wasting your money! The former is upsetting. The latter triggers outrage. It's odious to be forced to give our money to someone who squanders it. We're outraged, in part, because we had no influence on the process or events that led to this dissipation. Being forced to watch our money wasted is "not tickerteeboo"— the Cockney East Londoner's way of saying "not cool." It's a bit stomach-churning.

Our core understanding of waste is that of spending money frivolously and especially paying far more than what something is worth. That's what often characterizes government waste, which is measurable. The government builds a road meant to cost $2 billion. It eventually costs $3 billion. That's a billion wasted dollars. I sincerely doubt that many, if any, of you reading this book believe the government runs a tight ship. Maybe the more accurate description of government spending might be penny smart, pound foolish?

We'll get into specific examples of waste later. But there are a couple of significant and overlooked dimensions of waste I want to focus on here. First is the relationship between time and money. Almost every civil servant I've spoken to who migrated from the higher performing private-sector environment to government has complained about the public sector's culture of delay—the lack of appreciation that time is money.

Government organizations have their own laws of time, different from those Newton and Einstein arrived at. The public sector simply has far too many endless meetings for the sake of meetings, attended mainly by officials with no business being there in the first place. There's a readiness to push deadlines back and a momentum-stifling number of signatures required to order a box of pencils.

It all boils down to the same principle: "We have less time pressure here in government. We have all the time in the world. What's more, delays we create don't require a dozen signatures, a report by a consultant that may not be worth the paper it's written on, or the finance committee's approval. Oh, one last thing...we can't be fired for delays because nobody gets fired."

Taxpayers put up the cash to pay the costs that public-sector delays run up. The government continues to pay salaries, rent, utility bills, and numerous other fixed expenses during delays. Planning and parks officials still had to be paid salaries and benefits while my local Box Grove community park was being built—or rather not built—and government buildings still had to be maintained. The senior official who promised delivery by 2018 was still getting paid several years on. With extraordinary benefits.

Delays in carrying out initiatives also involve human costs. Young Samir missed out on the chance to enjoy a park opposite his house, with memories to be made and moments to cherish. Isn't the ultimate purpose of our government the well-being and happiness of the citizen population? Where does Samir, who paid his sales taxes and conducted himself in fine fashion, get recourse for the municipal government failing to get its act together? If Apple, McDonald's, or Truefitt & Hill had failed to perform, Samir would have had some way of being compensated, perhaps with a rebate or a discount on the next transaction. But if the City of Markham doesn't perform, we just have to swallow it.

Nobody in government has to sign off on the nonmonetary

costs extracted from citizens, whether they're associated with not using a facility or waiting two hours at a public-sector hospital because, *as always*, there was an unexpected emergency in the morning, which has delayed the attending physician from the scheduled appointment. Indeed, these costs don't attract a moment's attention. I've come across a "Finance Committee" but never an "Opportunity Cost Committee" or "Citizen Waiting Time Committee." Hundreds of citizen hours are wasted every single day in the waiting rooms of hospitals.

Some of these costs can be calculated. If we wanted to, that is. Let's say that a road is delayed by a year because a bunch of civil servants and elected officials were required to be at every meeting on its design and development when only a minority of those in the room ever really needed to attend. Let's assume at least a couple of attendees passed their time during the meetings by doodling on their photocopy handouts. They didn't necessarily share their doodling. But we're trying to keep it real here, so let's imagine a couple of discreet doodlers in the meeting.

Those who might have benefited from the road will now have to wait an extra year for something they ought to have had sooner. Instead of a thousand cars per day getting from points A to B via a direct road, these cars have to drive an extra six miles. That's a thousand cars driving an extra 6,000 aggregate miles every day. Our year-long delay ends up adding over two million miles of extra driving. The moon is only 239,000 miles away, to give you a feel for the number. The earth's circumference is about 24,900 miles.

At an average 404 grams of carbon dioxide per mile, that's also an extra 808,000 kilograms of carbon dioxide pumped into our air per year.[4] Thanks to our government's delay, we can all breathe lots of extra poison. The same thousand drivers, assuming twenty-four miles per gallon and a price of gasoline at US$2.50 per gallon, will have to pay an extra US$208,333 per year out of their pockets—after they've already paid taxes on their income to the public coffers. And of course, a big chunk of that fuel cost is tax, which is rather incestuously convenient.

And that's just for fuel. We haven't even touched on car wear and tear, increased driver anxiety and frustration, or the impact on drivers' bodies from sitting in their cars that much longer. Shall we include car accidents and harm to or loss of life? None of these costs are factored in when our public servants delay one project after another. Nobody in government is responsible for these costs. The doodlers are beyond oblivious, of course. Not one person will ever get their end-of-employment pay-slip as a result of these extortionate hidden taxes.

Government has a cozy relationship with waste in part because government spending is almost always far removed from its funding sources. Citizens are required to pay taxes to a central-ized tax collection agency such as everybody's favorite Internal Revenue Service or Inland Revenue. The tax collector may be aware of the effort that went into generating those taxes but has no idea how the money will be spent. In contrast, when a government agency spends those funds, it rarely, if ever, is in touch with its source—the hard work, sacrifice, and resources of the country's population and businesses.

Spending is quite impersonal and abstract, occurring at arm's length. An agency may have a budget that contains a line item of, say, $800 million. This is then spent on allocated overhead, including office space, equipment, supplies, and salaries for a predetermined head count. There is little, if any, sense that the money comes from citizens who paid taxes, including taxes from children, retirees, or those in serious cash-flow difficulty. Even homeless people pay sales tax on their purchases.

Not being aware of the citizens who are the source of these funds inevitably leads to a diminished sense of responsibility. If the citizens that our democracies supposedly serve were kept front and center, the government's use of money and time couldn't help but be more efficient. An agency's funds would be seen through a human lens, not as a series of line items in an abstract accounting budget.

In the private sector, by contrast, you're rarely far away from the reality of your income's dependence on satisfying customer needs. The vast majority of the private sector consists of small firms—the owner is the operator. In the US in 2018, 89 percent of all businesses employed twenty or fewer people.[5] In Canada, 74 percent of private-sector employees work in small businesses.[6] Most employees understand that if they don't satisfy customer needs or work well, not only will the boss be quick to find out, but they could be asked to move on.

When delivering goods and services, it's a shame that government doesn't consider citizens as customers—a term ironically derived from the medieval Latin for "tax collector." You might ask how government could, in fact, treat citizens as customers. After all, citizens don't have a choice as to where we get our passports, who will improve our roads, who will protect us from crime, and so on. Government can't have customers like the private sector does. We, as citizens, have no choice but to engage government on the government's terms.

Lack of performance pressure resulting from an uncompetitive environment is all too apparent in the public sector. Competition makes the private sector more efficient, less wasteful, and improves performance. Why wouldn't competition do the same for the public sector? Why can't we apply some thinking to introducing such competition? Why do we have such contradictory positions on "competition" in the private and public sectors? Could it be because government doesn't want to legislate a more demanding environment for itself?

I'm not suggesting that the public sector ought to compete with the private sector. Nor am I rabidly advocating privatization. This is important because the private sector can't replace many critical pieces of the public sector. We need a robust public sector. But why not introduce competition *into* the public sector? We can get a man to the moon, conceptualize the relationship between space and time, and do a thousand interesting things with our iPhones, but introducing competition into the public sector seems beyond our intellectual capacity. Really?

Are we waiting for an extraterrestrial life form to take us to the next level of intelligence? Or perhaps we don't have the technology yet? Or, more likely, is no one in the public sector incentivized to introduce competition, which will enhance government performance? After all, why would the public sector want to introduce competitive pressures within its ranks given its generally mediocre performance? Why would a public servant want to put himself on an uphill treadmill? Surely, the downhill one is just fine.

What we have instead is a legislature or executive allocating taxes into an annual budget and then asking an army of civil servants to get on with it. Whether these civil servants make efficient and effective use of the money in their budgets doesn't really affect them personally. And citizens have almost no way of finding out what these civil servants did, much less why and how. For the most part, the daily workings of the civil service, as we already know, are immune from citizen oversight. We get snapshots but nothing which is near comprehensive.

ACCOUNTABILITY

Parents regularly hammer accountability home. Did our kids do what we asked them to do—perhaps clean up after they played? It's an essential concept in every genuine journalist's lexicon. In the private sector, shrewd business leaders harp on accountability. It's so embedded in the private sector's culture that in most small businesses, accountability is a given, like the furniture. If you work on a task and it's not done well or on time, you'll be held accountable. Somebody, quite possibly the owner-operator, will ask you to explain yourself.

Likewise, customers hold businesses to account. In the private sector, if you pay someone to get something done—say, to clean your car—you agree, implicitly or explicitly, on a time frame for delivery and a price. You can watch the job being done and get updates. When the service is complete, you can review it and judge your level of satisfaction. If there's something you don't like, you can raise the issue with the person you're dealing with or their manager. For the most part, issues are quickly rectified. Sometimes, you'll even get your money back.

Accountability doesn't involve a trip to the summit of Mount Everest or using the Jedi mind tricks that Luke Skywalker and the rest of his type performed willy-nilly. Typically, a business doesn't want to lose you and then watch you blast them on social media before you eventually turn to a competitor. The business wants you back, typically. For the most part, effecting accountability is not an uphill battle. Welcome to competitive markets.

We stress accountability because it *encourages* performance, though it doesn't guarantee it. Let's be clear that performance doesn't completely depend on and is possible without external accountability. A small handful of people simply want or are driven to do a good job, perform well, and hold themselves accountable. Nevertheless, accountability is a powerful driver of performance, and less accountability typically leads to weaker performance.

In the public sector, an important part of accountability would be knowing what has actually been done with our tax dollars, especially in the context of and in comparison with what we were told would be done with them. We hired somebody to do something. We gave them money. They did it, didn't do it, or only half-completed it. We want to hold that person accountable. It's that simple. However, as you might begin to see a few patterns, this is not what happens—but more on that later.

A frequently overlooked but essential characteristic of taxes is that they are mandatory under the terms of not only our social contract but the law. I'm not going to roll out one of the most exhausted but nonetheless true quotes in history about "death and taxes." Let's not drive ourselves into boredom. Instead, with your help, I'm going to try to popularize Chris Rock's take on fiscal matters, because it gets to the pith of things: "You don't pay taxes—they take taxes." Bravo.

That we pay compulsory taxes as part of what's supposed to be a reciprocal social contract should make accountability even more essential from the public sector than it is from the private sector. We pay up front without choice in the public sector. We pay at the back end with choice in the private sector. When you also then consider that we constantly use government services, some of which are far more important to our lives than what the private sector offers, public sector accountability becomes critical.

Engaging with government is a multidimensional process. It happens frequently, every single day—every time we use the roads, for example, or rely on law enforcement to keep us safe. In most Western democracies, citizens also rely on government for vital healthcare services. When we're not in the hospital, we have peace of mind that a publicly funded nurse or physician is there lest we need one. Even in our homes, we typically rely on government, for instance, to supply us with water or electricity. Government is a colossal player in our lives.

Yet, most of our contact with government is with the faceless civil service that forms its vast majority. As we increasingly rely on government systems, that contact becomes more impersonal. Civil servants are accountable, but not to us, the citizens. They're accountable—or quasi-accountable, since public-sector employees are rarely fired for poor performance—to their superiors in the context of their own internal frames of reference, for what those are worth, and perhaps somewhere up the line, very indirectly to an elected representative. One who, it is unlikely, we voted for.

On the other hand, we expect that our politicians and elected officials, who propound a litany of proclamations and commitments during their campaigns, will also be accountable. They are, in theory, voted in partly on the basis of those commitments.

Once in office, we expect that they will do the honorable thing and deliver on what they said they would. And at election time, we can hold them accountable. Theoretically.

But those elected are elected primarily because they're good at... getting elected. This is such an important yet overlooked reality of our democracy. It's not the same as being elected because they're better able to get a job done or add value to society. Or even to represent a constituency. Race, gender, and even accent are just some of the many extraneous factors that influence our vote. The gift of the gab, name recognition, backroom deals, and plain, simple lies feed into almost every representative election. Selling hate is also increasingly fashionable. All this isn't some piece of political genius. This is all Political Marketing 101.

People who have a serious track record of getting things done usually don't consider running for elected office. Let that sink in for a moment. If you look around at the most accomplished people you personally know, they're not in government, and most likely they don't want to be. Legislatures are flooded, over-whelmed, in fact, with people who have achieved very little in their professional lives. Who have delivered nothing of note. But who are nevertheless great at getting votes.

Art, like poetry, often expresses truths in ways that prose can't. *Devolved Parliament*, a painting by the pseudonymous artist Banksy, depicts the British House of Commons with chimpan-zee MPs—behind the veneer, a bunch of noisy, high-energy folk who are great at making a commotion. This portrayal of many of our elected representatives—homogenous, and incapable—so resonated that it sold for an extraordinary £10 million in 2019.

And often the executive is no better. Ministers of state aren't selected because they know their subject or have a track record in getting things done. Often, they're simply close political or personal friends of the prime minister or the president. They have strong grassroots support, which isn't the same thing as competency. In many cases, they're selected because they heavily funded the CEO's election campaign. Linda McMahon contributed US$7.5 million to Trump's campaign.[7] The once-bankrupt French graduate was selected to run the Small Business Administration.

Shifting gears, if accountability really is integral to our democracy, how is it that government isn't obliged to consider what we, as citizens, believe to be important spending priorities? Where do we want our taxes allocated? Which spending is crucial, and which less so? What trade-offs are we comfortable or uncomfortable with? That rarely happens. A principal consequence of our broken social contract is that our government seldom aligns the spending of resources with what its citizens want.

As things stand, government is generally unaccountable, unrepresentative at its upper reaches and therefore outrageously capable of wasting time and large sums of money. I'm not suggesting that citizens detail budgets to the nearest thousand dollars. Even if there would be nothing ethically wrong with this, the process would be far too challenging and time-consuming.

But isn't it strange that in our democracies, despite all our techno-wizardry, citizens rarely have any input on what is taxed or what our taxes are spent on? We citizens are seldom, if ever, invited to make important spending decisions. Some governments, such as in Mississauga, Ontario, have made headway by inviting citizens for their view on the entire budget at a high level.[8] While this advisory basis tool is good, there's still no good reason why citizens of Western democracies have absolutely no say in how their taxes are spent.

The absence of citizen input into the key issue of budget allocation reinforces the distance between us and our democracy. If we're not invited to participate at all in the budget process, how can we know what our democracy is spending those taxes on and begin to demand government accountability? It's one thing to be presented with a set of numbers and another to be able to work with them, to get to know them, to at least get a basic understanding of them.

This lack of involvement in something so crucial helps explain why Americans are upset that their federal government spends 31 percent of its budget on foreign aid.[9] In reality, foreign aid is less than a single, measly, embarrassing 1 percent, and a significant portion of that is tied to buying American exports, which aren't necessarily what would be best for the country receiving the aid.[10] If Americans were aware of this, they'd be embarrassed, as they would be about their government's spending on the domestic impoverished.

This is not just about the US. In Australia, citizens think that their government spends 14 percent of the budget on foreign aid. I, too, would be annoyed if one in seven of my tax dollars went to foreign countries. That's a pretty steep number. In fact, as in the US, the aid is less than 1 percent, of which, again, a significant portion is tied to Australian exports when, in fact, the recipient country would often get better quality at a cheaper price elsewhere.[11] As it happens, the UK spends just short of 2 percent on foreign aid while Canada, putting their neighbors to shame, donates almost 3 percent.

The combination of the frequency and depth with which we

interface with government demands a level of accountability that is currently far from acceptable. In fact, describing the relationship between citizens and government as "accountable" does a huge disservice to the underlying reality we are living.

Our social contract is broken. But there are ways to repair it.

CHAPTER 3

THE BUSINESS OF GOVERNMENT

Government can learn a lot from the private sector.

Although there are exceptions, profound differences between public and private sector cultures impact both their efficiency and effectiveness. While there are high performance and poor performance cultures in both the private and public sectors, the unfortunate reality is that high performance cultures are usually found in the former, while far too much of the public sector is immersed in mediocre or poor-performance cultures.

Clearly, my perspective is going to jolt more than one civil servant, public employee, or elected representative. I did say I would speak my mind. And, yes, I'll back this up. But for now, and just as something of an hors d'oeuvre, suffice it to say that it's no coincidence that MBA students, who are among the most ambitious members of our societies, overwhelmingly prefer to join the private sector, even when it offers lower compensation levels than the public sector, as it often does in Canada.[1]

Put slightly differently, the private sector is more performance-centered than the public sector, irrespective of the exact measures by which that performance might be measured. Those who have moved between the two sectors will appreciate that in the public sector, a panel or committee often makes decisions in slow motion. Whereas in the private sector, responsibility and accountability tend to sit with the individual—the individual who, ironically, is conceptually the same bedrock of our liberal democracy.

Clearly, there are exceptions. A few government agencies have a high performance ethic—especially those close to the government CEO, such as the staff at 10 Downing Street in the UK or the Prime Minister's Office in Canada. Hands down, they're dominated by capable overperformers and work extraordinarily hard. Finance departments also tend to be a cut above the rest of the public sector—with longer hours, greater accountability, firmer adherence to deadlines, higher quality output, and dealings with the staffs of top-tier private firms. However, these are the exceptions and not the rule.

Irking many in the public sector, there's simply stronger performance management in the private sector. People's work is under greater scrutiny, and underperformers aren't allowed to remain for as long as they can in the public sphere. In the latter, it's close to impossible to get fired for underperformance. That luxury is much harder to enjoy in the private sector. Yes, we can find poor performers employed in the private sector. They're just nowhere as prevalent as in the public sector.

Let me repeat to be clear that I'm not advocating the privatization, and certainly not the blanket privatization of public services, which has become a rallying cry of some in the American right and, to a lesser extent, among British conservatives. I recognize that the neoliberal privatization agenda has caused considerable damage to the economically disadvantaged in society. Investing in our social infrastructure is really important for *everyone* in society. What I'm advocating instead is the application of business practices and culture, as well as the introduction of competition in the public sector to improve performance.

COMPARING APPLES AND ORANGES

Can we really compare the private and public sectors? Private-sector businesses typically focus on satisfying a relatively narrow range of customers with the aim of generating earnings, dividends, and revenues. In reality, it's not quite so simple since most private-sector businesses don't only focus on profits or revenues—issues of ego (biggest in the world), family (succession planning) and risk (avoiding too much reliance on one income stream) are some of the many other factors that dictate a firm's agenda.

But the overall bias towards profits and revenues is nevertheless especially true of businesses in Anglo-American countries. It's worth also recognizing there's been a recent movement among the very largest companies to try to broaden the definition of why and for whom they exist above and beyond profitability, but this is still at an embryonic stage.[2] It might get an added push from the coronavirus epidemic, but it's too early at this stage to preempt that.

In contrast, the public sector engages a broad spectrum of people—some departments engage every single person in the country—and has more complex responsibilities and targets. Government agencies don't aim to maximize profit or return on investment but to provide a broad set of social goods and services with consequences often across several departments or agencies. Government's much broader interests are social well-being, law and order, national security, economic growth, and keeping inflation down and employment up. Not just at a high level, but in minutiae detail.

How then can we compare the performance of the private and public sectors? What evidence do we have for doing so beyond tapping into the subjective experiences of people who have migrated between the two arenas? Isn't this like comparing apples and oranges? How did I come to assert what I did about the performance imbalance of the two ecosystems?

These are very important questions, and the failure to address the core underlying issue of comparison has undercut not so much our ability, but our willingness to compare the performance of the two sectors. They're so different, we tell ourselves, that we can't compare them. So, we don't even try.

Wrong! We should, however, admit that it's difficult to find hard proof or evidence when trying to compare apples and oranges. It's not as simple as comparing Microsoft and Samsung. Or Air Canada and Qantas. Or Messi and Ronaldo. Much of the financial, operational, or numeric data we might feed into those comparisons is publicly available. Even then, there are many who will cite any number of reasons why even those comparisons aren't fair or reasonable.

Nevertheless, if you looked to compare apples and oranges, if you actually made the effort, you would immediately note several similarities. They are both fruits, reside at rank two on the Licker Scale for sweetness, and grow from trees. There we go—

three easy similarities. Just as so, they also have immediately noticeable differences. Apples tend to have more fiber and a smoother texture, whereas oranges have more vitamin C and a peel we tend not to eat, despite being surprisingly nutritious. I only learned that last piece when researching for this book.

With the right mindset, we can, in fact, compare apples and oranges. Having neutered this metaphor, which originated oddly enough in England before Shakespeare's birth as a comparison between apples and oysters, let's bravely, without hesitation or doubt, without wasting time in a committee meeting, compare the performance of the public the private sectors.

We can present mounting and persuasive evidence that the public sector's performance ethic is inferior to the private sector's. While the two universes may have different performance criteria, we've just seen that comparison is possible despite such differences. The evidence that can be mustered may be more suggestive than hard and final, but it's still enough to steer us in a direction from which we can comfortably draw conclusions.

We can deploy different strategies to compare the two sectors. We could rely on credible third-party analysis. In the few such rigorous comparisons between the private and public sectors, the former has consistently done better than the latter. In 2019, McKinsey & Co published its survey of more than 2,000 private and public organizations, culled from five million responses worldwide, which highlighted the vast performance gap between the two.

The study found that not only were over 75 percent of public organizations below par with respect to organizational health, but that those organizations also had poor cultures.[3] The report cited particularly problematic components of the culture gap with the private sector: high levels of risk-aversion, and little reward for good or penalty for poor performance. Public-sector managers, the report found, were particularly poor at motivating and developing their most important asset—people.

As a second approach, we can rely on our own personal empirical experience. You can, in fact, feel the culture gap. I previously alluded to the noticeably subdued energy levels you find when you walk into any government space. Compare that to the energy level within a typical private-sector space and the private-public performance gap becomes clear. The reception area of the City of Toronto's main office has the energy vibe of limbo, as if it were a tiny sovereign land situated between the living and the dead. Walk a block south and you will be in the busiest and most vibrant offices in the country.

This energy can't be measured. And, true, as I've stated, there are plenty of dull private-sector environments and a few atypically energized public-sector ones too. It's easier nevertheless to find higher-energy, private-sector employees working longer hours than their public-sector counterparts. I work in an office building filled with private firms where almost everyone works more than eight hours per day. In contrast, eight hours maximum is the norm in Ontario's public sector.

A third area in which to substantiate the gap would be to focus on very specific performance measures. Consider calls to Canadian government call centers, meant to put citizens in touch with their government within two to ten minutes. In 2018, callers often had wait times of more than thirty minutes.[4] A million citizens waited so long that they hung up before they could be connected. Meanwhile, wait times for calls to the IRS, the US agency that wants to collect your taxes, regularly stretch beyond an hour, with an average wait time of twenty-one minutes.[5] No businesses can survive this sort of customer service.

All these measures have pros and cons, and I've opened the door to them for others to reflect and explore. In what follows, I'll focus on three further points of comparison between the two sectors, moving from the more specific to the more general.

The first example is extremely concrete, comparing the number of sick days taken in both sectors. Data here is readily available. While this comparison may not yield irrefutable proof, it is highly suggestive. It's an indicator of how one sector values the work ethic more than the other. It's a gauge of the commitment to turn up for work. To not look like the slacker. To the consequences for being seen as the idler.

The second example will be the adoption of performance management tools and concepts, which virtually always migrate from the private to the public sector rather than vice versa. This is a powerful indicator that the private sector values and demands performance, however defined and by whatever criteria, more than does the public sector. Business incessantly seeks ways to improve. The public sector, in contrast, resists or doesn't demand such innovation. It rarely has any competition. And where it does, it often loses.

The third example compares private with public-sector employment. Performance management and culture both feed into this. Who joins the public sector? Who joins the private sector? And, with respect to performance management, who is asked to move on in the public versus the private sector? The assumption is that high performance talent tends to prefer to work for high performance organizations. These scrutinize staff and remove those who don't make the grade. Yes, I know there are exceptions, but let's not let them obscure the general trend.

The irony is that our expectations of the public and private sectors should actually be the reverse of what they are now. Because the public sector makes us pay taxes, and as part of that makes the homeless and impoverished pay too, and pay on time, in advance, on trust, and without choice in the matter, my personal view is that it has an ethical obligation to outperform the private sector. Instead, we have this discomforting gut sense that the public sector is simply not as effective or efficient as the private sector.[6]

SICK DAYS

Let's compare the number of sick-time days private and public employees take each year. This is not a classic measure of efficiency, like output divided by input. But it's a powerful proxy for the two sectors' performance, in part because it involves both time and human capital, our most important resources. The relative desire of staff to show up for work or not speaks to the culture of the two sectors. It doesn't reveal what people do at work or how well they do it. It's just about showing up, but I don't believe this limitation invalidates the comparison.

Let's take a closer look. In Canada in 2019, full-time public-sector employees took off 62 percent more sick days than full-time private-sector employees did. That is "sixty-two," not "six point two"—an average of 14.6 as opposed to 9.0 sick days per year.[7] If this was a 10 or 15 percent difference, we could perhaps dismiss it as a statistical anomaly, but a 62 percent difference is shocking. It's hardly a small number, especially given the millions of people employed in each sector.

In 2019, Canadian federal employees took off an astonishing 16.4 days per year for illness, disability, personal days, or family responsibilities. This doesn't include vacation days.[8] Every year, if you're employed in Mr. Trudeau's federal government—and it was no better under the Conservatives so let's not play partisan politics—besides the vacations you are entitled to as well as statutory leave, you are taking more than three weeks off every single year for illness or responsibilities outside of work. How many small businesses would allow for this? Hey, how many could survive such a "sick" workforce?

There's more: many employment terms in the public sector are just unethical. Can you imagine a private business—not forgetting that most are small—whose employees have the right every single year to 120 days of short-term leave and disability at 90 percent of their salary? To be clear, you don't need to be disabled to receive this benefit. This is on top of eleven days per year for sick leave on full pay, as well as pregnancy-leave benefits. Any private-sector firm—Apple, Google, General Motors, or Bank of America—would fold under these conditions. How then do Ontario's public school teachers get this package?[9]

And who pays for this absurdity, among many others hidden in the vast crevices of the public sector? The taxpayer—who pays on time, every time. The aged pensioner, the downtown lawyer, the kid buying ice cream, you, and me. We're all paying for it, without much choice. Heck, all this is often so buried that, despite the magnitude of the expense, hardly any of us seem to be aware of it. It's nicely tucked away in an obscure clause in a two-hundred-page contract that unions, government officials, and lawyers have negotiated.

The Conference Board of Canada estimated that in 2011,

Canadian public-sector employees' additional sick time cost the economy C$16.6 billion, *excluding* costs related to paying replacement employees, delays, and missed deadlines.[10] Taking those into account, the number would be closer to C$20 billion. That was a decade ago. Between 2011 and 2018, there was a more than 8 percent increase in the average number of annual sick days taken by public-sector employees.[11] How that affects the C$20 billion lost is not difficult to imagine.

Let's bring home the data from 2011: public-sector absenteeism cost the Canadian economy the equivalent of more than C$500 per person—not per taxpayer but per person, per year. Put another way, if Canadian public-sector sick-day rates dropped to those in the private sector, if the government folk turned up like everyone else did, every Canadian citizen would save more than C$500, which for many hundreds of thousands of people is the difference between living in poverty or not, especially given that those citizens include children and those who are retired.

While comparing absenteeism to understand performance, we should keep in mind that, in some cases, public-sector employees earn more than their private-sector counterparts. According to one study, Canadian public-sector compensation in 2015 was typically 18 to 37 percent higher than for the same job in the private sector.[12] In 2015, the police force of York Region, a suburb of Greater Toronto, had 1,072 officers, of which 70 percent earned C$100,000 or more.[13] In 2017, another survey suggested that, on average, public-sector employees earned 11 percent more than their private-sector counterparts.[14]

Besides better earnings, Canadian public-sector employees are more than three times as likely to benefit from a pension package than private-sector employees are.[15] Furthermore,

80 percent of public-sector employees have defined-benefits pension packages, whereas only 10 percent of private-sector employees do.[16] Defined-benefits pension packages are notoriously expensive for those who have to pay for them. And really amazing for those who receive them.

Canada's public sector is not unique. In 2017, British public-sector employees were sick 2.9 percent of all working hours, while private-sector employees were sick only 1.8 percent.[17] In other words, if a private-sector employee takes off seven days in a year, their public-sector counterpart will be off sick twelve days. That's quite a noticeable gap. Accounting for weekends and vacations, five days per year per person for a public sector of more than five million full-time employees adds up to more than the hours that more than a hundred thousand employees work in a whole year.

Australia's story is similar, demonstrating that there's something very wrong with the performance culture, or lack of it, across the public sectors of all Western liberal democracies. Down under, private-sector employees took an average 9.5 sick days off per year during 2016–2017, while their public-sector counterparts took 11.6 days off. Overtime data in Australia reveals that private-sector employees are also, as it happens, far more willing to work extra hours without pay, whereas public-sector employees nearly always get paid for overtime.[18]

I don't think any of this is a coincidence. It's not as if working in the public sector makes people ill or that the government actively recruits immune-deficient employees. Nor can it be that private-sector employees eat more nutritious meals, have better access to fitness centers, or are forced to have their annual flu shots. You can dive deep into any statistic and find exceptions to the rule, but let's not kid ourselves about the big picture. Public-sector staff take off more "sick" days per year than do private-sector staff.

Why? It comes down to culture. A culture that holds people accountable, demands performance and bang for buck and keeps people on their toes won't stand for excessive sick days. In a low-performance and low-accountability culture, one where results and deadlines don't matter so much, neither do excessive sick days. It's not that sick days are welcome in government. It's just that there's greater tolerance and greater appetite to take them. And of course, it's extremely hard to be fired in the public sector for taking sick days.

The nature of taxation is a part of the problem. A lower-performance culture can flourish precisely because our money is taken from us with practically no accountability. That, in turn, trickles down, empowering public-sector employees to take off sick days without fear of reprisal.

Taxpayers don't deserve this. Some taxpayers can't even make ends meet.

PERFORMANCE MANAGEMENT CONCEPTS

Almost every new major performance management toolkit has originated or been adopted by the private sector before being transferred—if it ever is—to government. There are almost no notable cases where government took the initiative to create a significant new management toolkit that was then transferred to the private sector. This is no coincidence, but another indicator of the performance gap between the two sectors.

An argument can again be made that the two realms have different objectives that call for different toolkits. But again, despite their differences, we can still compare them. Returning to our apples and oranges analogy, consider rugby and football—called soccer in North America. Rugby is about running forward with the ball in your hands and then planting it beyond a line. Football is all about kicking or heading the ball into a net without using your hands. Yes, they are different. But both are team sports that involve physical activity, teamwork, and what's known as ball skill. Again, we dare to compare.

The toolkits of the private and public sectors also overlap. Management and leadership are needed in both sectors. Organizations in both universes require organizational design, marketing strategy, and key performance indicators (KPIs), all tools that, only after some time, are now used in government. Some tools originated in business schools before migrating to businesses themselves, and then, in a few cases, to the public policy academy and government. My issue is that the stream of management ideas and tools overwhelmingly flows in one direction—again, an indicator, but not itself final proof.

Take the pioneering works of Kenneth Andrews, Alfred Chandler, and Igor Ansoff, which were all adopted and adapted by the private sector before the public sector took any notice. Yet, all three wrote about issues as relevant to the public as the private sector. Chandler's work, for example, focused on the long-term health of organizations over and above the analysis of monthly accounts—a concept that readily fits into the public sector's complex mandate, which encompasses many factors besides finance.

The public sector's poor appetite for improved performance

is both the cause and effect of a related issue—its lack of an entrepreneurial ethic and culture. Entrepreneurship involves doing something different or unprecedented—to design, build, or distribute something people want for the first time or to do something better than anyone else. There is a wonderful small Daffy Duck bookend in my mother's home that captures much of the entrepreneurial spirit. The duck has his arms wrapped around a bag of money that sits atop a sign that says, "Bigger. Better. Faster." That's how entrepreneurs survive and succeed.

That spirit is largely absent in the public sector.[19] Government's motivation to improve and maintain its performance ethic is compromised accordingly. The public sector simply doesn't seek to develop the next big framework or idea for delivering better performance, spurring innovation, and meeting higher standards. The focus and hunger on wanting to do bigger, better, or faster is much less prevalent in the public sector than we need it to be.

My town of Markham has a significant private-sector technology presence, including the Canadian headquarters of IBM, AMD, and Huawei. Apple was here, too, until they moved downtown in 2017. In fact, the town self-identifies as "Canada's High-Tech Capital." Yet the government of Markham's website has the look and feel of something before the social media boom of more than a decade ago. It's stale. It's cumbersome. The information lacks structure, feeling more like a fire hose than a laser.

Because of this dearth of entrepreneurial spirit, the public sector also lacks a meaningful awareness of what entrepreneurs need. It's ill-equipped to recognize the challenges and issues of either starting a business or making the transition from a startup to a more stable enterprise. Entrepreneurs are arguably the biggest drivers of economic growth and change, and as such, are a critical part of society. Yet, with few entrepreneurs in government ranks, government seldom sees the world as entrepreneurs see it.

In 2017, I was at a dinner in London with some entrepreneurs and investors who were discussing a potential project. The talk turned to funding, some of which was to come from the "RDA." The RDA turned out to be Regional Development Agency, part of the British government. When we found what the RDA was, the atmosphere around the table turned from a Mary Poppins high to Jabba the Hut heavy. Entrepreneurs generally avoid working with government, because we know that government wastes time, the one resource which the private sector and especially entrepreneurs feel is in short supply.

Whenever civil servants have asked me what they can do to help entrepreneurs, they've always been startled and alarmed by my response: "Get out of our way." Their best first step in the right direction would be to go through every rule and regulation, every bit of bureaucracy, and ask if it is still justifiable. Do we really still need it, or is it just one of those lame "it's the system" relics? The last thing entrepreneurs need is energy-draining forms and approvals, especially those many that no longer serve any purpose or have unintended consequences.

PERFORMERS AND STRAGGLERS

We've compared sick days in the private and public sectors, as well as their contrasting appetites for better management methods. Now we'll turn to a third comparison—talent. In the private sector, management tends to recruit and retain high performers while getting rid of poor performers. If employees aren't performing, they're first taken aside for a polite conversation. If no improvement is made, the conversation often escalates quickly, and, if necessary, the employee is removed. The livelihoods of all those involved, employee and employer, depend on this dynamic.

Private-sector culture also gravitates to both organizational and individual accomplishments. You're given a job to do and typically the resources to do it. You're now expected to perform. The culture tends to be one of responsibility and empowerment, which don't depend on either soft or hard skills. It's a matter of expectation rather than, or in addition to, tools and systems. You'll struggle to climb the ladder in the private sector if you can't get things done on time to a high enough standard. If you repeatedly miss deadlines or deliver shoddy outcomes, you'll find yourself unemployed.

This is not the public sector's performance culture, which is more lax and indifferent. Yes, of course that doesn't mean every single body in the public sector is this way—hear me out. Not only does the public sector seldom aim to recruit and retain high performing individuals, but it's very difficult to fire unproductive staff. Underperformers find it easy to stick around and avoid getting pushed out. I have a friend working in a municipal government whose family repeatedly encouraged and cajoled her into her public-sector job precisely for this reason.

Attracting high performers is important for any organization. One of the largest surveys of its type, involving more than 600,000 respondents, concluded that high performing employees are typically four times more productive than average employees.[20] We can debate how that result came about and whether such increased productivity holds true for every type of job. But we can't deny the big picture result: a good consulting firm relying on 600,000 respondents concluded that high performers add multiple times the value of average performers.

How does the public sector fare in recruiting those top performers? Only 1 percent of the graduates from the University of Toronto's MBA class of 2017 chose to work in government. Only 4 percent of Harvard Business School's 2017 graduates went into government *or* the nonprofit sector.[21] Though these aren't necessarily the smartest kids on the block, they're among the most ambitious—the ones that want to do well, that demand and enjoy performance from themselves and those around them—and they don't want to join the public sector.

It's true that business school students innately lean towards business and the private sector, but let's venture a bit further. The top ten preferred employers of 20,000 Canadian college and university students in 2018–2019 were *all* in the private sector, despite some of Canada's largest employers being in the public sector.[22] The story is the same for the top tier of non-MBA graduates. In another recent survey, only 9 percent of graduates of the London School of Economics, with one of the largest government academic departments in the world, joined the public sector within six months after graduating.[23] In contrast, public-sector employment makes up 17 percent of all jobs in the UK.[24]

In the US, the number of graduates who applied to any government job fell 15 percent between 2001 and 2017, even as the national population increased 15 percent.[25] Graduates' interest in any government job has since fallen to only 5 percent.[26] Out of *Forbes*'s ranking of top 250 employers for new graduates, only six were in the public sector.[27] None were in the top ten, and not a single US federal government agency was in the top one hundred. Not the CIA. Not the FBI. Not the Treasury.

The ability to recruit has consequences. Let's not forget the profound impact that the public sector has on society, from safety to vital infrastructure. With these at stake, in theory, the public sector deserves the most capable and outstanding talent. Why aren't graduates from Auckland, Oxford, or Stanford hustling to join government the way they currently are to join Google, Goldman Sachs, and McKinsey? Part of this is compensation levels. Part boils down to the lack of performance culture and opportunity in government.

Just as it's lagging behind in recruiting high performing talent, the public sector struggles to remove low performers. It's very difficult to fire civil servants. In the US federal government, of the two million civil servants under the Merit Systems Protection Board, only one in two hundred is fired every year for poor performance or misconduct.[28] Nearly half of those are in their probationary period, which means that, once past probation, it's incredibly rare for a civil servant to be dismissed for performance problems—just one per 400. Those numbers do not inspire a performance culture.

By contrast, Goldman Sachs, a high performance investment bank, removed 5 percent of its staff in the second quarter of 2016.[29] The chances of being fired at Goldman Sachs during that quarter alone were one in twenty. To those who don't keep track of the health of the financial services economy, 2016 was neither a good nor a bad year, so the firings can't be attributed to broader economic issues. 2008 was a bad year. 2020 is turning into a bad year. 2016 was neither here nor there.

Some might ask, why compare one of the world's premier

firms with government? Isn't that unfair? I agree because most private-sector firms aren't one of the world's top investment banks. So let's look at a broader cross section of the private and public sectors. Employees in the US private sector were three times as likely to get fired in 2016 than those in the public sector.[30] Does that help? In that year, the US economy grew at a sensible 1.5 percent, so as I said earlier, we can't attribute the private sector dismissals to an economic crash as we might for 2008 or 2020.

Meanwhile, north of the border, the Canadian federal government, which employed 380,700 people in 2006, fired an average of 127 employees per year between 1999 and 2009 for misconduct or poor performance.[31] That's less than one in 3,000 employees. Between 2005 and 2015, that increased to only 132 employees fired per year.[32] One leading national newspaper hit the mark nicely: "Canadians are correct to assume that it is almost impossible to fire a public employee, even if that employee was found guilty of a violent crime offense while on duty."[33]

I want you to understand this statistic. You'd have a greater chance of being recruited as an astronaut by NASA than of being fired by the Canadian federal government for poor performance. A record 18,300 people applied for the fourteen vacancies in NASA's 2017 astronaut program—one vacancy for every 1,307 applicants.[34] Even if the number of applicants to NASA doubled, in other words, twice as competitive, you'd still have a better shot at becoming a NASA astronaut than getting fired from the Canadian federal government. It's utterly embarrassing.

This goes some way to explaining why Canadian governments

employ police who have criminal convictions, prison guards who have been convicted of violent crimes, and teachers who have been convicted for sexual offenses.[35] When Toronto policeman James Forcillo was charged with the death of Sammy Yatim in 2013 and eventually found guilty and sentenced to six years in prison, he was suspended with pay—not fired.[36] Unable to do any police work, he received a salary and benefits of about C$100,000 per year for several years, which the taxpayer fronted.

One Ontario teacher made lewd remarks to his female students, drank alcohol with students at parties, used profanity while in the classroom, and slapped female students on their buttocks— only to get a one-month suspension by The Ontario College of Teachers.[37] Whoop-de-do. This isn't an isolated case. Another Ontario teacher was found guilty of physically grabbing and pushing elementary students, kids who haven't reached their teens.[38] Some were so traumatized that they need psychological counseling. The College of Teachers threw the kitchen sink at the teacher—a six-month suspension and the costs of the hearing. Whoop-de-da.

Across all tiers of Canadian government, there's also a soft collusion between unions and government regulators. The former back their members to the hilt, even when the member is guilty as sin; the latter are often staffed by former union executives or members. In this context, it's unsurprising that government uses our taxes to retain staff who simply aren't good enough. In contrast, in 2017, Canadian private-sector employees were five times more likely to be removed from their jobs than public-sector ones.[39]

How does our government get away with this? Well, let's say I was working at a private firm and got fired either because

I wasn't doing a good job, or the firm simply didn't need me. These being solid reasons for my job loss, I'd be unlikely to raise a legal fuss. I would take severance pay, read a book, and watch some football. If I were a civil servant, though, I'd be speaking to my union representative, lawyer, and even the press. The private and public sectors have sharply contrasting approaches to talent because one group prioritizes accountability and performance. The other does not.

TACTICAL CHANGES

What sort of intervention is needed to repair the broken social contract? The answer may be counterintuitive, since there are so many problems with public-sector waste, representation, and accountability that the issues seem overwhelming and intractable. In fact, many are. And I don't want to remotely suggest that a single magic wand will make everything better. I'm not a business school professor. I don't think everything can be resolved by a single reductionist panacea…to sell books, become famous, and then do lucrative consulting work.

However, one lesson I've learned in business is actually that you don't have to change everything at a fundamental level to have a significant, even huge, impact. To use business terminology, the most effective changes are often tactical and relatively small-scale rather than big strategic interventions. Even so, if they're permanent and persist, they can be immensely consequential. We're awake for some sixteen hours a day. If we allocated a mere twenty minutes, or 2 percent of our day, for rigorous exercise, we'd make a big difference to our health and well-being.

My intention is to focus on equally small but powerful interventions. This is not to say that our governments couldn't benefit from some more fundamental, wholesale changes that would require more consideration and be more difficult to implement. For instance, what exactly are we asking our elected representatives to do? Do we want them to represent and advocate for their constituent's communities? Or toe the party line? Focus on the national interest? Do we need wholesale structural thinking, a redefinition of their roles, or something else? To be honest, at this point, I don't know. And I don't want to go there either.

People often think you need drama to have an impact. Earlier, I pointed out that I'm not a business school academic. I'm also not a Hollywood producer. We don't need frightening changes. We don't need, for instance, to halve or double our taxes. We often forget that just tweaking things can have an impact, which is essentially the "theory of nudge" that James Wilk and D. J. Stewart, among others, articulated.[40] If we could only just see the breach of the social contract, recognize its toxic consequences before we therefore inevitably decide to act, a great deal can be achieved with seemingly disproportionate means.

So, let's pick the proverbial low-hanging fruit first. I had wanted to avoid using that expression in this book, but c'est la vie. None of us has all the answers, but again, as I've learned in business, that doesn't mean that we can't act. In fact, we can and should act because not only is time money, but we can always start on a small scale, learn, refine, and then expand. Immediate tactical changes are the easiest place to start, which is why I'll focus on them and invite you to focus on them as well.

To set the tone for what's to follow, one such micro-change we'll be exploring in greater depth is requiring elected and unelected officials to share their work calendars online. This one adjustment would give us a basic sense of what they're doing and maybe even have accomplished on a daily and weekly basis. It's far from an impossible proposal and can be managed so as to accommodate security and privacy issues.

This change would also force the entire public sector to fundamentally rethink how they're spending their time and approaching the job of governing. Politicians would behave differently if they knew that the public and media could now see what they're doing—if they knew that you could merely click on a link to an MP's or senator's agenda to find out what they focused on or accomplished last week. Might meetings with big-business lobbyists be replaced by meetings with local constituents?

Another change we'll be exploring in greater depth is establishing a policy of mandatory dismissal of the weakest performing 2 percent of employees in government every year—no ifs, ands, or buts. This involves managers defining and communicating performance metrics, evaluating staff against them, and then having the authority to act. This will light the kind of fire in the public sector that private-sector culture has long used to improve performance.

I want to make one tangential point here. Earlier, we compared absenteeism in the private and public sectors to point out the latter's relatively poor performance. However, comparisons can be applied more positively. In fact, there's no good reason why we can't more frequently benchmark and compare the public and private sectors to make government more accountable and representative, as well as to reduce waste. At least in some respects, government can be measured against the private sector.

For instance, why can't we measure, compare, and advertise the time it takes to connect with a human being over the phone? Or basic customer service satisfaction levels for simple two- or three-minute transactions? Surveys would include such questions as: How long did you have to wait before talking with a representative? Was that representative polite? Helpful? If you were an employer, would you hire the person that you just spoke with? And then there needs to be meaningful consequences to these survey responses.

Some of the challenge lies in government being a monopoly. Since citizens can't go elsewhere to get their needs met, why do you need friendly telephone operators who answer calls within a minute? A business in a competitive environment might fold if it responded to calls like the IRS does. Government, in contrast, can't fold. The public sector doesn't prioritize improving performance, nor does it want to do so with anything like the gusto of private-sector businesses, which consistently benchmark themselves against each other, even if sometimes only at a basic level, to ensure survival and success.

Because benchmarks are ubiquitous, it wouldn't be challenging to establish and implement them in government. It wouldn't be difficult to research the top fifty Dow Jones companies in terms of customer satisfaction and leverage their metrics and benchmarks in the public sector, and then publicly communicate the results. After all, we as taxpayers have a right to know how our government is faring. Our delegating our right to govern to elected and unelected officials does not dilute our ownership of the state or our right to know what's happening in government.

Without data, it's quite difficult to hold government to account and say, "Why aren't you doing this as well as these private enterprises are doing it? Why aren't you recruiting top-tier talent?" With such data, accountability—perhaps not of a person or team, but certainly of a government department or agency—becomes much easier to determine and enforce. Hello! We now have the technology to collect and analyze such data. Oh, right, yes, we've had it for years.

CHAPTER 4

DISRUPTIVE TECHNOLOGY

The impact of today's communications technology on the political landscape in which government functions has already been mentioned, but it's almost impossible to overstate its importance. This influence is so significant that it warrants deeper examination.

Both communications and machine-learning technology vastly increase the scope of what's feasible. They're sometimes associated with the concept of "creative destruction," meaning tearing down past and current ways of doing things in favor of alternatives that may unlock greater potential. We seem to do that at an extraordinary pace and scale nowadays. Information technology has opened and enabled a whole range of productive possibilities, including the potential to make government less wasteful, more representative, and truly accountable.

Technology is a double-edged sword, however. Much of technology's influence on the social, political, and economic landscapes has been negative. Before moving forward, we must take account of how technology is contributing to the break-down of our social contract. Web and mobile-web usage in particular have transformed communications. Even the way we walk has been influenced by our addiction to handheld devices. Our IT revolution has facilitated the fastest rate of large-scale social, political, and economic change we as a species have ever seen—welcome to technology's law of accelerating returns.[1]

THE NEW, TOUGHER MEDIA

If anything, government was probably even more wasteful, unrepresentative, and unaccountable thirty years ago than it is today. We now use Microsoft Office, Google, and email—all of which are deeply embedded in the functions of modern government—to get things done more quickly and efficiently. More women, ethnic minorities, and disabled people are in senior government positions.

The ability to probe into slivers of government, not quite the same thing as accountability, has been enhanced by the internet explosion as well as the introduction of Freedom of Information acts that have opened more of the public sector to inspection. Before the internet, few could scrutinize the government the way we can now, even if we still lack robust, meaningful accountability processes. An important part of that has been the increasing power, independence, and even belligerence of the fragmented press.

So, what's changed? Why are we losing confidence in government?

To begin with, picking up on the last point, the media is more adversarial. Once upon a time, there existed the media. And the media folk were few, obedient, and trusting in government. Our understanding of how our government worked was far more rose-tinted. Citizens generally, perhaps naively, assumed government was working as it should. We trusted government more, and it had very few critics in the public sphere. Yes, we had government scandals such as the Profumo affair in the UK and Australia's constitutional crisis of 1975, but critics were troublemakers, the bad guys.

Beginning in the late 1960s, even before the internet's boom, Western media became increasingly independent, critical, and probing. That's not to say that it was a government propaganda mouthpiece until then. In 1915, Viscount Northcliffe, the leading publisher of newspapers in the UK, had no qualms about going after Asquith's government during the Shell Crisis, when British ammunition supplies fell short on the front line, which was "coincidentally" where Northcliffe's nephew died. There was little obedience or trust there.

Even so, the media's critical posture and independence before and after the 1960s were quite different. The *Washington Post* didn't just criticize Nixon's Vietnam policy or the Watergate burglary and cover-up. It, along with a few others, including the *New York Times*, engaged in a gladiatorial contest that practically battled the titular head of the federal government to the death. But this was nothing compared to the disruption to come.

Let's just remind ourselves of the pre-web media and communication landscape of thirty or forty years ago, going back to when the original *Ghostbusters* came out or when the likes of David Gower and Ian Chappell graced the Ashes, the series of cricket matches between England and Australia. I just need to throw in Ian Botham at Headingley, 1981. How did we learn about and relate to our democracies in that era, which some may feel to be long past? My kids, in fact, see it as part of the pre-iPad prehistoric era. My youngest hasn't yet come to terms with how I lived a childhood without any Apple products.

The UK of thirty years ago had four television stations, a few radio stations, and a countable number of newspapers and magazines. In 1982, I remember watching the first televised program on Channel 4, Britain's fourth TV station. This was a big deal, much talked about in the community and beyond since it was the first new television station in the country since 1955. It's interesting that the station's first program, *Countdown*, is still going strong and now has something of a cult following.

In the early '80s, there was still a fairly tight range of perspectives on what was news and what was fact. This was true in the UK, Canada, Australia, New Zealand, and the US—even in the cable era that followed the dominance of the "big three" American television networks. But the days when the vast majority looked to the likes of Walter Cronkite, James Dibble, or Judy Bailey as the voices of reason are long gone.

Popular web usage really only began in the mid-1990s. In 1992, there were only 130 websites. Five years later, there were more than a million, and today, there are over 1.5 billion. There are so many information outlets, we don't know what to believe, which makes it relatively easy to assert the pseudo-truths and lies now known as "fake news" all along the political spectrum. Many government officials, let alone media sources, put out stories knowing full well that they're either distortions or outright falsehoods.

We now live in an era of information chaos, one of the most sinister dimensions of the late-modern era.[2] Our media universe has burst into millions of websites, including online newspapers and magazines, inescapable social media outlets, and thousands of streaming "television stations."This is all omnipresent, thanks to our mobile phones. We can't help but be pummeled by information—fake, real, or somewhere in-between. Most of our species seems to be hunched and staring into their mobile phone screens. We've never been flooded with as much information as we are today, and we're gasping for air.

Incessant, proliferating critiques (both fact-based and fiction-based) of government reach us instantly. We bubble immediate emotional reactions, made without a pause for thought or reflection. If a government project can't account for almost a million dollars, this will no longer be kept secret. Somebody on the inside will leak the news. Before long, somebody else will falsely assert that in fact, ten, not one million dollars was stolen—not temporarily unaccounted for—to fund the migration of the entire Turkish population to the UK. To get attention, nothing does the job like blaming foreign ethnic groups.

Debates in national legislatures are now broadcast, so, on top of everything else, we're constantly reminded that our legislatures don't look particularly representative. In fact, we can also discover that our representatives may not deserve the respect we've been accustomed to giving them. Note, for instance, during Trump's impeachment trial, that we saw senators napping, making paper airplanes, solving crossword puzzles, and reading books. All this in the middle of a trial in Congress's upper, more esteemed chamber to determine whether the US president should be removed from office.[3] I'm not making this up. It was broadcast live on national television.

What's the culmination of these trends? A gradual disillusion-ment, drip by drip, with government. In the US, the proportion of Americans who trusted the federal government fell steeply from between 60 and 70 percent in the 1950s and '60s to below 30 percent since 2006.[4] Some of this is because the stories that come to us through the media, especially social media, are inevi-tably conflict- or tension-based. A sizeable chunk of online news is simply false, and most citizens at some point have accepted some of this fake news as authentic.[5] We give it our attention because bad news is interesting or aligns with our prejudices.

If we were still using the communications technology of the *Ghostbusters* era, we would, I'm convinced, have a very differ-ent perception of current political, social, and economic issues. With less access to detailed and often false information, we'd accept government's perspective far more, be much less aware of what government did or did not do, and find it much more diffi-cult to coalesce and organize into small groups that feed on each other. In Western democracies, today's technology has played a starring role in eroding governmental authority, uncovering government inadequacies, and fanning citizen dissatisfaction.

Our democracy now operates within an environment it wasn't designed for. And this isn't going away. We, unlike Marty McFly's DeLorean, can't go back in time. The ground we live on no longer feels stable. Instead, we seem to be living without gravity, in a far more dynamic system than what we're used to. Greater access to information seems like it is or should be an advance. But access to so much information and disinformation has become confusing and disorienting. That our democracy's processes and systems are broadly what they were a century ago—let alone when a bunch of Columbia University scientists took on New York's ghosts—is not good.

CONFIRMATION BIAS

Today's fragmented media has fundamentally changed the way people see the world and engage with one another. Our tendency to accept only the facts we are biased or predisposed to believe has had real and wide-ranging consequences. Search the internet for "The Mafia Shot JFK" and you'll find more than a million websites. Look further, you'll find evidence demonstrating that almost every country, religious group, or ethnicity—even aliens—is to blame for Kennedy's assassination. Whatever bias you have can be supported by Aunty Google and then calcified.

Some of my fellow Britons believe the UK's social and economic problems are fundamentally due to immigrants who have come in and taken over healthcare and education. It's easy enough to find selective evidence to support this belief. Indeed, it's easy enough to find selective evidence that Elvis Presley is still alive. The truth is that not only do second- and third-generation immigrants feel as British as anyone else, but they're an integral part of the country, to which they greatly contribute. The first three physicians who died from contracting COVID-19 while caring for the sick were Dr. Adil El Tayar, Dr. Habib Zaidi, and Dr. Amged El-Hawrani—hardly the most typical Anglo-Saxon names.[6]

The recent spike in immigration to the UK was driven by migrants from other EU countries, especially Poland, and was after the A8 Eastern European countries joined the EU in 2004. One significant study in 2016 concluded that not only were these immigrants younger, more educated, more likely to be employed, and less likely to claim benefits than British citizens, but they actually paid more in tax than the benefits that they claimed.[7] Did that matter to the anti-immigrant section of British society? Nope.

The study also revealed that immigration had little effect on the employment or compensation levels of other Britons. Most anti-immigrant Britons seem to be completely unaware that the regions most affected by immigration didn't suffer high unemployment or lower wage growth.[8] Aside from the benefits of a pluralistic social culture, the economic benefits of immigration are in fact, considerable. Again, the anti-immigrant posse held to their beliefs.

Likewise, the UK health system depends on immigrants at all levels, from nurses to physicians to administrators. In 2016, 26 percent of physicians in the UK weren't even British.[9] Ten percent were from other EU countries.[10] In 2019, only 56 percent of medical staff in the NHS were categorized as ethnically "white" (I'm not sure that's an ethnicity but still).[11] Thirty percent were Asian, mostly from South Asia. In fact, 31 percent of senior physicians were Asians. The latest national census has Asians constituting less than 7 percent of the national population.

Even if only non-British immigrant employees in the NHS were sent back to India, the Philippines, and the EU countries they came from, the healthcare system wouldn't have the manpower to deliver its services to nonimmigrant Britons, let alone what was needed during the coronavirus outbreak. Years before the epidemic, the British Medical Association, Royal College of Nurses, and Royal College of Midwives all expressed serious concerns about Brexit's impact on medical talent.

Despite this reality, the popular outcry for Brexit grew and coalesced quickly, achieving legitimacy and critical mass. The disinformation campaign around Brexit was both fascinating and appalling. Pro-Brexiters told a lot of lies so quickly and in concert that there was no opportunity for proper examination and analysis, and this disinformation fed into many discontented citizens' prejudices. Hit the audience hard through multiple media with a degenerate lie, pummel it for a good few hours, then concoct another lie and repeat.

The web both allows and encourages people to confirm and reinforce their biases. When you create an echo chamber, that's what happens. A third of those who voted for Brexit ranked immigration as their main reason for doing so.[12] No doubt, some online media sources convinced them of what they wanted to believe, making claims that would never have stood up to sensible scrutiny. The fact that the current prime minister himself was treated for coronavirus in ICU by British-Asian medics was a peddler of this disinformation and is a damning indictment of Britain's political ecosystem.

Citizens had neither the time nor opportunity to reflect and say, "Hold on! Where did you get this information? Is it complete rubbish?" Lies, especially those that appeal powerfully to our deepest emotions, can reign over facts. Indeed, they often do.

ANONYMITY AND ASSOCIATION

Just prior to Trump's election, an article in *Politico* entitled, "Trump Is Pat Buchanan with Better Timing" argued that Buchanan's brand of conservative populism, which Trump's mirrors in many ways, would have had much more of an effect during his presidential bid in 1992 if he, like Trump, had been able to amplify it through social media.[13] There's something to that argument. We've always had disturbing politicians and we've always had citizens with a penchant for unpleasant positions. I say that without needing to be blasted as a Hillary fan because I'm not.

Technology both enables confirmation bias and quickly brings people together in ways that can fuel what's harsh and nasty. In the past, if you wanted to start or join a political or social movement, you had to do so in person and in real time. To join up, you usually had to travel somewhere, walk into a room, register, and pay a membership fee. And you did so in public, with others witnessing your actions, even if they only saw you enter or exit the building. Under the circumstances, keeping such associations secret or anonymous was basically impossible.

This was particularly inconvenient for people whose beliefs might be considered alarming or unacceptable. Your actions would declare your beliefs or identity and, to some extent, determine how your neighbors, colleagues, and other members of society engaged with you. You might think twice about walking into a transgender or polygamist club. In our liberal democracies, identified homosexuals were incarcerated and are still, to this day, murdered for their sexual preference.

It was challenging to connect such individuals into groups, however marginal, and those groups to politicians, but that's changed. Online communication simultaneously brings people together and tears them apart in ways we've never had to deal with before. Using only two mouse clicks to unfriend someone on Facebook can have significant consequences in the real world. Social media enables like-minded individuals both to unite and fragment unnervingly fast.

Echo chambers are not unique to the internet era. What's different today is that social media has enabled a far wider range of groups—from "Arsenal Supporters in Canada" to "Readers of Serious Nonfiction"—to coalesce. Lunatic fringes that once would have struggled to crawl out of their caves can unite in minutes, taking comfort from their comrades' support. The online echo chamber has empowered those who were once on society's margins. They feed off and confirm each other's perspectives instantly.

That is not entirely bad since being outside society's norms was quite isolating until recently. The pressure to conform is not an innately good thing—just ask anybody who was homosexual a couple of decades or more ago. Today, people can more easily connect with others who share their interests and worldviews, however much outside the mainstream they may be. The individual within each of us has been immensely legitimized. But, on the darker side, this allows people with nasty and violent agendas to unite, quite often at the expense of those least able to defend themselves.

Things have indeed changed. In many cases, you'd find not only that you weren't alone, but that, although still a minority, there were a fairly substantial number of other people—perhaps one to ten million in a world of almost eight billion—who also believe what you believe, no matter how taboo or "politically incorrect." Not only are you no longer isolated, but critical mass can be developed to the point where your movement and others like it gain their own kind of legitimacy, as happened with Nazism in the 1930s.

To use a relevant worst-case scenario, it's very possible to go online, sign up for, and participate in a neo-Nazi group. All in the anonymity of your living room, possibly in London's Golden Green, a neighborhood with a large Jewish population. Or you might join the Jewish Defense League, a fiercely Islamophobic organization, while living in Mississauga, Ontario, which has a large Muslim population. You can then articulate and develop beliefs that your online "friends" will be all too willing to reinforce. You can help fund the group anonymously and stay behind the scenes until the movement gets big enough to come out from hiding.

The next step is cross-fertilization between your movement and the public at large. Now that you're part of a larger group and armed with more disinformation, you're emboldened to chat about your xenophobic views. Perhaps with a seventeen-year-old who has never heard of Auschwitz and can't locate Indonesia or Pakistan, the fourth and fifth most populated countries in the world, on a map. It doesn't take long before the teenager, catalyzed by misinformation, begins his own journey to the Dark Side of the Force.

Online connection and then physical association can so easily lead to action. The 2017 racist "Unite the Right" rally in Charlottesville, Virginia, is an example of many such gatherings in recent years, especially in the US. A white supremacist drove into a crowd of counterprotesters, killing one of them. Trump then made the event infamous, shocking many by saying there were "very fine people on both sides."[14]

Anti-immigrant, racist perspectives that would never have gained social currency a couple of decades ago—because they were both politically incorrect and fundamentally wrong—are now able to gain traction. They've become normalized enough to enable white supremacists to self-identify as such in many American neighborhoods, despite the movement's associations with mass, race-based murder. According to 57 percent of Americans, this stance has become more respectable due to the current incumbent in the White House.[15] I don't know if the coronavirus epidemic has changed perspectives given that 28 percent of physicians and 25 percent of healthcare support staff are foreign-born, in contrast to 17 percent of the population.[16]

But the real problem for Western government isn't really lunatic fringes, though that's certainly a concern that deserves more attention than it gets. The more existential question revolves around the loss of confidence in the democracy that we have and the citizen body's ability to unite to change this. Australian owners of gas-guzzlers can amalgamate in huge numbers just as easily as down-under climate change activists can. They develop their perspectives and then act, with emails, phone calls, protests, boycotts, and much more at an unprecedented scale and speed.

SQUEEZING OUR EXPERIENCE OF TIME

If I wanted to join a fan club for the late Nusrat Fateh Ali Khan, one of the great mystical musicians of recent times, I would have been hard-pressed to find one thirty years ago. I would probably have had to first find a specialist magazine in a niche record store that covered his genre of music. I might also have attended one of his concerts to find a contact. Both approaches would have involved at least a few hours of effort, and my work might have gotten me nowhere. I risked simply wasting a fair chunk of time.

Now, I can do a web search and find any number of such clubs, including several in Canada alone, in five minutes, about the time it takes me to make a cup of tea. I can do this without spending a cent on transportation, slouched on my sofa, dressed in my pajamas, eating a Rich Tea biscuit. (And biscuit is what it is—not "cookie.") Communities that previously could never have gotten together, because it took too much time, can now do so easily, without incurring meaningful costs.

We can also communicate just as instantly. In one study of American white nationalist Twitter accounts, researchers found that for the twelve months beginning May 2017, each account tweeted on average eleven messages per day. Each follower received the messages in real time.[17] No postal delay, no waiting. A comment on an event in Paris could be sent and received anywhere in the US in a flash.

In the early nineteenth century, the fastest communication between New York and Liverpool took twenty-one days.[18] If you had a message to relay across the Atlantic, at best it would take three weeks to get there, assuming you were at the New York docks and your recipient was at Liverpool's docks. It was no doubt going to cost much more than a free email, which, in contrast, is almost guaranteed to get to its destination. Even if the early nineteenth-century message did get through, it could have become outdated by the time the recipient read it.

As an aside, I'd just like to acknowledge that pigeon carrier postal service was officially used in some parts of the world up into this century, that's right, century number twenty-one. Although a faster communications medium than a ship, carrier pigeons cannot fly across the Atlantic, which is why it's not particularly useful to use them in our earlier New York to Liverpool example. Just a useful bit of trivia to share.

In June 2014, Donald Trump had 2.6 million Twitter followers to whom he could instantly tweet his comments. By May 2020, that was 80 million—still 37 million less than his predecessor's following.[19] Trump immediately reaches a community equivalent to almost a quarter of the American population several times a day, without any third-party media intervention. Thus, between March 11, 2019 and September 11, 2019, the White

House didn't give a single daily press briefing. It held only one briefing in all of 2019, in contrast to the typical two to three hundred briefings per year in the previous two decades.[20] That though, changed briefly in 2020 to help stem the debacle of the *management* of COVID-19.

It's as if we and our social and political environment have transitioned from a solid to a gas without passing through the liquid stage. Particles in solids have a limited ability to move and change, while gas particles have far fewer restrictions. Like the political landscape of which we're increasingly a part, they can head off in any direction instantaneously. Our democracy evolved on land, but information technology seems to have made much of that gravity irrelevant. The era we're living in is fundamentally unprecedented.

We have less time to mull things over and think critically. In fact, we have almost no time before the next bit of information demands our attention. We have to consider our next position, assuming we can do so at all, before the agenda again moves on. We're then hit with another instantaneous communication, miraculously and addictively tuned to our interests, which we don't dare ignore if we suffer from fear of missing out and don't want to fall behind.

In 2015, the average US office worker received 121 work-related emails per day.[21] They also got personal emails, social media messages, news media pop-ups, and notices about blogs to read. This is true not just in the US. A planet of less than eight billion people is sending out 294 billion emails per day.[22] That's an average of thirty-seven emails per day, per person. And let's remind ourselves that many living in poverty or in premodern or traditional societies still don't have internet access, and many others are illiterate or simply too young for email.

For those living in the internet age, where's the space to think and assess? By the time you've even begun, you're into the next day—and another 121 emails from work, as well as all the rest. The coronavirus lockdown temporarily changed our relationship with time—many of us found, even if for a few weeks, that we had a lot more time than we're accustomed to. But we still live in the uncharted territory of the immediate sound bite, where we're nearly always connected, and last month's news is history. Instant reactions and reflexes are increasingly the norm. Technology has changed human behavior, and the journey is far from over. Yet, despite the scale of the change, the processes of Western democracy remain fundamentally stuck in the nineteenth century, if not earlier.

GOVERNMENT AND TECHNOLOGY: THE FLIP SIDE

The government lags far behind the private sector in its use of technology, with the obvious exception of national security and defense. Although the internet was originally developed back in the 1960s by DARPA, the US military's research arm, public-sector use of technology in general and communications technology in particular is notably behind the curve. Government's record in pioneering the use of technology to engage with ordinary citizens is virtually nonexistent. Instead, it relies on the entrepreneurial dynamism of the private sector and typically follows only many years later.

Technology allows us to shine a light on government failures, enabling us to react to specific waste, representation, and accountability problems and express our general frustration, saying, "Look, we're done with this system." But neither government nor we citizens have used it to meaningfully improve our relationship with one another. Technology hasn't energized or mended our social contract. Quite the opposite. It may have made things a whole lot worse.

There's nothing inevitable about this, however. We're rightly concerned about technological surveillance and invasion of privacy. Many of the same underlying technologies could also be used to make government officials more accountable. Certainly, what's currently being done is far from enough. We can significantly improve the quality of government. We've focused on some of the challenges that technology now poses to our Western democracies. In the chapters to come, we'll focus on solutions to the challenges brought about by current and developing technology.

Just for a moment, imagine, for example, how much we would learn if we used our techno-wizardry to develop and distribute a tool that gives citizens the opportunity to directly express their fiscal spending priorities to government officials. Such a tool might also be able to generate graphical predictions of the effect such allocations might have in the real world. This would be a real eye-opener to the millions of Western citizens, who would now learn that their governments don't spend even one percent of their budgets on supporting the world's most impoverished people. Or that much of that aid supports oppressive dictatorships and their military spending.

In that spirit, we'll first more closely examine the problems now gnawing away at the foundations of the democratic social contact—government waste, lack of representation, and lack of accountability. Then, one by one, we'll look at the levers and fulcrum points—possible tactical and targeted solutions—which can improve our social contract.

PART II

WASTE

CHAPTER 5

WASTE NOT, WANT NOT

In 2011, the New Zealand customs department began linking their IT systems with those of the Ministry for Primary Industries.[1] The NZ$75 million project was due to be completed in 2012. The project was completed in 2017 at a cost of NZ$104 million, an additional NZ$29 million. That's the equivalent of having every New Zealander, not just those earning an income with a roof above their head but every single person, pay an extra NZ$6.60 in taxes to get something that was delivered five years late.

Nobody compensated the taxpayer—not even the multibillion-dollar giant IBM, which did the work. The government minister didn't pay a dime. No dimes were extracted from the civil servants involved. Nor was there any compensation or tax refund for the five-year delay. No government official got their head handed to them on a plate. Heck, that's a bit extreme—firing someone for gross incompetence. Every New Zealander paid more than they should have for something delivered five years late.

So few of us believe that government doesn't waste our taxes, that we have become inured to what is, when all is said and done, a fundamental and often shocking violation of the social contract. If a comparable violation were taking place with a contract in the private sector, we would have long walked away from our vendor and perhaps sued it for wasting our money.

Economists define efficiency as the optimal use of resources and production capacity. Accountants define it as using minimum input to generate maximum output. Neither of these technical approaches, however, really touches what we're getting at here. Ordinary people don't use an economic or accounting lens to make sense of government. Maybe it's not even "efficiency" of government. Something much deeper is going on.

Wanting our government to be good with our money, we're thinking about something far more elemental and meaningful than economic resources or balance sheets. Something ticks us off that a financial statement doesn't really get at or an economist can't get all worked up about. We're really thinking about waste. We don't want government to waste our money.

In Canada, all three tiers of government—local, provincial, and federal—charge tax. Businesses pay corporate tax on profits they make, as well as taxes just for making products to sell. The average newly built detached home in Toronto carries with it C$222,652 in taxes and fees, most of which the developer pays.[2] And which is then passed on to the home buyer. This informs Toronto's housing affordability problem. In 2018, median home prices in Buffalo, Cincinnati, and Augusta were all less than the taxes alone Toronto charged to build a new house.

Employees pay taxes on their wages, and nearly all adults, retired or not, pay taxes on any other income. Everybody, including children, the sick, the elderly, and the destitute, pays sales tax on practically every good or service they purchase. We pay taxes for bringing items into the country. We pay vehicle taxes to drive our cars. We pay property taxes for living in our homes. Even the homeless pay taxes on the hot coffee that warms them in tough winters. This isn't just about Canada since practically the same holds true in all Western democracies.

What would you do if somebody took $1,000 of yours and just burned it or fed it to the cat? (Of course, if you fed it to the cat, you'd have local animal services and the police to deal with, assuming the cat actually ate the currency which ordinary cats don't do. But you get the point.) In the UK, stealing that sum is a criminal offense with a sentence of as long as two years. Okay, let's just say Apple or McDonald's charged you for absolutely nothing. You get nothing back. Now or later. It's inconceivable that you'd sit content the way we so often do in the face of government waste.

Just like courts that have tried the same type of defendant too many times, taxpaying citizens have become "case-hardened." We're so accustomed to government waste that we rarely notice it anymore, much less try to do anything about it. What would make us sit up and really notice would be a government project coming in under budget and delivered before deadline. We'd all be a bit curious about what just happened.

Governments waste our taxes far too often, irresponsibly, and without meaningful consequences. A million dollars or pounds wasted simply doesn't ensure somebody's job is on the line. Even hundreds of millions wasted doesn't take us to that door. It's true that a project on budget and on time can still be useless and a complete waste. That's a Pandora's box we won't open too wide, even if I do want to briefly illustrate what I mean.

In 2013, the US Government Accountability Office (GAO) found that tens of billions of dollars were being spent on duplicate federal government programs.[3] Sometimes, eleven agencies were doing the same public policy job without coordination—an example being dealing with autism.[4] More recently, two federal agencies with different workstreams were trying to keep arsenic out of the rice-supply system, and six separate providers were in chaotic fashion being used for the Defense Department's human resources work.[5]

There are more than four hundred US federal departments, agencies, and subagencies. Each has multiple functions which overlap other federal organizations, including human resources, information technology, and finance and accounting. And they're not competing with each other. That's potentially an awful lot of waste in procurement, duplication of work, and lack of alignment. We shouldn't be surprised that Americans feel their government wastes more of the country's taxes than it uses responsibly.[6]

Across the Atlantic, one study estimated that public-sector waste in 2009 alone cost British taxpayers £58.4 billion, the equivalent of 42 percent of the country's income tax.[7] That works out to just under £1,000 per citizen, including children and those unemployed and retired. Even if the waste was half that number, it would be extraordinary. I'd think that taxpayers are entitled to do more than raise an eyebrow about this.

The story's the same everywhere. In 2015, one consulting firm estimated that the Australian government could save A$2.5 billion through just a handful of better procurement policies.[8] An independent think tank estimated that the New Zealand government wastes an extraordinary one-third of the country's taxes.[9] Another study suggested that the Canadian government wastes a quarter of its spending.[10]

Yes, there's a truckload of waste. I want to target two manifestations of that truckload—project delays and cost overruns—because they're easier to crystalize. We can count the direct cash cost of a project against its budget. We can also count how many days late it is delivered. Let's look at some specific illustrations and case studies of government waste which, while far from reaching the impossible goal of being completely inclusive, might help dispel our apathy and give to us a sense of the problem's scale.

CASE STUDY: ONTARIO POWER PLANTS

In May 2005, Ontario's Liberal provincial government signed an agreement with Eastern Power to build two 280-megawatt natural gas-fired power plants in Mississauga, a Toronto suburb.[11] One of the plants was soon canceled because Eastern Power couldn't arrange financing—no surprise given that each plant was significantly bigger than anything Eastern had previously proposed or built. Let's not even go into how they won the contract in the first place—suffice to say that I'm not remotely surprised that this came about.

In any event, local opposition to the remaining second power plant from both residents and elected representatives soon picked up—opposition based on supposed health and safety issues. Even Erin Brockovich, the activist portrayed by Julia Roberts in the film biography of the same name, pitched in from the US. It would have been quite something if Ms. Roberts herself had joined in, arm-in-arm, shouting among the protestors, but she was conspicuous by her absence.

In September 2011, during the provincial election campaign, the government, wanting to remain in power, relented and announced that the remaining Mississauga plant would not proceed as planned, but would be relocated more than 200 kilometers away. Ms. Brockovich could put a feather in her cap. (Ms. Roberts couldn't.) As it happens, the Liberal Party then won eight of the nine provincial seats in Mississauga and nearby Brampton and Oakville, while garnering fifty-three of 107 provincial seats.

Despite the cancellation, construction on the plant, now one-third complete, continued apace as late as December 2011, two months after the election. The mechanics of government were so poor, and the importance attached to saving tax money so small that large checks were still being written for the construction of a canceled project.

The agreement to relocate the plant was signed in July 2012. The government said the cancellation cost was C$180 million. The province's auditor general later disagreed, saying the cost was, in fact, C$275 million. A cost of C$180 million, let alone C$275 million, is not insignificant for a population of thirteen million people, especially given that less than two-thirds of that population earns a salary. In fact, it's an incredible waste of tax money, causing hundreds of thousands of Ontarians extra work for absolutely no good reason.

Meanwhile, in October 2009, the same provincial government signed a different but parallel contract with TransCanada Energy to build a 900-megawatt natural gas-fired power plant in Oakville, another Toronto suburb. As in Mississauga, residents protested. I'm sure you're beginning to feel a sense of déjà vu here, albeit minus Erin Brockovich.

In October 2011, two years later and just before the election, the government announced that the Oakville plant would also not proceed at the proposed location but would be relocated more than 200 kilometers away in the other direction. Could even Monty Python have written a more surreal script?

The government agreed to compensate TransCanada Energy for its losses. But, as in Mississauga, many argued that the contract did not require the government to use taxpayer money to compensate TransCanada because that vendor had failed to meet major contractual obligations. But it didn't occur to the custodians of our taxes that they should do their utmost to avoid squandering our money.

The provincial premier's office insisted the cost of this cancellation was only C$40 million—as if such a huge sum was irrelevant—despite privately knowing that TransCanada had rejected compensation offers as high as C$712 million. The province's auditor general again later chimed in, calculating that the cancellation's cost was between C$675 and C$815 million, and rebuked the government for failing to exercise the option to cancel the contract without penalties, given TransCanada's alleged breach of contract.

Every person in Ontario—working or not, sick or able, child, elderly, or homeless—had to pay for this Oakville misadventure to the tune of an average C$53 per person. They had no choice. The tax was obligatory and had to be paid on time. If you didn't comply, you could have your possessions taken from you. The government could kick you out of your home, which would then be sold to collect the taxes. If you didn't have a home, the tax was already collected on your coffee. But who wants to pay C$53 for a government debacle?

In September 2012, with elected representatives from the opposition, the media, and a tiny minority of ordinary citizens all demanding answers, the government, finally acceding to pressure, released *all* thirty-six thousand relevant documents. As if this Monty Python sketch needed another twist, a month later, the government then released *another* twenty thousand equally relevant documents beyond the "full" set of documents released earlier.

Premier Dalton McGuinty resigned the next day, but not for failing to do some basic arithmetic. In 2013, the province's privacy commissioner ruled that McGuinty's office had broken the law by deleting emails relating to the plants' cancelation. Even now, we don't entirely know why the government wrote out fat compensation checks when it didn't need to. I won't comment on that. Not one bit.

McGuinty was replaced by a cabinet minister who had served him for six years, Kathleen Wynne, who, after winning the 2014 election, in 2018 led the Liberals to the worst defeat of any governing party in Ontario's history. And as a reminder, neither was elected premier by the citizen body. McGuinty was elected by Liberal members of the provincial Parliament, and Wynne by delegates at the party's January 2013 convention.

The commissioner's ruling precipitated a criminal investigation. In 2015, McGuinty's chief of staff and deputy chief of staff were charged with breach of trust, concealing data, and misuse of a government computer system. The commissioner added that Wynne's staff had also "misled the public" about their ability to recover the deleted emails. McGuinty's chief of staff eventually received a four-month custodial sentence, not because of the extra cost taxpayers shouldered, but for his criminal activities.

There was obviously an attempt in Canada's most populous province to cover up the decision-making and financial mismanagement underlying the relocation, at great taxpayer expense, of two power plants. But this wasn't just a cover-up. The government repeatedly lied about the costs of its decisions, with the subsequent deletion of records being yet another attempt to hide its fiscal malfeasance.

The people of Ontario have no prospect of getting almost a billion of their dollars back. Neither McGuinty nor any of the senior civil servants involved will compensate them in the way that the private sector might be forced to. Very few taxpayers would have objected if those dollars had instead been used to support the more than half-million children in Ontario who live in poverty. The wasted funds could have provided almost C$2,000 for each of these children, helping them and their families enormously. Instead, nobody was held accountable for the waste.

CASE STUDY: US DEFENSE SPENDING

We pay our taxes in part so that our government will defend us. However, I can't be the first or only taxpayer who thinks there was something seriously wrong when Canada, a country that has only a marginally greater chance, even in the Trump era, of being invaded than of relocating to the moon, spent C$22 billion on its Department of National Defence in 2019–20.[12] C$423 million per week is a lot to protect borders nobody intends to attack. Especially when the same government also told us that nearly one in eleven Canadian children were living in poverty.[13]

Of course, Canada's defense budget pales in comparison to the US's—by far the largest in the world—and the nonchalance with which that budget is deployed is an eye-opener. Let's take a couple of "small" examples to help illustrate why one US federal government audit agency breathtakingly concluded that, "In DoD [Department of Defense], there can be few consequences if funds are not used efficiently."[14] That is something no taxpayer should ever have to read.

In 2008 and 2009, the US Navy placed orders with Northrop Grumman Shipbuilding for the USS *Gerald R. Ford* and the USS *John F. Kennedy*, two nuclear-powered aircraft carriers. The *Ford*, the world's most expensive warship when it was ordered, was scheduled for delivery in 2015 at a cost of US$10.5 billion, while the *Kennedy* was scheduled for delivery in 2019 at US$9.0 billion.[15] It's easy to guess what happened to the delivery dates and costs. The only hint you need is that these were public-sector projects.

Delivery of the *Ford* is now running six years late, with the ship costing US$2.6 billion more than budgeted.[16] The *Kennedy* is currently running five years late and will cost at least an additional US$2.1 billion, for a US$11.3 billion total.[17] The late Senator John McCain, chairman of the Senate Armed Services Committee at the time and somebody who understands a thing or two about the US Navy, described the multiple delays and cost overruns as "entirely avoidable."[18]

The point is that American taxpayers are being asked to pay an extra US$4.7 billion for these two ships, when in fact they shouldn't have been asked to pay a single extra dollar. In fact, that's many "extra dollars," because the actual forecast cost—which will rise again no doubt—is at US$24.5 billion. If the public sector had properly managed the projects, taxpayers would have kept a lot of money or at least seen it spent on other, more deserving projects.

A third nuclear-powered aircraft carrier, the USS *Enterprise*, is being planned for 2025 or later. It's inevitable that it too will come in late and over budget at a time when, as it happens, many defense experts are questioning the need for or efficacy of aircraft carriers in the current era of drones, information warfare, and small-scale, dynamic conflicts. I think we can admit that if the *Enterprise* came in on time and on budget, we'd all have to question if we'd heard or read the news correctly.

Who exactly is paying for this US$4.7 billion in extra costs? The American taxpayer. Every single person in the US. The homeless included. Since paying an extra US$4.7 billion is a financial catastrophe, who in government is having their head handed to them on a plate? Who owes us the overage? Nobody. It's even more telling that CNN didn't issue an urgent news alert, nor was the press camped outside the Secretary of Defense's home. These sorts of things are so common that they barely make the news.

Wasteful defense spending isn't just about big-ticket items. In Afghanistan, for instance, the Defense Department spent US$28 million more than it had to on camouflage uniforms for the Afghan National Army, because a single Afghan official liked the proprietary design pattern.[19] The decision came down to personal taste. It certainly wasn't made because the camouflage design, a lush forest pattern, was appropriate. It made Afghan soldiers highly conspicuous, given that Afghanistan is almost entirely mountains and deserts with virtually no forests.

Even mundane spending, which allows for more planning and is less rushed than in a war zone, carries significant waste. A 2015 Pentagon report stated that the defense department was wasting US$125 billion on bureaucracy.[20] Every year. This isn't a one-off. That's about US$389 per citizen being wasted by just one department. Every single year. To avoid Congress reducing defense spending, the report was buried until the *Washington Post* dug it up.

How is it that so much is being wasted on bureaucracy? More than a million people are employed in the Pentagon's administration alone, just 30 percent fewer than the total number of troops on active duty. Worldwide, McDonald's employs less than a quarter of what the US military bureaucracy alone does. We may as well relabel the institution the Department of Defense and Bureaucracy.

CASE STUDIES: TRANSIT IN TORONTO

Toronto is the fourth-largest city in North America and covers more land area than London. However, it today has fewer metro stops than the London Underground had in 1939, and the municipal and provincial governments are unable to do much if anything about the transportation problem in the country's most important city. I was tempted to say that governments *seem* unable to do much, but upon reflection, I realized that they *are* unable is a far more accurate description.

In 2018, the average one-way commute time in Toronto was forty-two minutes, up from twenty-nine minutes in 2013.[21] The average Toronto commuter spends eighty-four minutes per day getting to and from work. Those who use public transit typically spend 104 minutes per day commuting. Compare this to London's commute time, which is seventy-four minutes per day.[22] One study suggested that Toronto had the longest commute times of any major city in the world, with the exception of Bogota.[23] Toronto's citizens have a major transportation problem.

That problem has multiple consequences. Lengthy commute time involves fuel costs, car wear and tear, and having to work more to pay taxes for those costs, which involve more taxes. Carbon emissions also do phenomenal damage to the environment. Then there's sheer frustration. One study demonstrated that a twenty-minute increase in commute times was the equivalent of a 19 percent drop in job satisfaction.[24] We've been there earlier in my hypothetical example of the delayed road project.

Why has practically nothing been done? In Toronto, a study is initiated, and then, either before the results can be submitted or an irrevocable commitment is made to its recommendations, the local government changes. Any decisions one municipal government mandates are quickly rescinded when the new legislature takes over. That new government then busies itself making other plans that are equally unlikely to be followed through, possibly because another tier of government, provincial or federal, is going through its own roller coaster. That's part of the problem. There's also simple ineptitude cultivated by a lack of accountability and a poor performance culture.

Let's focus on some of the key players and specifics. In the last twenty years, the Toronto Transit Commission (TTC), which operates Toronto's subway, buses, and streetcars, has initiated one study and consulting assignment after another, practically all of which have been a waste of time and money, although transportation consultants might beg to differ. If the purpose was to reward consultants, many of whom once worked in government, then mission accomplished!

The few public-sector projects that do get through are late and wildly over budget. You order your food at a restaurant. It comes to the table after many hours. And you pay more for it than is advertised on the menu. The restaurant slips in a 30 percent bump as "Miscellaneous Costs." Are we good with that? Do we extend our credit card to make the payment? Or do we raise a storm first about the delay and then the stupid price? Does this analogy help you understand the basic problem? It's true of practically every single major TTC project.

The TTC's Automatic Train Control project for Line One began in 2008 and was meant to be completed in 2019. The forecast for completion has been changed to 2022 and is C$98 million over budget.[25] That means the project's benefits have been delayed by three years. Between now and 2022, the cost overrun will certainly increase further. That's already been established, even if we don't yet know how far above the nine-figure mark it will be.

Then, there was the Toronto-York Spadina five-mile extension of Line One, which was C$550 million over budget, coming in at C$3.2 billion.[26] For a city with a population of 6.2 million, an extra C$89 per person (not per earner) for a project is tough. The project, approved back in 2004, was completed in 2017—two years late.[27] Pay more for something that comes late? This public-sector model would never work in the private sector. A restaurant that did this would shut down within a week.

There's also Metrolinx, which operates most of Ontario's public transportation, aside from what the TTC runs. Metrolinx incurred C$438 million in unrecoverable costs from 2009 to 2018 because of changes in transit planning and the way the agency operates.[28] That's almost a million dollars per week for a decade. Its Sheppard Light Rail project is now a decade behind its initial completion date of 2013 and C$125 million over budget. Its Presto charge-card system cost more than C$700 million, making it the most expensive public transport charge card in the world.[29] The initial budget was C$255 million.[30]

We also dare not forget the Union Pearson Express linking downtown Toronto to its airport. Its contract was first awarded in 2003, but the link was only completed in 2015 at C$456 million. That was almost four times the budget that was revised and increased in 2012.[31] Not four times the original budget—four times the *revised and increased* budget.

Go to a restaurant and order a $10 hamburger. When the hamburger arrives extremely late, you're charged $40. Would you be tempted to shout at the manager? Why then aren't we outraged when government is just as inept? We're now, with just a few examples, close to a couple of billion dollars of audited waste, not including the costs society shoulders for transportation project delays. And let's remember that the province of Ontario has only thirteen million people to it—far fewer than Sri Lanka, Malawi, and Niger.

And we have the Ontario Ministry of Transport, which is responsible for the province's roads. Ontario's auditor general noted in 2016 that not only were taxpayers paying an extra C$23 million for repairs on new roads, which had been guaranteed for fifteen years, but that policies in the ministry had been changed to benefit the Ontario Road Builders' Association at the expense of both taxpayers and the ministry itself.[32] What's more, the contractors who had delivered work proven to be shoddy were nevertheless being offered substantial new projects. That's a nice arrangement. Deliver rubbish and get offered a new contract.

Almost nothing has been achieved in twenty years of Toronto

transport, despite the massive growth in both Greater Toronto's population and size during that time. Key organizational stakeholders have burned through extensive resources and achieved worse than very little. Lodge a complaint or even an inquiry, and the consistent response is: "We'll get back to you. The issue is being researched and investigated."

In April 2013, the City of Toronto government estimated that its cost overruns on just the Toronto transit projects still in the planning or early construction phases had reached C$224 million and rising.[33] Josh Matlow, a Toronto councilor, didn't hesitate to use the words "fiasco" and "scandalous" to describe the situation. It appears he didn't think that the structure of the government of which he's a part may be the underlying cause of this waste. He's now been in office for almost a decade, and things have only gotten worse. Josh Matlow is now part of the fiasco.

The federal government is also embroiled in wasting transportation funds. In 2017, it set up the Canada Infrastructure Bank to support infrastructure projects through partnerships with the private sector. At an operational cost of C$1m per week, the C$35 billion fund made just two significant investments in its first three years.[34] It has *pledged* C$3.3 billion to Toronto's and Montreal's transit systems, and another C$375 million in smaller investments. This is far below what it set out to do—C$3.2 billion of financing *per year*. In its first three years, it should have distributed C$9.6 billion to meet Canada's infrastructure deficit, which experts estimate is between C$110 billion and C$270 billion and rising.[35]

Of course, public transit and transportation cost overruns are by no means limited to Toronto. Shifting to the US and just outside Washington, DC, a bus stop, hardly the Taj Mahal, cost a million dollars to build.[36] The Seattle Sound Transit light-rail line saw its costs jump from US$1.7 billion to US$2.6 billion.[37] California's High-Speed Rail, that state's bullet train, has been delayed in an ironic twist of fate, and its costs have increased from US$33 billion to US$80 billion.[38] In fact, the most common theme of every American metro project between 2010 to 2019 has been cost overruns, with delays running a close second.[39]

More recently, across the Atlantic, a 58-kilometer (36-mile) bypass in Aberdeen, Scotland was set to open in February 2019, ten years later than promised, at a cost of £1 billion rather than £745 million.[40] Why the delay, and who is going to pay the extra £255 million? In 2020, Britain's High Speed 2 (HS2) rail line has seen its forecast costs rise to between £70 billion to £85 billion.[41] The original cost, forecast in 2017, was £24 billion.[42] In three years, its costs have tripled. And no stakeholder's remuneration has been adversely affected—except that taxpayers continue to pay more tax than they should have.

Such instances could be cited *ad infinitum* and *ad nauseam*, which is why we as taxpayers simply shrug our shoulders over each incident, put on the kettle, and switch the TV station from cricket to rugby. Or basketball to baseball. With or without Rich Tea biscuits. It's the system; it's the way things are, we are repeatedly told.

Sheer scope makes the problem more significant. In the public sector, projects can run up to billions of dollars or pounds. Therefore, even a small percentage of inefficiency and waste can still add up to huge amounts of money. That's no justification for government's failure to hire the requisite talent and craft the right culture, systems, and processes to ensure that we actually spend the £745 million originally budgeted, instead of spending £1 billion. Nor is there any justification for roads to be completed a decade later than originally scheduled.

CASE STUDIES: IT AND COMMUNICATIONS

Communications technology is another focal point of Western democratic government waste. I'll only touch upon a select few examples. In 2016, the US Internal Revenue Service (IRS) spent US$12 million on a new cloud-based email system that it soon found was unusable.[43] That's a helpful bit of spending. Cheap change, you might think? Well, how about the Pentagon and Veteran Affairs Department's joint venture to build an integrated health record system, which disbursed US$1.1 billion before the entire project was canceled?[44] That's right, funds went from taxpayers to government, and US$1.1 billion of those funds were then spent on a project which was canceled.

In Australia, the Victoria government initiated a A$25 million Infringement Management System project, which, six years after its supposed completion date, was canceled because the guardians of Victoria's tax spending realized the project vendor couldn't actually complete it.[45] The loss to Victoria's six million residents? A$60 million had already been spent on a project budgeted at A$25 million. You do have to wonder what is going on.

Similarly, in 2018, in New Zealand, a major government IT project was nearly NZ$30 million over budget and three years behind schedule.[46] The project, which was meant to merge the computer systems of New Zealand Customs and its Ministry for Primary Industries, had increased in cost from NZ$75.9

million to NZ$104.1 million. Projected benefits from the project will now take fifteen years to realize, as opposed to the forecast ten years—meaning that the completed project's economic value is significantly less than originally intended.[47]

In the UK, the government's Emergency Services Network project, begun in 2015, was supposed to be completed by 2019 at a cost of £6.2 billion. Its current completion forecast is 2022, and its projected cost has already increased by more than 50 percent to £9.4 billion. I predict that costs will almost certainly exceed even that latest revision.[48] This isn't cynicism. I haven't even read through the detailed scope of works and procurement plan. We know that almost every large public-sector project will be late and over budget. At the same time, we know that this is very wrong.

GOVERNMENT MONOPOLY AND ACCOUNTABILITY

I could multiply the instances of government waste indefinitely, but the point has no doubt been made. The bigger question is why waste in our democratic governments is pandemic. Such waste is closely tied to lack of accountability, so the two feed off each other. The intra-governmental accountability that exists is fundamentally meaningless because government isn't substantively accountable to its citizens.

Government takes money at multiple points from the poor, rich, aged, and young, on time, every time, and sometimes with devastating consequences to both businesses and individuals. I've said it before, and I don't mind saying it again: government has a greater responsibility and moral duty than the private sector to make sure that money is used properly and effectively. That fiscal responsibility is not emphasized nor taken seriously enough, as the earlier examples show.

First, note the conclusion of an infrastructure expert who extensively studied government infrastructure projects: "I am absolutely convinced that the cost overruns and patronage overestimates were not the result of technical errors, honest mistakes or inadequate methods. In case after case, planners, engineers, and economists have told me that they had to "revise" their forecasts many times because they failed to satisfy their superiors. The forecasts had to be "cooked" in order to produce numbers that were dramatic enough to gain federal support for projects whether or not they could be fully justified on technical grounds."[49]

The superiors to whom he referred are not accountable to citizens. No government department in Western liberal democracies is directly accountable to its citizens. Government, especially the unelected majority of civil servants, may as well be working from Saturn. Or Jupiter. Although the public pays taxes, government superiors are insufficiently motivated to deliver value for money. Who is checking on government on behalf of the citizen body, a bit like boards of directors do for shareholders of large private-sector companies?

There's a second essential factor. Government is a monopoly and behaves like one. A monopoly is defined as a single supplier to a market, and government is the sole or practically only supplier of a great many services to its country's citizens. The public sector makes a significant effort to prevent and disband monopolies in the private sector but says little about the elephant in the room—the public sector. It does feel hypocritical. In fact, when it comes to the services that the public sector offers, the elephant is usually the only one in the room.

With rare exceptions, government is responsible for many

goods and services that are off-limits to the private sector. Government manages the development of roads, bridges, and similar infrastructure. You can only get a driver's license from the government. You can only make a criminal complaint to the police, a government agency. You can only get a license to construct from the municipal planning department. We can't go anywhere else except this all-pervasive leviathan.

In Ontario, a government-appointed monopoly supplies electricity to homes. The regulations are such that there is only one supplier people can turn to, whether you like it or not. Whether the services are expensive or cheap, effective or ineffective, or the people you deal with are polite or rude, you must get your power from the public agency. And if you don't like what they offer, your home has no electricity. You can burn candles, send smoke signals, and watch the black of your TV screen.

In the UK, Australia, and New Zealand, you can go to the public or private healthcare sectors for medical treatment, but the public sector is far larger and, for much of the population, the only affordable option. For emergency services, you really have only one choice—the public healthcare system. In Canada, for all practical purposes, you must go to the government for most of your healthcare needs. Which is part of the reason why almost every hospital appointment is late "because of the overnight emergencies."

Most government services are provided to consumers by organizations or agencies that have no competition. Imagine you're an athlete who runs 100-meter track races. But there's nobody racing with you, so, at every race you run, you win, and get a gold medal. Typically, you clock in at an impressive 11.3 seconds. Your personal best is 11.05 seconds. Bear with me, since the point is not that you will soon have a cabinet of gold medals or be featured on the cover of *GQ*.

Now introduce four other runners into your races. Let's imagine that one of them has it in for you personally and has perhaps insulted your girlfriend by comparing her to his own pet. And then compared you to his grandmother's pet. To keep it real, he also supports Manchester United. Collectively, these four runners force you to change not only what you do when running the race, but how you train—what you do before and afterward. The enemy runner adds still more wind to your sails. Out go the Big Macs. In comes the kale, broccoli, and grilled fish. You get serious, researching how to improve your technique to achieve better performance, and you beat your personal best by a margin.

You now have to compete and give it your best, which you were less incentivized to do when nobody else was competing against you. You also feel biologically compelled to beat the runner who has insulted you. This is not a major new insight into human behavior. Some competition is always healthy and sharpens performance. Where there's no competition, performance nearly always dulls, even if only marginally. But even a marginal lowering of performance standards in a government that spent US$4.4 trillion in 2019 is still a big deal.

We all know and have known for some time that monopolies are less efficient and responsive than businesses in competitive markets.[50] Government is tasked with preventing private-sector firms from creating monopolies, as was the case during the breakup of AT&T, which was for many decades effectively the US's sole telephone provider. When British Telecom was privatized, it became subject to competition for customers, finance, talent, and much else.

But even with government oversight, private-sector monopolies are often less subject to interference than public ones. Private-sector firms can make and execute decisions more quickly because they typically don't require multiple tiers of authorization and can embrace an entrepreneurial work ethic. Private-sector monopolies rarely embrace a public-sector culture fully.

A private-sector monopoly's focus on profits, earnings, or market capitalization is admittedly more precise than government's. Decision-making is clearer. We can recognize that's an advantage the private sector nearly always has. However, since the vast majority of private-sector firms are small businesses, I do want to stress that these firms aren't only looking at financial return. There are also issues of work-life balance, appetite for risk, and the role of family members in the organization's present and future, all of which broaden the private sector's goals. For example, many businesses are run with a view of keeping things in the family, and often an entrepreneur will groom his kids into the firm irrespective of whether the labor market offers better talent.

In contrast, government monopolies must pay attention to a wider spectrum of issues that private-sector monopolies are usually unencumbered by. In the UK in the 1970s, government-owned monopolies were also focused on generating employment. However, there comes a point where you either generate employment or make money, but not both, which is part of the reason that so many British government businesses in the 1970s and 1980s ran at a loss and went under—so the job creation wasn't quite what it had seemed. This is why so many either went bust (British Leyland) or were sold (British Gas).

Indeed, it's hard enough for an organization to generate positive cash flow or deliver a positive return on investment, let alone be burdened with an equally important, if tangential, objective, such as generating and maintaining jobs. About two-thirds of small businesses fail in their first decade. Try to run that 100-meter race against those four athletes while stirring cookie batter at the same time, and let's see how well you perform.

Lack of consumer and financial competition is culturally debilitating for both public and private monopolies. Consumers pay extra for products and services in both cases. The difference is that, in the first case, the taxpayer covers the costs of inefficiency, and, in the second, the shareholder pays. However, shareholders can benchmark management's performance with precision by looking at share-price appreciation, earnings growth, or dividend yield. All this can be plotted on a graph. If management doesn't stack up, out it goes.

This luxury is not afforded to taxpayers. We don't have such clear-cut data to work with. In any case, we're hit with such a fire hose of information and misinformation at practically every election that it's hard to separate fact from fake, let alone decide what's important and what's not. We certainly can't replace the core management, the 99.5 percent, from government. The vast majority of the public sector is so far removed from us that we wouldn't know where to start investigating.

Nevertheless, there are possible solutions that we can consider.

CHAPTER 6

REDUCING
GOVERNMENT WASTE

Instances of democratic government waste are as prolific as they
are disheartening. The last chapter's specific instances, examples,
and case studies of necessity only scratched the surface. They
were meant to specifically illustrate the existence and extent of
a problem of which we are all too well aware. Instances could be
extended beyond the Anglo-American sphere to other Western
European countries and others across the world.

What is to be done, given the enormity and seeming intrac-
tability of the problem? As I've mentioned, the main reason I
wrote this book was to get us seeing things differently, to get
us thinking so that we can then act. Just as the examples in the
last chapter were limited if representative, the solutions I'll propose in this chapter aren't meant to be comprehensive. Rather,
they're my recommendations for dealing with the problem in
ways that are viable, even if they may require fine-tuning. Or
at least so I believe.

I hope these suggestions will get you to do exactly that—see things differently, think, and develop your own or refine my proposals. These proposals, like those in later chapters addressing the problems of representation and accountability, are tactical suggestions. They don't require major constitutional reform, nor would they, relatively speaking, be expensive to implement. But if put into practice, they'd be able to effect significant change in relatively short order. We'd see some pretty serious improvements quite quickly.

The overall intention behind all these proposals is to reinvigorate our social contract—let's keep that front and center. To give citizens what's theirs before yet more generations are disenfranchised from government and its processes. My proposals are designed to bring the governed closer to governance and to impress upon all stakeholders the public sector's moral responsibility to outperform the private sector. If you're going to force even the homeless to pay taxes, you'd better work every dollar and cent rigorously.

My hypothesis is that these proposals could reduce public-sector expenditures by 20 percent, while at the same time improving performance and efficiency by another 20 percent. These are, of course, not meant to be exact figures, but they try to convey a general sense of both the scope and direction of what I am proposing. I'm absolutely convinced that we can get government to perform a lot better for a lot less.

How do we improve government performance? How do we reduce waste? In the private sector, performance is rewarded and the lack of it is penalized, as it should be in the public sector. What can we do without having to redraft our constitutions or apply a few billion dollars to reducing government waste?

REVIEWS AND CONSEQUENCES

If human capital is what you might consider the flip side of time, it's our most important resource. If it's what distinguishes good from bad organizations, it's important that we start there. If we can get the right people and develop the right culture, there will be a substantial impact on processes and systems. Without getting the right talent, we'll struggle to design, sustain, or refine systems or processes to generate higher performance.

Let's tackle the waste associated with the management of public-sector employees. My first proposal is that, each year, 5 percent of the best performing civil servants should be given meaningful recognition, bonuses, and promotions with greater responsibility and decision-making authority. Not just a lame certificate which goes straight into the recycling bin, but something that friends and family celebrate. If they're good, we need to value them and make them feel valued. We need to give them jobs that stretch and energize them and take advantage of their superior performance—for the government's, the citizen body's, and their own sakes.

We should also remove the weakest performing 2 percent from their positions. We need to stop protecting staff who are underperforming and move them out in much the same way the private sector does. Otherwise, taxpayers will continue to bear the cost of poorly performing talent. I once worked with somebody so inept that not only did this person achieve almost nothing, but also continuously vacuumed chunks of productive time from many colleagues. Again, 5 and 2 percent figures are not meant to be literal, but to give a general sense of the scope and direction of the change proposed.

This is, of course, easier said than done. I've built and am running my own business and have worked with a number of firms in both the private and public sectors. In all cases, I've found the best and fairest way of managing staff performance is through a regular review and evaluation process. Such reviews have to be meaningful, rigorous, and carry weight. They can't be conducted in an elevator with off-the-cuff feedback. They need to be thorough and comprehensive.

Some of this is a matter of checking off boxes on a standardized form, which helps formulate a clear, stable, and broadly consistent basis for reviews. That way each person in the organization knows there are criteria that sets forth what is expected of them. What's expected of a department head will not be what's expected of a newly hired associate. Both, however, ought to be given a review form setting forth what they need to accomplish as soon as they're hired or promoted.

But an evaluation is obviously more than a completed form with boxes checked off and comments made. Even if most boxes on someone's form have been checked, it's possible they still haven't performed well. There are many qualitative factors, such as someone's attitude, that quantitative evaluation forms don't easily capture. It might also be the case that, although someone has only dropped the ball twice in a year, both those times were critically important. What you consistently want and need during a review process is a frank exchange about what's going on, what's gone well, and what issues and problems need to be considered.

This review process must be protected from political and relationship pressures and run by the department's top civil servant. Having it run by a human resource manager would be disastrous. Top public-sector management must not just oversee performance-management reviews but actually sit in the driver's seat. And if they can't see that, they are neglecting their most important resource.

I'm not saying that the department head should attend everyone's appraisal. I'm saying that everyone needs to know that the department head is deeply involved in and committed to performance reviews. It's not just that they signed off without really being aware of what they're signing, but they fundamentally ran the process. They challenged those involved. This sends a powerful signal that reviews are being taken seriously. Having the department head be the central player on all decisions protects the outcomes' integrity.

This is extremely important, since protecting the review process protects the entire department's performance, lifting its culture as a whole. It enables the department to recruit better people because they can trust that it's a meritocracy. And it protects taxpayers, who no longer have to subsidize underperforming staff. If we compromise or make exceptions, we lower the organization's performance, and that costs us more than we should pay.

Reviews must lead to the immediate and meaningful consequences now missing in the public sector. Consequences drive improved performance for both individuals and the organizations they work for. They deliver better value to taxpayers. Without such consequences, neither reviewer nor reviewee will take the exercise seriously, and the review process protections won't matter. And every single citizen pays for it.

At the end of each calendar or fiscal year, the top 5 percent of staff will be selected for recognition. They'll value what they have earned, whether it's a large cash bonus, a medal, or some other reward. Their colleagues will also share in this recognition. Because the review process was robust and protected, there will be a general sense that the outperformers did well, that they deserve what they got, and that they should be proud. Bravo!

In contrast, the weakest 2 percent who are let go with no ifs, ands, or buts are told, "You've tried, but it hasn't worked, and that's the end of it." I'm not suggesting that they are then asked to leave the building with their belongings in a box, security guard in tow. There are many reasons to be supportive and helpful during an exit, one being that it maintains goodwill and another that it sends a positive signal to potential new employees. Above all, it's the right and human thing to do. But the message needs to be clear, firm, and irreversible. You were part of the lowest 2 percent, and that's that.

Even if the performance management process was robust and protected, there will still be a sense of disappointment, even shock, for those let go. That's to be expected. Deep down, though, those let go need to sense that there was no massive miscarriage of justice, but a sensible process with pros and cons, and that they didn't do well, even if they may not articulate it. Without a robust process, however, expect mayhem, because everybody in the bottom 2 percent will be up in arms. They got fired due to a bad process.

What could the unintended consequences of introducing a meaningful performance management framework be? Clearly, it would shake up all staff somewhat. Anybody thinking they could sit at their desk for a couple of decades without trying will need to jettison such notions. Another obvious consequence is that government will need to sharpen its strategy and value proposition to recruit staff. If it's going to remove 2 percent of its staff every single year, it has to replace them with employees it can retain. Government must be competitive in securing talent.

There once was a time when the diplomatic and intelligence services recruited at the country's top-rated universities to fill sought-after positions. James Bond graduated from Cambridge, Jack Ryan from the London School of Economics, and Ethan Hunt from Pennsylvania. Something of this spirit needs to be recaptured and brought from the big screen into the real world. This needs to be done across all government agencies if for no other reason than that government's mandate is greater, more important, and more complex than that of any other organization.

Will this mean higher government expenditure and, therefore, taxes? There will be redundancy packages to pay out. In some countries, average salaries may have to rise to recruit better talent, especially in the US and UK, since both countries have underpaying public sectors. In Canada, as noted earlier, this shouldn't be a significant barrier, because the public sector is paid more than the private sector and has greater benefits and job security. The same is true of Australia.[1]

However, if a single outperformer can deliver many times what an average performer can, let alone what an underperformer can, this salary arithmetic might be moot. Aggregate talent costs may not rise, and yet still we should expect a disproportionately higher increase in output or value. For now, at a high level, my hypothesis is that this set of measures should have both a positive fiscal and performance impact, neither of which we can fully calculate without more specific national details.

Recruiting and retaining talent also means considering non-financial factors that attract employees. The civil service may need to raise its game on work-life balance and opportunities for growth and learning, as well as for empowerment and responsibility. Or any combination thereof. In short, in becoming a more competitive employer, it needs to rethink its human resources philosophy. High performing talent needs challenging, compelling, meaningful work. There are few things as debilitating as working without impact. Capable people don't tend to stick around for very long to push paper clips.

Another unintended consequence of introducing a meaningful performance management framework involves unions and litigation. Getting fired in the public sector is often hard because civil servants rush to their unions to protect them. That doesn't even speak to those countries where public-sector workers have stronger *legal* rights than private-sector employees when confronted with dismissal.

The proportion of public-sector employees who are unionized varies in Western democracies—from 34 percent in the US to a stifling 76 percent in Canada in 2019.[2] That's one reason why it's statistically harder to be fired for poor performance by the federal Canadian government than it is to join the NASA astronaut program.[3] There's little doubt that, without belittling the legitimate benefits unions provide, especially against irresponsible management and shareholders, they also protect low performance, even sexual and violent abuse at the workplace by their members.

One unionized employee was remarkably candid about this in a piece for the *Guardian*: "To say I'm underused would be an understatement—this is written at my desk. I will stay here for a long time because the benefits—as you would expect from a trade union—are incredible. Short hours (and no one would dream of doing overtime), ample holiday, a very good salary (especially given the amount of work I have to do), a great pension and being able to attend any course I wish."[4] That's hard to read if you're paying taxes. We are all paying taxes.

If government wants to reduce fiscal waste of ordinary citizens' hard-earned taxes, the legal and other barriers to removing poor-performing staff have to be eliminated. Citizens do not deserve and did not sign up to support underperforming public-sector staff or the costs associated with dismissing them. If this means new legislation to curb union powers or to enable government to get rid of underperformers in much the same way the private sector does, so be it. The public sector needs to protect citizens, including those who can't even afford shelter but are still taxed, from being taken for a ride. After all, it's the job of the public sector to focus on the public interest.

AUDIT AND COMMUNICATIONS UNIT

My second proposal to reduce government waste is the creation of a citizen-centric audit and communications unit. This would be an independent government agency, in some ways like the Bank of England and the US Federal Reserve—notwithstanding Trump's attempts to restrict the latter body's independence, and for that matter, many federal and state government agencies and departments. Another example is internal affairs units, whose function is to monitor police departments.

This unit or agency would be given complete autonomy and power to investigate the government. It would need to have the authority to thoroughly examine all government files and personnel, and interview or monitor whenever it chooses, across the board. It would therefore have a high level of clearance and power, meaning that nobody and nothing would be able to put roadblocks in its way.

One way this sort of works in the private sector is that shareholders in large firms appoint a board of directors whose job is to keep management on its toes. The directors rarely comb through details, but they have a fiduciary duty to shareholders. In the Western corporate structure, the purpose of boards of directors is to protect these shareholders, who are too removed from the business to look after its or their own best interests.

Boards of directors are not meant to be ceremonial officials. And their primary aim is not to encourage gender or ethnic diversity, though they go down this rabbit hole way too often. The purpose of a board is to protect stakeholders from management abuse, conflicts of interest, and underperformance. That's why, in small firms, boards are largely redundant, since the owner is also the operator or CEO as well as sole shareholder. It makes no sense for owner-operators to appoint a board to monitor themselves.

In government, despite its being much bigger and swampier than even the largest corporations, nothing like this exists. Not even close. We as citizens don't have a board of directors who can say to other government branches, "We're independent of you, and this is what we want to investigate on the taxpayers' behalf. We want to assess your performance and double-check what you're doing. We're working for the citizen population and no one else." If we outsource our legislature and the rest of government, surely we need to keep a tab on what it's doing. Instead, we citizens are stuck with our own limited private resources against the backdrop of our daily work and family responsibilities when we try to figure out what's going on in government.

And yes, I can already sense the pushback. We already have bodies such as Auditors General, National Audit Offices, and Comptrollers. Therefore, we don't need more of the same. We do, but not quite. We need something far beyond what's currently available, something with an entirely different philosophy. Perhaps these existing bodies can be improved and adapted to deliver the value taxpaying citizens deserve. Perhaps not.

What's missing from existing bodies? Most obviously, the ability to communicate. When typical government audits take place, almost no effort is made to relay findings to taxpayers. There's little value in conducting a detailed investigation only to then communicate it in a report that's nothing more than an archaic tome, set in a small font, with a generous amount of gobbledygook, jargon, and legalese. A tiny number of ordinary people find these reports palatable or even comprehensible.

For example, the Australian National Audit Office's annual reports are similar in format, size, and style to the voluminous audit reports that large accounting firms prepare for companies listed on stock exchanges.[5] They aren't easy to scan, with their long sentences, technical speak, and an unrelenting amount of data to absorb. They may not be quite as difficult as philosopher Martin Heidegger's works, but they're still nothing like what people want to read, which defeats the whole purpose. Let's be honest—it's what you might read to help you fall asleep. And if you were stuck on a desert island.

This is quite strange, is it not? Why publish government audits that are difficult for the vast majority of government's primary stakeholders, the citizens, to understand? It's left to a handful of journalists to publicize key summaries and recommendations, if they choose to do so. And if some other big story hits the media radar, the audit agency's findings may get buried in the back of the paper or dropped altogether. Let's not even flag the reality that many people don't get their news from traditional media.

The audit and communications agency that I propose has to radically break with this approach. We just don't deserve or need the nonsense we have. Given how critical government is in our lives, and that its current machinations are so removed from us, we need an independent evaluation agency able to get its message across. We need a body that acts as a public-sector supercharged board of directors, able to communicate its findings to the vast majority of the population unfamiliar with verbose jargon just as well as to those with advanced degrees in public policy and accounting.

Any such agency's mandate is to investigate, evaluate, and communicate. Without the latter, there is little to be gained. We may as well watch paint dry. We need to bring the citizen back not only into government, but into the process of checking in on government. The full spectrum or vast majority of citizens must be able understand the audit's analysis and conclusions. The audit agency's communications therefore need to be sharp, snappy, and eye-catching because there's so much information out there which is being presented so well.

The agency should work with leading communications and advertising talent and methods, whether in-house or outsourced. The agency would have to compete with other strong communications teams for consumer mindshare. It needs to be as good at getting its messages across as the people who do this work for Apple, Coca-Cola, and Unilever are. It must be able to publicize its findings to all citizens. It needs to inform the general public about the issue at hand, what went wrong, what went right, why, what should be done about it, and who is or should be held responsible.

In an era of constant distraction, these findings, unlike what government audit agencies currently produce, need to stand out, using graphics, video, or any approach that gets the message across. If the agency needs to rap its information to a segment of the population, let's get rapping. If the agency needs to present with satire, let's go down the road of Horace and Juvenal. The unit must be aware that it's competing for public and not just elite mindshare, against other compelling, clever, and creative content providers.

And this can't be an annual report. I want this audit body to communicate at least every day, maybe more. There's a lot happening in a government that's doing so many different things. Let's not wait to dazzle citizens once a year. Get those social media accounts pumped with meaningful information about the government's performance every single day. It will help rejuvenate our ownership of our democracy and light a Bunsen burner under every public official's chair. The people will love it.

We need to know, for instance, what proportion of patients have to wait more than a month for surgery in the state healthcare system. Who are the officials managing projects delayed by a year, and who are their supervisors? Which politician went on a trip abroad that a foreign government paid for and why? Just as we want the bad news, we want to know which civil servants led projects that came in on time and budget, and how the government reduced hospital wait times.

These will not be snap reviews or one-offs. They'll be ongoing reports on a scale government hasn't seen before. It's applying the Board of Directors concept to government and pumping it with steroids to defend citizens from waste.

Much of this goes back to recruitment. Our new agency needs to attract and retain quality talent. Factual and analytical integrity must be the foundation of the agency's findings. The work has to be rigorous, which brings us back to an earlier point—the public sector needs to reward high performing talent and let go of stragglers more aggressively than it now does. A mandate this consequential can't have a mediocre staff prone to absenteeism and adamant on clocking out at 5:00 p.m. every day hell or high water.

Something else needs to change—current audit agencies' accounting bias and culture. Ontario's auditor general, as of 2019, was a chartered accountant who had spent nearly her entire career in public-sector auditing. Aside from being a male, her predecessor had exactly the same profile, as did his predecessor too. The vast majority of government audit agency chiefs have the same or similar backgrounds. It's not that difficult to see why these agencies can't get their message across to ordinary people.

The purpose of the proposed audit agency will be to report to citizens on government performance. It's not to report to fellow auditors. Furthermore, important aspects of government performance don't lend themselves to analysis and problem-solving with financial and accounting standards. Any organization is so much more than its ledger. If you only lay out a set of accounts, your insight and understanding of an organization will be extremely limited. Which is exactly where we are today with government audit agencies.

Take, for instance, organizational culture—a department's mood, ethic, and expectations. These are important organizational characteristics you can't meaningfully capture on a balance sheet. You need emotional intelligence, operational experience in different business cultures, and perhaps an education in organizational theory, anthropology, or sociology to even see let alone and tackle these issues. You'll get just as much insight on cultural psycho-dynamics from a chartered accountant as you would from a fisherman. The accountant and fisherman simply aren't trained. The current obsession with accounting hamstrings the broader, more comprehensive audit required.

The proposed audit and communications unit needs a spectrum of technical skills and experiences comparable to the talent diversity at bespoke management consulting firms—although not perhaps those that grew from and are appendages of accounting firms. Someone biased with a narrow focus on financial performance can't be at the helm. Nor does the agency need to be headed by somebody already so ingrained in the public-service system that their expectations are skewed, and their established relationships with colleagues potentially compromise their work.

These executives would also have to be thick-skinned and, frankly, bloody-minded. Any job is partly defined by its occupant's personality and character, which must be factored in. There's no point bringing someone on board who doesn't have the intellectual horsepower or critical thinking skills needed to challenge and push back when required.

And they'd have to be tenacious. These executives should expect to be told that what they are trying to do can't be done. They'll get defiance and stonewalling. They must be able to respond to such positions ideally by subtle influence, or if necessary, by asserting, "I don't really care what you say. I want to see what I want to see." For which of course, they need the legal tools as well. I can't but help think of Steve Jobs here, because he had an exemplary ability to challenge naysayers and get things done.

Given how vital the functions of the proposed unit would be, as well as the work's seriousness and sensitivity, the first order of business is recruiting the right person to head the agency. I'd be inclined to push for someone with a strong private-sector background who has a fast-paced, no-nonsense, delivery-oriented approach. And please, let's go beyond accountants. We just don't need their tightly focused agenda anchoring this role.

The way to get the right people on board is to assure them they'll have the authority and responsibility to do an important job—to keep government in check. To make sure that elected representatives feel a fire under their seats not just at election time but throughout their terms. For that matter, as I noted earlier, let's turn up the heat under every public servant who's paid with our taxes. Let's not exclude them from this accountability process.

Let's brainstorm a bit about how the agency's top brass could be chosen, postulating that the team would consist of a dozen people. The senior executive from the private sector would be invited to choose the team. This might consist of a senior civil servant reassigned from another department; an academic expert in public policy, government, or management; and maybe another top-ranked executive from the private sector. It couldn't be exclusively or even primarily comprised of accomplished sixty-year-old white men. Women are, after all, majorities in all

Western democracies. As for slicing the pie differently, middle, middle-lower, and lower economic class citizens need to be just as involved.

Also, such an agency can't be civil servant heavy. That's not to say that civil servants don't or can't add value. At the very least, the proposed agency needs an awareness and understanding of the beast that it's engaging with, so it must have public servants in its ranks. But it needs to look at the public sector with fresh eyes, its view unhindered by the way things are being or have been done. It needs staff willing to question and probe the public sector through multiple filters, and who aren't dependent on public-sector professional and personal relationships.

This senior management, whose mandate will be to create a workable agency capable of holding government accountable, would be told, "Your job is to protect citizens against government and specifically to ensure that government is accountable, representative, and efficient. And where you find it isn't or needs improvement, your job is to inform the citizen body." That's an extremely meaningful role.

If we successfully form our agency either from scratch or by transforming those that already exist, what should we be wary of? What could some of the unintended implications be? To start with, this unelected agency would wield extensive power. That's a big deal. It could probe the entire public sector and report its findings daily to citizens through any media outlet. That's a lot of power, for which we need safeguards to prevent abuse.

I'd encourage applying special criminal sanctions to agency staff who commit such abuses, which should at least act as a deterrent.

Limiting terms of office to three, four, or five years may also prevent staff and management from becoming too comfortable in their new roles. Finally, let's have citizens evaluate the quality of their research, recommendations, and communications as a key factor in determining staff-exit compensation packages. After all, this is being done on the citizen body's behalf.

Both functions of this proposed agency—investigation and communication—will undoubtedly be difficult. But I'd far rather we deal with such challenges than those associated with current audit agencies. These myopically focus far too much on accounting and financial analysis, fail to communicate usefully to those they serve—we, the people—and leave an awful lot of value on the table.

PARALLEL COMPETITIVE GOVERNMENT DEPARTMENTS

My third proposal to reduce government waste is the creation of parallel competitive government departments. ("What is the world coming to?" you're asking, and wait—I can hear the Four Horsemen of the Apocalypse just around the corner. They're ordering some food from the McDonald's drive-through.) That's right—have government departments compete with each other to better serve citizens. Competition makes private enterprises more efficient and effective, and the rationale behind this proposal is to inject a measure of that competitive spirit in the public sector.

Some will instinctively push back. "What? How on earth would that work? How can you make the public sector compete against itself?" Others may even be appalled at the prospect, perhaps wrongly thinking my next suggestion will be to privatize the entire government. And yet another group, those who love their undemanding government jobs, simply don't want to feel compelled to perform.

How could competition be brought into the public sector? The same way it's done in the private sector—by first entertaining the prospect. Much has been achieved that way. Einstein alluded to imagination's priority over knowledge. We make progress by imagining what we had dared not. What if we could kill bacteria? What if we could fly? What if we could land on the moon? Going down that same road, what if we could introduce competitive forces into the public sector?

Now for a proviso, which is that I don't think it's possible to create parallel, competing government departments in every instance. We wouldn't want two prime ministers. I can sense the opportunity to mention that even a single PM is too much to handle, but it's best not to take that one up. However, there are departments, as well as functions within large departments, where this proposal would be feasible. We clearly need to find the right spaces to introduce competition that encourages better performance.

Having competing, parallel government departments may also lead to a positive culture transfer. If two highly competitive, high performance government departments interact with other departments that are lackadaisical or haven't been split, the latter will be affected by the former units' pace and achievement. Raising the game in a handful of agencies will impact other agencies as well. Culture, like mood, is infectious.

A concrete example of how this might be done is the enormous US Department of Agriculture, which employs more than a hundred thousand people in more than thirty agencies, not to mention a small army of permanently embedded so-called consultants. For argument's sake, let's split the Food Safety and Inspection Unit into four entities carved out from what already exists. They would receive the same mandate and accountability standards, robust performance indicators, and similar resources.

Each new unit would have its own CEO, human resources department, brand, and head office. Let them compete not just for customers but for talent and in many other respects. If one department wanted to offer laundry services for employees on site, as Google does, they could do so. If another wanted to offer cost-free online credit card payments for customers, that's up to them. They can do what they like as long as they deliver the outcomes we expect.

While each competing department now has more autonomy, their targets and goals would have to be identical, perhaps allowing for minor nuances. Each department might choose its own key performance indicators (KPIs)—which is neither a small nor simple job and not to be taken lightly. In reality, KPIs are far too often not key, performance-associated, or meaningfully measurable—so they have to be crafted with care. Each department and its staff will dedicate their time and energy to meet its KPIs and accomplish the goals it shares with its competitors.

The aim would be to motivate each agency to perform better and more efficiently than the others. Not only do performance indicators tell agency employees how their team is doing, but they may be able to compare themselves with other teams. Citizens can also see who is and isn't doing well and choose which agency they want to work with. The staff at the agency that does best would be rewarded appropriately.

Such rewards might take many different forms. The winning agency could be given a bonus, a pay raise, a week off work, or another recognition. Send the team to Disney World with a Disney Park Hopper ticket for a weekend, if that's what's needed to help generate a 20 percent improvement in results with 20 percent fewer resources. There are obviously any number of different means of rewarding achievement. But they need to have gravity.

In some cases, it would be easy to identify which agencies should be split in two. Passport services is an obvious choice. Law enforcement might be another, putting pressure on police to tackle serious crime. In 2017, US police arrested or identified a suspect in only 62 percent of murders.[6] In 38 percent of homicide cases, the police failed to present a suspect to the courts. When the victim was black, the percentage of murders solved was lower still. No surprises there.

These figures are discouraging, given that "solved" does not mean "convicted." It just means that the police sent a case to prosecutors, regardless of whether it was taken to court or the accused was sentenced. If police services had to compete and measure up against parallel police services, wouldn't they put more thought and energy into their work? They might share certain resources, such as databases, and be rewarded for assisting rival agencies, but the emphasis would be on a competitive culture.

Certain agencies might never be subject to competitive pressures. Or we could wait to see what sort of ripple or follow-on effect there is from splitting up a small number of agencies before determining if it should be done to a greater number. Whatever the details may be, this innovation is intended as a

permanent and ongoing rather than temporary means of rein-
forcing the benefits of competition in the public sector.

These proposals are intended to make government less wasteful
and more efficient and productive, a foundation of the social
contract. Let's now look at the second of Western democracy's
eroded cornerstones: that government must be representative.

PART III

REPRESENTATION

CHAPTER 7

OUT OF SIGHT AND OUT OF TOUCH

Representation is the essence of Western liberal democracies, which are "people power" governments. Of course, that's unfortunately only in theory. Since the direct democracy that existed in ancient Athens may still be impractical, especially in countries with large populations spread across an extensive land mass, a small number of officials are elected to represent constituents. And the rump of government stays put. That's the way we've set up our democracy.

There are at least two meanings of the word "represent" in a political context. First, the people who run our democracy should be similar to or reflect the people on whose behalf they govern. Our government should be *representative of* its people. This means that people in government should instinctively see the world through the same lens we do, however diverse we may be. They shouldn't have to learn about how we see the world with reminders and CliffsNotes. They should instinctively get it.

The second connotation of "represent" isn't about identity, but instead proxy as in *representatives for*—who do our elected advocate for or defend? Our communities choose a person to promote and problem-solve on their behalf in the national government. The idea is that we ordinary citizens choose not to spend our days in Parliament or the Capitol, attempting to secure our wants and needs. Instead, we elect somebody to do that for us. This meaning as *representative for* and not *of* is perhaps more pertinent to the elected end of government than it is the unelected 99.5 percent.

Government officials rarely represent their constituencies in either sense. In Western democracies, neither elected officials nor the upper strata of the civil service reflect the population they supposedly serve. Rather than truly representing the needs of their constituents, elected politicians are too often disturbingly influenced by other factors both inside and outside government. In both key senses of the word represent—mirroring and advocating for a constituency—there's not much to brag about.

Representation is a fundamental characteristic of the democratic social contract. Distorting or diluting it potentially undercuts the contract so fundamentally as to nullify it. Let's explore the principal ways that our government isn't what we mean by "representative."

UNREPRESENTATIVE REPRESENTATIVES

The few people we elect to represent us too often don't share our identities and all that comes with them. They subsequently struggle to understand the issues that matter to us and the challenges we deal with. They're often out of sync with our priorities and aspirations. In other words, neither our elected representatives nor, for that matter, the silent majority in senior ranks of the civil service are especially representative.

Let's start with socioeconomic status. There's a reason why exclusivity is as stubborn a hallmark of Western democratic governments as persistent poverty and homelessness. No head of government in any modern Western democracy has ever been homeless. Ever. Only one British MP in the current legislature, Melanie Onn, has been homeless, as has only one member of the US Congress, Kyrsten Sinema. It's a fair assumption that the vast majority of the upper echelons of Western civil services haven't experienced homelessness either.

The US Congress has 535 members whose average net worth is US$4.5 million.[1] Their Congressional salary alone—exclusive of campaign "donations," advisory positions, lectures, consultancies, and many other fringe benefits both legitimate and of the "nudge, nudge, wink, wink" variety—puts them in the top 6 percent of earners. Between 1999 and 2008, only thirteen out of the 783 legislators in the US Congress came from blue-collar backgrounds.[2]

Members of Congress represent and legislate on behalf of American citizens whose *households* have a median worth of slightly under US$97,300 in net assets.[3] Depending on how this is measured, each American household has, on average, about three people.[4] There's a 138-fold disparity in net worth between elected representatives and the individual Americans that they represent. Some 39.7 million Americans, or almost one in eight, live below the poverty line, which for a single person means an income of slightly more than US$12,000 per year.[5]

America's poor lack not only representation in government but influence over how their problems are solved. A 2014 US House Budget Committee hearing convened by Representative Paul Ryan entitled, "A Progress Report on the War on Poverty: Lessons from the Frontlines," absurdly failed to invite testimony from a single person living in poverty.[6] Not one. Imagine if we had a legislative select committee investigate domestic violence against women yet didn't invite a single woman to testify. There's almost a déjà vu here—remember the Saudi conference on women that only men attended?

This goes some way to explain why the US's spending per capita on its domestic poor is among the lowest in the OECD (Organization of Economic Co-operation and Development) countries.[7] US poverty levels have hovered at 11 to 15 percent for more than half a century.[8] Meanwhile, the US has been at war with one or more countries mostly thousands of miles away who haven't threatened the US, let alone have the means to do so, almost every one of those years. It's a skewed interpretation of national defense.

The lack of representation really hurts. Epidemiologists at Emory University concluded that if the minimum hourly wage in the US had been a mere $2 per hour higher between 1990 and 2015, there would have been 57,000 fewer suicides in the world's most powerful country.[9] That's six suicides fewer per day, with all the related grief and emotional trauma for hundreds of thousands, over a twenty-five-year period. Families in which a suicide occurs seldom recover. Two dollars per hour matters, but not to America's legislators.

In 2020, we only had more of the above during the coronavirus outbreak, the worst pandemic since the Spanish Flu of 1918, with a worst-case forecast suggesting an American loss of life of between 480,000 and 2.2 million people, not to mention a 10 percent per annum drop in GDP for the second quarter of 2020.[10] On March 18, 2020, the Senate declined to pass a motion "to provide Americans with paid sick time and paid leave so that they can address their own health needs and the health needs of their families."[11] Wealthy Senators don't need paid sick time. They don't really understand what typical Americans face.

There's nothing reasonable about a country that's still the world's economic superpower, with more than a fifth of global output and an unrivaled appetite for fighting costly wars far from its borders to have such persistent poverty rates. American poverty is due in part to the lack of representation of lower socioeconomic classes, including the homeless, in government and especially its decision-making strata. It's not a difficult cause-effect to grasp.

There's a stark contrast between the incomes of elected representatives in other Western nations and those they represent. For instance, one in seven Canadians live in poverty.[12] In contrast, Canadian MPs in 2019 earned C$178,900, which was three and a half times the average national salary. Ministers received another C$85,500 plus a car allowance.[13] Economists currently consider a middle-class household with more than one income earner to be one that brings in almost C$100,000 a year. Canadian MPs also receive a generous pension, despite often having a career track record that reflects little more than the ability and drive to get elected.

The socioeconomic divide is just as pronounced in the UK. A third of British MPs attended private school and a quarter studied at Oxford or Cambridge, as opposed to 7 percent and 1 percent respectively of the general public.[14] Two of the last three British prime ministers attended Eton College, where tuition fees alone were £42,000 in 2019—some 20 percent higher than the average pretax salary of a British full-time worker. That's right, Eton's annual tuition fee is significantly higher than the British average gross annual salary.

British MPs command an annual salary nearly three times that of ordinary citizens, as well as a range of benefits including the costs of a second home in London, hardly the world's cheapest city. Ministers are also far wealthier than those they govern. In 2010, just 2 percent of Britons were millionaires. In 2012, more than 65 percent of the British cabinet hit the seven-figure mark.[15] It may not be so extreme today, but that slant is still very much there.

As a result, such representatives can only be less aware of, interested in, or responsive to poverty. This is why, despite more than 0.5 percent of Britons being homeless in late 2018, the government wasn't and still isn't much interested in confronting the problem.[16] In 2017, a few months before Heather Wheeler became the Minister for Homelessness, she disparagingly referred to the homeless as "old tinkers, knife cutters."[17] A couple of years later, a fellow Conservative MP called them "undesirables."[18]

More generally, you're not going to see much excitement in the Commons when MPs discuss poverty—if any even bother to show up. Indeed, in 2019, only fourteen of Britain's 650 MPs turned up to a parliamentary debate to discuss a UN report on the 14 million Britons—more than a fifth of the population—living in poverty.[19] You might want to mull that for a few moments. In essence, the MPs saw little sense in attending. A debate to reduce their salary by a measly percent would have seen the entire house in attendance.

Is it sheer coincidence that homelessness in Britain increased by an astonishing 134 percent between 2011 and 2017?[20] I can promise that if Britain's MPs, most of whom say an awful lot to present themselves as ordinary citizens, had each lived homeless for a month, Britain would now have a tiny percentage of the homeless people it has today. Let me go further—the country may not have any homeless people.

The tragedy is that those communities rarely, if ever, represented in elected or senior public-sector positions suffer from the most persistent social, political, and economic problems. This, again, is no coincidence. Lack of representation isn't an abstract problem. It undercuts both our social contract and the social fabric on which we all rely. On June 14, 2017, a fire at the Grenville Towers low-income housing estate in London ended with seventy-two deaths. In the aftermath, an investigative report came to the following conclusion:

> "Theresa May [the Tory prime minister] has admitted the initial response was not good enough. It goes much deeper. This is the culmination of years of Tory cuts and neglect. Addressing the systematic failures requires a systematic overhaul in how the poorest and most vulnerable are treated by government."[21]

Should we therefore be surprised that the lowest socioeconomic stratum is significantly less likely to vote in general elections than the highest stratum, who typically need government less?[22] Poorer communities don't feel government is concerned about them, and, unfortunately, they're not far off the mark. A government not representative of its people, rich and poor, black and white, male and female, damages the entire society. This is corrosive not just for those on the margins, but for those who think they benefit from the system.

Ethnic minorities are another constituency underrepresented in government's upper reaches. They make up 13 percent of the UK population, yet occupy only 3 to 4 percent of top civil service jobs.[23] In the House of Commons in 2019, 8 percent of MPs hailed from ethnic minorities, while in the Lords it was 5 percent—far from representative.[24] It's worth flagging that the Labour Party typically has several times the number of ethnic minority MPs as the Conservative Party, a point for another topic.

Most British government departments' senior executive management teams are not just mainly male, white, and Christian, but *entirely* so. One 2015 government study pointed to palpable discrimination and borderline racist abuse in Whitehall's culture.[25] Subsequent research from a recruitment firm suggested that the UK's mandarins were becoming alarmingly *less* representative of the country's ethnic makeup.[26]

This has consequences. The British government's attempts to tackle fringe Muslim extremism are a failure in part because the senior officials who make policy are disconnected from the Muslim community. They can't see the problem of the lunatic fringe, which gets a massively disproportionate amount of media coverage through the lens most British-Muslims see it through. This has eroded trust with successive governments, who have tended to instinctively see all violence by Muslims as terrorist acts while failing to make the same connection with political violence non-Muslims commit. Far-right political violence barely gets on the political agenda and is rarely called terrorism.[27]

Having British Muslims as an integral part of the core problem-solving team would have allowed "Prevent," the UK's counter-extremism agency, to empathize with the community's fears and come to grips with how the lunatic fringe's violent extremism coalesces and emerges. I've been stunned by the ignorance of senior British officials who struggle even to pronounce "Islam" and "Muslim" correctly, let alone try to tackle what is a nuanced and complex problem.

The even more ethnically diverse US population has long struggled for representation in the national legislature, with reverses frequently offsetting advances. Entrenched interests consistently and often successfully try to stymie attempts at ethnic minority representation. America's racial problems are too well-known to require detailed substantiation or analysis here. The country's WASP (White Anglo-Saxon Protestant) elite's hold on government power may be more tenuous than in the past, but it persists.

The first Afro-American president—who is, in fact, half-Caucasian—was elected only recently, in 2008. The 2016 Congress, deemed the most diverse ever, was still less than a quarter non-Caucasian, quite short of the 38 percent of non-Caucasians in the national population. Some religious minorities remain grossly underrepresented in Congress, especially Muslims, Hindus, and Sikhs, with a paltry six members in total. Of course, this has consequences for political legitimacy, government effectiveness, and overall societal well-being.

The problem has taken a twist in recent years. Not only can't Trump bring himself to name far-right acts of political violence "terrorist," but more broadly, much of the American media is biased, almost xenophobic as well.[28] Between 2006 and 2015, attacks by Muslims received 357 percent more press attention than attacks by non-Muslims.[29] No wonder so many Americans are worried about Islamic extremism. Media sources massively overplay the violence of Islam's lunatic fringe, while overlooking that of other groups.

A white terrorist is usually presented as a lone wolf with mental issues. His racial and religious identities are unimportant. But a lone wolf with mental issues who happens to be Muslim is seen very differently. I have to remind my many American friends that the world's most populous Muslim country, Indonesia, has a per capita homicide rate twelve times *less* than the US does.[30]

There is also a lack of ethnic minority representation in Australia. In 2016, despite Chinese-Australians constituting 5 percent of the population, Victoria's state Parliament had only one Chinese-Australian MP among a total of 128. Hong Lim, an isolated figure, had a few choice words about this: "We have an entrenched culture—whites feel entitled to enter politics, born to rule. Both political parties are only interested in raising funds from the Chinese communities but are not interested in considering them for safe seats."[31] And there's also New Zealand, where the country's native Maori, 15 percent of the population, make up only 5 percent of its civil service.[32]

Gender is another obvious area of underrepresentation, despite the gains made in recent decades. There may be more female legislators and executives in Western democracies than there once were, but a serious disparity remains. We simply don't have enough women with influence in our governments. As a result, they will continue to struggle to see the world from the female perspective, which is to the detriment of everybody. That's not to say that women's perspectives are homogenous, but they tend to focus on and interpret issues in ways most male perspectives do not.

The 116th US Congress had 131 women—less than a quarter of both chambers. In the UK in 2019, the House of Commons had ninety-one female MPs, a total of only 29 percent. In Canada, there were ninety-two female MPs or 27 percent, and in Australia—you get the picture. The percentage of top civil service jobs occupied by women in 2014 was slightly better but still far from equal, with Canada and Australia leading at 46 percent and 40 percent, and the US struggling at 34 percent, which is below the levels in either South Africa or Brazil.[33]

Active sexism reflected in the lack of gender representation continues to contribute to significant miscarriages of social justice and poor policymaking. The power vested in unrepresentative legislatures has any number of baleful consequences. Notoriously, in 2019, the Alabama state legislature passed a "near-total ban on abortion, making it a crime to perform the procedure at any stage of pregnancy."[34] The measure passed by a twenty-five to six vote, with men delivering all twenty-five yeas. Saudi women's conference—need I say more?

WORKING ON BEHALF OF CONSTITUENTS (OR NOT)

Then there is the second use of "representative." Are our elected representatives working for their constituents, the entire country, their political party, a few lobbyists, a foreign country, or their own personal interests? Or are they paying back favors owed to their election campaign team or funders? Some elected representatives in the UK, Canada, and the US are dual citizens, including until very recently the British prime minister, who also held American citizenship. Which lens do they view the world from? And under what circumstances does that change? It's a blend of these and other factors, which means that calling them "representatives" is grossly misleading.

Representation in this sense is often compromised in fact right at our democracy's starting point, the election process. The five biggest donors to each of Donald Trump's and Hillary Clinton's 2016 presidential campaigns contributed an extraordinary US$187 million.[35] Surely these donors expected something in return? Please don't tell me that the donors loved America so much that they spent on Donald and Hillary enough money to eliminate homelessness in its entirety in the US for almost two weeks. How many large donors did Trump subsequently appoint as ambassadors or give special contracts and awards to? Doesn't this undercut the president's mandate to do the best for all citizens?

This reinforces our government's leaning towards wealth, big donors, and special interests. One reason the public is unable to hold government accountable is because there are wealthier and more determined forces who see to it that they, not the public good, hold significant sway. Within government's hidden daily work routines, meetings, conversations, and endless documentation, there's plenty of room for intervention and maneuverability. In fact, more often than not, the problem is far more blatant than that.

Let's recognize that self-interest influences those who represent us in varying degrees. Some will lean just a little toward personal gain and furthering their careers, others a lot more. David Cameron, the former prime minister, had no doubt that Boris Johnson campaigned for Brexit only "because it would help his political career."[36] Most Britons share Cameron's view. A week before Johnson was appointed prime minister by Conservative MPs, a mere 20 percent of Britons were prepared to trust Johnson, or even, for that matter, describe him as "honest."[37] No surprise, given that he was, as I said earlier, fired twice for lying.

Though most people have a jaded view of politicians, for reasons which I can't totally pin down, some examples still challenge our cynicism. Oddly enough, we only have to visit the same Johnson family. In 2019, for instance, Boris Johnson's younger brother, Jo, resigned as both an MP and a minister in his brother's cabinet on principle. He couldn't reconcile his commitment to his country with one to his brother. In other words, he thought having his brother as prime minister was bad for the UK. Interesting how siblings can be so different.

Donald Trump has clearly redefined presidential norms in this space. A US federal watchdog agency, part of the executive branch he leads, noted that Trump had more than 1,400 conflicts of interest, two per day, in his first two years as president.[38] For example, both domestic politicians and foreign governments dramatically increased booking hotel rooms and renting space at Trump's private properties. In 2017 alone, no less than seven foreign governments leased luxury apartments in Manhattan's Trump Tower...which is a four-hour drive from Washington, DC, where foreign governments tend to rent real estate.[39]

Our awareness of the diluted nature of this type of representation has risen dramatically in recent decades. We've become quite cynical too. In 1964, 64 percent of Americans felt that the government was run for the benefit of the people. In 2015, only 29 percent held that opinion, feeling instead that elected officials put other interests ahead of citizens.[40] An extraordinary majority of Americans don't have much faith in their federal government but still, for the most part, pay their taxes. That's a serious warning.

Is such self-dealing simply human nature? Possibly. Let's not kid ourselves; we all do our jobs for our own benefit. We get paid, after all, and many of us enjoy our work. However, in part, because there's someone we regularly report to or we have specific tasks to complete, we don't use our work to benefit in personal privileges, especially those off the books. Our representative's *job* is to do what's good for those they represent—us, but they are not monitored one bit to challenge the daily conflict between selfish and selfless interests.

We need to be aware of this and think about countermeasures that will make it more difficult for our representatives to bend to self-interest or ignore the interests of those they claim to represent. As is, there's very little stopping an elected representative from furthering their own or their political bosses' agendas, while giving scant attention to their constituents. This is especially so in constituencies where the candidate's party has a huge hardcore following. In the UK, Walton in Liverpool might well remain a Labour seat even if the party selected a horse as its candidate.

Another force that dilutes our representational power is lobbyists, a career path taken by many a retired or ousted government official. Many elected officials are beholden to special interest groups who help finance their campaigns, "charities," or trust funds. An elected official may be confronted with a thousand constituents, none of whom are prepared to finance their next campaign. Most of the constituents may be urging their representative to vote a certain way. Then the official meets with the representatives and lobbyists of a major corporation or industry that, if they vote the opposite way, will fund 98 percent of their campaign.

Our representatives are often not strong enough to ignore the wishes of such lobbyists rather than honor the agenda of those they're meant to represent, and thus the dry comment by one former Canadian MP, "CEOs no longer know who their MPs are, but they sure know who their lobbyists are."[41] More than one former lobbyist has described their job as legalized bribery.[42] Nicky Hager's book *Dirty Politics* is a good expose of New Zealand lobbyists bribing several tiers of government. Such bribery consists of both the legal and the not-at-all legal.[43]

Clearly, lobbyists prey on human frailty and the weakness of the political mechanisms counteracting that frailty. And those lobbyists do so with considerable resources. For instance, in the US in 2018, lobbyists spent US$3.46 billion.[44] Pharmaceutical firms alone spent US$281 million.[45] That's more than US$1.1 million per working day spent lobbying government on behalf of drug companies—the equivalent of eleven Porsche 911 Carrera luxury cars every single day. With those resources, you could influence an awful lot of people in government whose job it is to oversee the pharmaceutical industry to dilute or modify their obligation.

Other, similarly resourced lobbying groups have enjoyed brilliant successes. The Sugar Association, formerly the Sugar Research Foundation (that's right, "Research"), has done an excellent job through the decades defending the nutritional value of sugar while protecting giant corporations like Coca-Cola and PepsiCo.[46] It's only now that we the public know what independent nutrition scientists have known for some time: consumption of refined sugar is poisonous, and sugary soft drinks are a major cause of the rapidly increasing number of Americans who are obese or suffering from diabetes or heart disease.

The gun lobby also has as much to answer for. In 2016, it spent US$10.5 million on lobbying and an additional US$5.8 million on campaign contributions during that year's election cycle, 98 percent of which went to Republican candidates.[47] Meanwhile, between 1991 and 2019, although numbers regularly shift, between 44 and 78 percent of Americans have wanted tighter gun control, including background checks and preventing mentally ill people from purchasing weapons. Most Americans also want a full ban on high-capacity ammunition clips and assault-style weapons. Instead, they have had to make do with a tragic diet of "thoughts and prayers" in the face of remarkably regular mass shootings.

The hydrocarbon industry may have lost its fight to stay under the radar, given the rising concern about climate change, but oil and gas executives are still working hard with their lobbyists. In 2018, UK petroleum giant BP spent US$53 million on climate lobbying.[48] That's a big sum for a single firm—a million dollars every week on climate lobbying alone. In terms of Porsche 911 Carreras, given that's a whole new currency, that's a couple per day. Shareholders didn't complain about this outlay, because they understood that giving a couple of 911 Carreras every single day is not wasted money. BP got benefits that didn't align with the needs of ordinary citizens.

In 2017, the Australian coal industry spent more than A$5 million on climate lobbying, outspending by a factor of twenty-seven to one Australia's four biggest environmental groups combined, who only put up A$183,000.[49] Again, big coal, like its siblings, big oil and big gas, clearly thinks this investment pays off. It will be interesting to see how Australia's devastating fires of 2019-20 affect such lobbying efforts going forward.

Another big spender in this space is the defense and aviation world. There is Boeing, and the controversy surrounding its new 737 Max aircraft. Lion Air flight 610 crashed in Indonesia on October 29, 2018 with the loss of 189 lives, while Ethiopian Airlines flight 302 crashed in Ethiopia on March 10, 2019 with another 157 people losing their lives. Some American nuns and friars have been on Boeing's case to disclose its lobbying of the aviation regulator. Did Boeing lobby the regulator to soften its standards? According to the Chicago-based manufacturer, such disclosure "is not in the best interests of our shareholders."[50]

Bribery is too strong a word for every single thing that lobbyists do. Often their work is about greasing the wheels, both financially and in the sense of "you scratch my back and I'll scratch yours." Favors range from taking politicians and senior civil servants to big sports events to finding an influential politician's lazy son a good job. With their significant resources, lobbyists indeed dilute the representative nature of our democratic governments. You simply can't entirely and faithfully represent two parties with different goals on the same issue. It's what lawyers and others call a "conflict of interest."

Although this major crack in the social contract is no secret, most citizens don't seem compelled to deal with lobbying's effects. What I find tragic is that we really don't have anybody fighting to prevent or challenge a vast swathe of activity that compromises the relationship we citizens have with our government. It compromises our democracy. Which again raises the question, who is protecting our democracy? As it is, we have outsourced it to elected "representatives" and a permanent but unelected public sector.

Of course, constituents can come together and organize into groups demanding that their representatives vote a certain way or take a specific action. However, grassroots movements are rarely, if ever, a match for well-funded, disciplined corporations. What's more, we shouldn't need to fend off lobbyists' work. The taxes we pay are the citizens' "lobby money," which in aggregate is far more than what lobbyists pay.

Lobbying may be less of an issue in Canada because corporations are not entitled to finance political campaigns, even if some do get around the rules by "inviting" their employees to donate and get something in return from the employer—another case of "nudge, nudge, wink, wink." Corporate influence is much more of a problem in the US and, to a somewhat lesser extent, the UK. But lobbying involving behind-the-scenes arm-twisting and favors takes place in every Western democracy.

The representative nature of our government is diluted from within as well as from outside the system. In reality, political party leaders and whips dictate most of what elected representatives can do on important issues. If a representative wants a career promotion, they have to toe the line. A party or legislative hierarchy, or the government CEO, can also severely curtail our representatives' roles. Our elected officials often stop representing us to instead follow orders. In fact, the government's chief executive probably does more than any other single person to dilute our democracy's representative nature.

The British Conservative party typically has more than a dozen whips whose job it is to remind, push, encourage, and bully

Conservative MPs to follow the party leader's line. The term "whip" originates from hunting. It's the term used to describe the huntsman's assistant, who would whip stray hounds into the main body of the pack. That ugly etymology parallels the enforcement measures whips use to scramble the messages constituents send to their representatives. On big issues, our representatives have little wiggle room. They are hounds to be whipped back into shape.

In fact, even on petty issues, I've become aware of instances where the government CEO directly intervened on a constituency matter. In one case, an MP was to present a local award—not even a particularly prestigious one—to a constituent for community work. The prime minister's office intervened on the morning of the presentation and told the MP not to present the award because of negative comments the constituent made about the PM several years back. The MP excused himself from the ceremony due to poor health.

This is party politics, which undermines democracy and people power. I know every party official is shaking their head at this because I'm undermining the very apparatus on which they've built their careers. After all, it's the system, the same one which all party politicians helped to build and now rely on. Even if we accept that people power can be outsourced or delegated to representatives for four or five years, what good are the representatives if the party chief or government CEO makes them turn a deaf ear to our needs? This happens every single day. Who, then, is representing us ordinary citizens? And why is our representative effectively taking orders from somebody else?

PUBLIC SERVICE LIFERS

Another aspect of representation that deserves attention are officials who stay in government as long as possible. Welcome to the age of the career elected official, who doesn't understand or, more likely, chooses to overlook that in holding their seat for so long, they do the representative nature of our democracy a real disservice. To put it bluntly, many of our elected politicians need to emerge from their political bubbles and get jobs like the rest of us. And national politics is precisely that—a bubble that politicians seldom emerge from during the time they "represent" us. More ordinary people need to have an opportunity to represent us instead.

In the nineteenth century, the average tenure of US senators was five years, while that of representatives was less than three. At that time, almost 40 percent of representatives did not seek reelection. Only one percent of congressmen and not a single senator in the Sixteenth Congress (1819-1821) served for more than sixteen years.[51] Representatives legislated for a brief period and went back to their regular jobs, to be replaced by fresh faces with new perspectives. After all, the government belongs to and consists of ordinary people, not an elite sliver.

In contrast, the average tenure of senators in the 116th congress, which ends in 2021, is about eleven years, more than double what it was in the nineteenth century.[52] The average tenure of representatives has more than tripled to nine years.[53] Since 2000, an astonishing 89 percent of representatives have sought reelection, many because they would struggle to get a better job.[54] They also have no intention of doing so, having developed real skill and expertise in campaigning and winning elections.

The 115th Congress was not much different. Forty-two percent of representatives and 46 percent of senators had served for more than eight years.[55] It's not entirely clear to me who they served. "Served" has connotations of doing a service to the public and society, an interpretation that's often a stretch. It's extraordinary that 22 percent of the members of both bodies kept their jobs for more than sixteen years. In fact, reelection rates in the House haven't dipped below 80 percent in the last fifty years, while those in the Senate have hovered at rates only marginally lower.[56]

The connection between citizens and representatives is not only compromised by the latter hanging around for too long but also by demographics and simple arithmetic. The US Constitution was written in 1787, when America's population was four million, and each congressman represented 30,000 people. Today, the US has a population some eighty times larger. On average, each elected official in the Capitol now "represents" more than 750,000 people. Not only do their lengthy terms limit everybody else's opportunity to participate in government, but the number of citizens they claim to represent is so much larger.

I analyzed the employment histories of the three leaders of the Conservative Parties of Australia, the UK, and Canada as of September 2019. Of the combined seventy-nine years they had worked to date, fifty-four were in politics—68 percent of their combined experience. If we then included experience as a journalist covering politics, which Boris Johnson did for years, that would mean sixty-eight years, totaling 86 percent of working in or reporting on politics.

With this unimpressive track record, why is it that Conservative MPs elected them to manage entire governments with budgets in the hundreds of billions of pounds or dollars? No intelligent

Conservative MP, when being honest with themselves, could justify nominating someone who has never managed any organization in their entire life to then manage a multibillion entity. Would the same MP entrust their party leader to manage the family business? Of course, a large majority would not.

How did we arrive at Career Politician Land? First, it's so much harder to dislodge incumbent representatives than it used to be. They have a huge advantage in raising campaign cash. To win a House seat, a candidate typically needs to spend US$1.5 million and given recent trends, that number is rapidly rising. Winning a Senate seat typically costs more than US$10 million, and that too is on upward trajectory.[57] That's a lot of money for a nonincumbent political aspirant to try to raise. The vast majority of citizens can't even see that hurdle, let alone try to jump it, which reflects not at all on their ability to work on behalf of their constituents if they were allowed to do so.

Another reason is that elected officials now constantly seek reelection, since many aren't capable of any other sort of work as financially rewarding or interesting as wielding political power, with all the trappings. Part of this, of course, reflects the ongoing workplace specialization, as we move from traditional to modern, and then to postmodern societies Yes, the minister of finance might eventually end up in a bank, and the minister of industry might go on to head a manufacturing group, but most representatives who aren't reelected don't like their new jobs. Not only do the vast majority have little expertise or experience beyond performing in the political circus, but their skills aren't easily appreciated.

I have a private-sector business. If I needed somebody to manage a piece of it and a career politician walked in with his resumé in hand, the first questions that would go through my mind would be: "Have you ever achieved anything of substance?" "Have you ever managed teams against deliverables?" "Have you ever led, inspired, and enabled an organization to get a job done?" "Besides these soft skills, do you have up-to-date technical skills?" The typical politician will try to sweet talk their way out, smile, shrug shoulders, and desperately camouflage the real answer: "No, but I can do lots of politics. And I can orate, too." Well, that's obviously incredibly useful.

The one core competency elected officials have is electioneering, which has nothing to do with the ability to get the public's or any business done. They're also good at being interviewed where they ignore questions by answering ones that weren't asked. They deflect and defend with their public-speaking skills and emotional intelligence. It's more than a little interesting that "politician" translates to "orator" in Latin. Who needs to hire an orator? I've said it once and I'm saying it again, because it's critical to coming to terms with what's wrong in our democracy—it's rare to find a representative who has actually achieved anything of note before or during their elected tenures.

That's why a sizable number of those who aren't reelected try to get elected again. Twenty-nine MPs booted out of Canada's 338-MP Parliament in 2015 campaigned again in 2019.[58] The obvious alternative to another run at an office that would allow former representatives to remain in the political industry is to become a lobbyist, a seemingly incestuous state of affairs and a real loss of face. They couldn't get elected, so they ended up lobbying. What thirteen-year-old ever aspired to be a lobbyist? It's not the job that politicians signed up for.

Is there any doubt that both these factors have diluted democracy? And let's remind ourselves that there's absolutely no mechanism or agency tasked and no movement or energy inspired to narrow the gap between citizens and the state. Politicians sticking around a lot longer and representing twenty or thirty times the number of people that the system and process of our democracy were designed for—there are profound real costs to this disconnection. Earlier we learned of legislatures' lack of interest in the plight of their homeless citizens. It doesn't, of course, end there.

Career politicians, as well as former bankers and lawyers, dominate the British House of Commons, creating a cocooned reality which doesn't instinctively see the universe of the citizen body.[59] In 2019, only 4 percent of MPs came from a healthcare background, in contrast to the 10 percent of the national population that works in healthcare.[60] If more MPs were former physicians and nurses, the legislature might properly support the country's National Health Service (NHS), an institution that an extraordinary 82 percent of Britons are worried about. The British government may have been better prepared for COVID-19. It might also help if British MPs were banned from using private healthcare, a luxury afforded to only 11 percent of Britons.[61] That would really get things moving in the NHS, wouldn't it?

I'm now going to make what may seem like a tangential point that may be surprising only because of my emphasis thus far on bridging that gap between citizens and their democracy. I am largely in favor of Britain's unelected and unique second house, which might seem a very undemocratic position. Canada may have legalized the use of marijuana but I have neither smoked nor inhaled. I'm quite sober, so please hear me out. The British House of Lords has a very limited role in national government, but it's also an institution that has come to play a vital role, and one that citizens benefit enormously from.

Members of the House of Lords are not elected. Citizens have no say in their appointment. Mind you, citizens don't elect their prime minister or cabinet members, either. I can and will go on, but we don't need to belabor this further. But it's so tempting— neither a prime minister nor a cabinet minister needs to be elected as an MP by the people. If the Commons or the party with the most MPs decided I should be prime minister, I'd head to 10 Downing Street and be entitled to take the famous drive to Buckingham Palace, with my Sainsbury Red Label tea bag at the ready.

Despite 99.5 percent of the British government already being made up of unelected civil servants, a lot of people want to abolish the similarly unelected Lords. I'd rather keep the nonhereditary component of the Lords, because it provides a platform for bringing some of the country's most accomplished, experienced, and capable people into government, including many who are not interested in a full-time, 9-to-5 job or running in our election circus. These individuals benefit both the government and citizens immensely.

For a cost of up to £305 per day in 2019—and they're paid on a per-day basis—British citizens get the input of a brilliant range of renowned experts who have valuable insights and expertise to offer. These include James Dyson, the founder of the Dyson manufacturing, David Craig, the former chief of the defense staff, and David Attenborough, the documentary filmmaker and environmental campaigner. That's not a particularly high price to have such people support or inform better government.

And, given that the same chamber has a largely advisory role with extremely limited power to reject legislation from the Commons, its ability to dilute representation, which has already been diluted almost out of existence, is also minimal. The citizen body doesn't lose much in granting the Lords limited influence and gains a lot by having a level of stability, accomplishment, and expertise at the heart of government that MPs, who are focused on electioneering and following their whips' beck and call, can't hope to match.

Unlike the members of the Commons, nonhereditary members of the Lords have usually achieved something spectacular and been at the head of undertakings. There's a huge difference between sitting in the passenger seat giving advice, which is what many lawyers and accountants do, and actually driving. As a citizen, I want our society to have the input of drivers, not passengers. And I definitely want to avoid having the chimps in Banksy's "Devolved Parliament" sitting in, much less driving, my car.

The Lords detour aside, the issue of government employees becoming fixtures is not confined to elected representatives. Civil servants also overstay their welcome. In 2018, the median job tenure in the US private sector was 3.8 years.[62] In the federal government, it was 8.3 years. In the UK in 2017, the numbers, although a little more balanced, followed the same pattern—6.7 years in the private sector versus 9.8 years in the public.[63] In Canada in 2016, 16.4 percent or one in six federal civil servants worked in the government *for more than twenty-five years*.[64] A quarter of a century is time enough to usher in a new generation.

It's unhealthy for our democracy and people power when unelected officials are stuck in civil service for that long. They need to refresh their perspective on government, aligning it with that of the majority of citizens. They should see government not primarily as an employer but mainly through a consumer's or financier's lens. Those who pay taxes and use government services also deserve greater opportunity to take ownership of the state and inject it with fresh ideas and experience. It's their country, too.

ENTREPRENEURS

There's one type of underrepresentation in the public sector that seldom receives the attention it deserves—the absence of entrepreneurs. Having been employed by and a consultant to both the private and public sectors, my current vantage point as an entrepreneur gives me insights very few public-policy thinkers enjoy. I have a set of experiences that those in government rarely possess. During my interactions, I've come to realize that if they do understand, it's only in intellectual sense.

It's difficult to nail the exact number of entrepreneurs in society, partly because of conflicting definitions. Are all sole proprietors of businesses inherently entrepreneurs? Can somebody—for instance, Facebook's CEO Mark Zuckerberg, who started as an entrepreneur—evolve out of the role as the business matures? It's now hard to see Zuckerberg, Bill Gates, or Warren Buffett as entrepreneurs, even if that's how they started their careers.

Despite problems of definition, the literature suggests that between one in ten to twenty people in society are entrepreneurs. Some sources suggest the world has 400 million entrepreneurs, and the US, a relatively entrepreneurial country, has between 25 and 30 million of them. Even if only 5 percent of a population is made up of entrepreneurs, that's a sizable number. Considering the proportion of Caucasian men in the US is 30 percent, 5 percent is not insignificant.[65]

That percentage, however, doesn't convey the disproportionate effect entrepreneurs have on the world around them—getting things done, driving change, and innovating. They have a widespread and marked impact on society, the economy, and even politics if we look at social media's role in recent elections. They build businesses, generate jobs, and create and fulfill needs and wants. Entrepreneurs, as the word's French origin suggests, "undertake"—they commit and begin. They build cars *and* put themselves in the driver's seat.

The entrepreneurial mindset, the willingness to take calculated risks and sensitivity to cash and time costs, are a life source to the private sector and drive a significant portion of economic, political, and social change. Entrepreneurs are good at seeing opportunities and estimating costs and benefits on the back of an envelope. They see how an opportunity can be developed and how to seize it. They've got a tendency to focus on what can be achieved, without letting the challenges and obstacles suffocate their enthusiasm. It's a mindset.

Here's one clear example: Steve Jobs fought for the iPad. He didn't want or need a marketing study before undertaking the challenge. In fact, if he's to be believed, what triggered the final decision to build the product was his getting back at someone who was badgering him over dinner about a Microsoft product.[66] Who would have thought that Bill Gates had a role, however passive and distant, in the iPad's launch? Jobs got his iPad. Since 2010, more than 400 million have been sold, and it's now a significant part of many people's lives.[67]

Not every entrepreneur succeeds. Many, many fail, some of whom try again. But let's not ignore that in 2016, self-made entrepreneurs made up almost two-thirds of all America's billionaires.[68] Entrepreneurs started America's largest six companies as of 2019. In fact, it might be more accurate to say that entrepreneurs founded nearly all large corporations. This aligns with the driving role which entrepreneurs had in both the industrial and technological revolutions. We don't find elected representatives or civil servants at the heart of either.

You may be surprised to learn that public-sector entrepreneurs are "not an oxymoron," as one *Harvard Business Review* article felt compelled to state.[69] Given their rarity, though, they may as well be. That entrepreneurs are so poorly represented in the public sector isn't good news. We don't have enough people in government who "undertake," commit, and begin. I found not a single government employment program that prioritized entrepreneurs within its ranks in any of our five Western democracies. The risk-averse culture stifles the oxygen which entrepreneurs need. There's also the issue that working with people who can't be fired does nothing for the entrepreneur's operating environment.

Nearly all organizations benefit from a blend of expertise, experience, and personality types. Existing government culture is basically that of its civil servants, who, in many ways, would be a good complementary counterbalance to entrepreneurs. Without a greater representation of entrepreneurs as agents of change and innovation, the public sector will struggle to perform or to meet the needs of both society and entrepreneurs operating in the larger economic landscape.

However, a government consisting only of traditional civil servants will struggle to see opportunities to improve and innovate. This reflects the civil service personality type, with its aversion to risk and obsession with systems and processes. Rather than looking to make things better, faster, or cheaper, or rushing to get a project off the ground and operational, they play it safe. Too many of those who succeed in the civil service don't rock the boat.

Such caution resists taking ownership and responsibility. Slow decision-making by committee, with meeting after meeting and multiple reports, often from one-person consulting firms, is the daily menu. Decisions often require sign-off from many officials, killing momentum, reducing everything to the lowest common denominator, and sucking away the energy and initiative that innovation thrives on. If Steve Jobs had faced the civil service sign-off gauntlet, the iPad would never have been developed. He might have shot himself in frustration. Welcome to an entrepreneur's nightmare.

The civil service culture is unlikely to change of its own accord. What I'm suggesting is putting these two different cultures into the same mixing bowl. One of those may be more volatile and impatient than the other, but citizens deserve and desperately need a public sector that values time, can innovate and make things happen, and reflects the members of society who are able and want to "undertake."

What then can be done to make our governments more representative? Let's look at a few proposals, which, if properly applied, could have a significant effect.

CHAPTER 8

MAKING "US" "THEM"

How do we make our democratic governments more representative? Before answering the question, let's focus on a specific point. Historically dominant groups—in Western democracies this means Caucasian men—are now feeling the pinch of demographic change. For a substantial minority, their response roughly translates to: "Our country was basically made up of whites and Christians (at least nominally). The women stayed home and did as they were told. And men married women. Now, nothing makes any sense!—transgender (whatever that means) folk marrying each other willy-nilly; Indians hijacking the cabinet; and women demanding equal pay on the football field!"

This reaction parallels what my friend felt when he saw major ethnic changes in our old hometown of Edgware. Rapid societal change, especially if visible and obvious, can be hard to digest. It's not just a white person phenomenon. And it probably becomes even more difficult after a couple of decades of income stagnation and the effect of rapid technological change, especially in social media, where half-truths and lies feed prejudices.

Dominant identities feel anxious and unnerved that their

countries are changing so quickly. They ask, "How did this happen and happen so fast?" Do once-dominant ethnicities now feel underrepresented? Under siege? Possibly. Although the Canadian population is some 80 percent Caucasian, the prime minister's cabinet, as we've seen, is multiethnic and includes ministers who wear turbans. It's not difficult to understand the feeling in some quarters that, while things were great twenty or thirty years ago, they're not so great now.[1]

Ethnic majorities, despite their ongoing privilege, increasingly feel threatened. In 2017, more than half of white Americans felt they were discriminated against.[2] They want things to stop changing and to go back to the good old days. They don't want to see turbans in their federal cabinet. They don't want to see gay men kissing in movies. And they definitely don't want a black head of state. It was an open secret during Obama's presidency that many Republican representatives and senators cringed at having to shake hands with an African-American president and first lady at social gatherings. And thus the "Make America Great Again" campaign, which pointed to a more racist and sexist America.

At the same time, despite their growing presence and stature in government, women and minority groups feel the pushback and counterattack. It's a vicious cycle. Elements of once dominant groups are striking back, as demonstrated by the return of white supremacy in mainstream American politics. Xenophobia and misogyny unfortunately command a significant and growing presence in Western democracy. We need to remain aware of this dynamic.

None of this, however, should stop us from demanding a representative government if we are to avoid an even worse vicious cycle. Without true representation, any sense of government accountability to "other" members of society will remain disingenuous and merely cosmetic. After all, why should government be accountable to groups of outsiders? This in turn dampens performance across the entire public sector. If government does not feel accountable to those segments of the citizen body which are different from the influential end of government, why should it feel an emotional obligation to perform for them?

With government's diminished sense of accountability and therefore performance, comes a persistent failure to reshape the state apparatus to be more representative of its people. Underrepresented groups on the margins of national influence, feeling less connected, further distance themselves from their government, which does even less for them. This cycle is vicious and has real consequences. It's not just something that we should merely shake our heads over. It's a very serious problem.

Preliminary results in March 2020 suggested that a staggering 42 percent of American coronavirus deaths rate were of Afro-Americans (they're 13 percent of the population).[3] Lack of meaningful representation has impacted their economics. They disproportionately worked during the epidemic, live in more crowded accommodation, have underlying health conditions, and are unable to pay for healthcare. This tragedy for underrepresented ethnic minorities is true across Western democracies.[4]

To break this circle, here are a few proposals. As a reminder, these suggestions are not meant to be a manifesto. There's nothing final or comprehensive about them. By the same token, they're more than a first stab at some potentially viable ideas. They involve tactical interventions in government and are not meant to uproot the current system. We're not trying to knock down the Death Star (I'm not saying government is the Empire). Nor do the proposals require redrafting national constitutions. What they're meant to do is effect improvements in our democracy through instrumental shifts in government.

Here's a personal analogy. I recently wanted to figure out how to incorporate a set of stretching exercises for improving mobility into my everyday routine. In executing this plan, I found ways to combine some of these stretches with work tasks. I had to think about this, and I've had to remind myself to follow through. But I didn't have to give up much of the rest of my life to incorporate new, important, and useful routines. These small changes have made a big difference.

Let's move on to some suggestions for mending the social contract by making our democratic governments more representative.

CAPPING TENURE

The first proposal is to cap the tenures of elected and unelected government officials by instituting and enforcing term limits. This, in my opinion, is a no-brainer. I suggest elected officials should have a maximum tenure of twelve years and civil servants a maximum of twenty years. These limits would be in effect whether the years served were consecutive or not. We'd need to find a mechanism to prevent civil servants from circumventing the rules by working as contract "consultants." Once the limit was reached, officials could no longer be employed by the state.

These time periods are long enough to allow the government to benefit from the experience and expertise individual officials accrue. After all, it takes time to settle into a new job and learn the ropes, and more time to master it. Then there comes a point where things get too comfortable, the learning curve diminishes, and people become somewhat too complacent. More importantly, they stop prioritizing ordinary citizens' needs. It becomes more about the status quo, and less about innovating.

I'm less focused on the exact duration than the underlying principle of capping overall tenure. I'm not quibbling about adding or removing a year, especially since what's best for New Zealand may not work for the UK. The key idea is to force those who have been in government for too long to move out. It increases the number of people able to access and fill government positions, which will help to better align public-sector representation with the broader population. The public sector's ability to empathize with and understand citizens' needs can only increase when new faces have greater opportunity to enter government service.

Someone who has been a representative for twenty or thirty years has become too much of a fixture in government's fabric. Peter Bottomley became a British MP and Patrick Leahy a US senator when *Jaws* was released. It's 2020. Am I the only person who thinks nobody should be in elected politics for that long? Their ongoing presence does nothing for "people power." Nothing. It's corrosive. It's fine if our very specific election process is our priority. It's not if our democracy is more important than that process. I don't expect our "representatives" will surface this issue, which raises the question of where in our democracy this proposal might take root? I ask again, who is protecting the citizen body here?

We have enough—far too much—deadwood in the system. If we bring in someone new to replace an MP after twelve years, in many cases, they'll bring with them the fresh perspectives of a different socioeconomic background, gender, or ethnicity. Yes, there's something to be said for the institutional knowledge elected officials possess. But we don't need them to stick around their entire lives "doing politics" or being part of the bureaucracy at the expense of citizens who own the state just as much as anyone else does.

Most countries have term limits, at least for their government CEOs. If US presidents can have term limits, why not members of Congress? Why the different approach? We want elected representatives to limit the amount of time they sit in a comfortable seat. In this, we're asking them to legislate what they personally don't want—the haunting specter of life beyond politics. Clearly, we have a gap: we citizens are missing an advocate in the system. Let's not forget that in 2018, 74 percent of Americans wanted congressional term limits.[5] Another political landslide that "representatives" ignore.

One objection to term limits is that new recruits won't have experience. But I'm not proposing that twenty-two-year-olds directly out of college be brought in to fill positions vacated by department heads. In the civil service, for instance, it would be quite possible to focus on recruiting from within or hiring those who have spent fifteen or twenty years in the private sector.

There are, for instance, lawyers, accountants, designers, managers, and urban planners in both the civil service and the private sector. When a government urban planner leaves after a twenty-year tenure, someone with private-sector, urban-planning experience could be recruited to take their place. Or perhaps another civil servant with fifteen years of experience might be offered the job. You'd both hope and expect these fresher faces to bring new ideas and approaches, as well as a more vigorous culture, with them.

The increased propensity to switch jobs and even careers in contemporary society aligns with this proposal. Instead of spending one's entire life in a single organization or career, there's a trend toward greater career diversification, which imposing term limits could leverage. Different sets of valuable career and life experiences can't help but benefit government. I am quite convinced that my previous work in government has helped my work as an entrepreneur.

There's another obvious pushback to term limits. If the people want a representative in the legislature for fifty years, so be it. Heck, if they want to a cat as an MP, let them. Why should we deny them that right? Why should we interfere with a perfectly sensible process? Well, the people's rights are already denied. The people didn't want Donald Trump in office, yet they got him. And the people in Australia, New Zealand, Canada, and the UK never elected a prime minister. There's no proof that they wanted those prime ministers. The "process" is far from perfect. Let's not ignore what's obvious.

There's a bit of tongue-in-cheek in that response. The more serious answer is that we need to remind ourselves of the massive systemic advantage that incumbent elected representatives have over their challengers. It's not a level playing field. Representatives already elected have a significant advantage in generating the resources needed for a campaign. It's an advantage that ordinary folks struggle to compensate for or filter away. The incumbent representative starts the election race several feet ahead.

The other thing is that we must protect our democracy. It's more important than the voting process, which, without sounding tautologous, is a means and not an end. We, the people must govern, or get as close to it as we practically can. Voting in representatives may be a step to that end. However, just as so, we can have a democracy, we can have people power, *without* electing representatives for five years, without mentioning that 99.5 percent of our democracy isn't elected. In fact, some would argue that outsourcing the legislative function of government is itself antidemocratic. The process of voting for representatives can undermine "people power."

If we replace our misguided obsession with voting for representatives with an obsession for democracy, term limits become a no-brainer. The mechanics of our particular form of democracy is that we have chosen to elect a tiny sliver of representatives for two, four, five or six years—don't ask me why three years is excluded—while maintaining a permanent rump majority. But we need to recognize that the way we have chosen to effect democracy, meaning people power or the power of self-governance, has limits, one of which is that we have outsourced democracy for so long that in fact we no longer self-govern.

There's a good case to exclude certain categories of government employees from this limit. The obvious ones include members of the armed forces, physicians, and other professions that have a long, specialized training period. Each country will have to determine its own exceptions. However, the idea isn't to provide blanket exceptions for a majority of, let alone all, categories. The aim is to enforce the rule that once you've been on a government paycheck for long enough, there needs to be a powerful set of reasons why society should keep you there for longer.

What are this suggestion's unintended consequences? First, as already mentioned, if we're going to remove civil service staff, we need to replace them. The value proposition that government offers to talent—not only financially but in other factors such as career progression, empowerment, work-life balance, impact, and challenge—needs to be sharpened so that we don't have public-sector staff shortages. Some recruitment and retention strategies may need fundamental enhancement; others may only need to be tweaked.

Another potential unintended consequence is that introducing term limits for elected representatives might encourage them to ingratiate themselves with potential employers in the final year or two of their terms. If you knew you'd be out of work next year, might you spend the final months job-hunting? Might you do favors for your next employer? This is something to anticipate and prevent. It needs management, but that's not an impossible task. Perhaps we could introduce strict criminal sanctions to dissuade such conduct? Or transfer staff to the nonprofit sector and local community projects for a year at 85 percent of the full salary?

Setting term limits also makes representatives more vulnerable to third-party influence. An experienced elected official will know how to handle civil servants, lobbyists, and special interest groups better than a fresh-faced, rookie representative. Experienced representatives know who to lean on, who to ignore, and when. They're aware of hidden pitfalls. Inexperienced legislators might be more easily manipulated, both by outsiders and by senior members of their own party. These possibilities should be anticipated.

In the end, if those elected truly represent constituents, which is, after all, the fundamental basis of our democracy, there really isn't much that lobbyists and others with self-interested agendas should be able to do. And we'll get into protecting that representation a bit more a little later. It's only when our public servants' objectives don't gravitate around those they represent that things get messy.

CAMPAIGN SPENDING CAPS

Capping or putting limits on campaign spending is another slam-dunk strategy for increasing representation. The problem is particularly acute in the US, because enormous amounts of capital flood its electoral processes, especially at the federal level. Unlimited campaign spending is destroying America's democracy, an institution polluted with so much money that the ordinary citizen has been obscured. Money has drowned out the people's voice.

As we've seen earlier, without campaign-spending caps, incumbents have a tremendous advantage. Legislators who favor oil and gas companies, big banks, or unions during their terms find it relatively easy to raise millions of dollars to market their electoral campaigns. This legalized bribery, which incumbents have almost no incentive to scale back, significantly curtails citizens' ownership of and influence over the state. Price tags of US$1.5 million for the House, US$10 million for the Senate, and hundreds of millions of dollars for the presidency are akin to an element of political prostitution.

Fundraising is critical to campaigns. In 2018, the winning candidate raised the most money in 83 percent of Senate contests. The figure was even higher for House candidates—89 percent.[6] It's not always the case that the largest fundraiser wins—there always glaring exceptions—in the three months after November 8, 2019, Michael Bloomberg spent an extraordinary US$452 million in advertisements alone to earn the Democratic Party's nomination in the US presidential election.[7] His total final spending hit almost a billion dollars, and he still didn't win the nomination.[8] This was a frankly immoral burning of wealth and felt like an attempt to buy the presidency.

But 83 percent and 89 percent are still pretty high numbers. Money affects who gets elected, what policies they put forward, and whom those policies benefit. Without this funding advantage, incumbents' seats would be challenged left, right, and center. The way things currently stand eliminates nearly every citizen from seeking office since they don't have the money.

Instead, citizens should be able to say, "You know what? I might want to run for the legislature in six years. I don't have to raise a million dollars to have a real chance for that seat. I have to raise five thousand, which I have or can save or borrow from my brother. Five thousand is doable." The extraordinarily steep financial prerequisites to meaningfully enter election races are an embarrassment to our democracies.

The absence of fundraising caps mirrors the absence of spending caps. The wealthiest citizens sharply increase their prospects of becoming elected "representatives." It makes no sense to give candidates seats in legislatures on their fundraising ability. This is as callous as rewarding ambassadorships to campaign donors. With tight spending limits, fund-raising becomes a less serious bar for those who could do an amazing job at working for their constituents. Citizens have a right to choose candidates on a level playing field, based on their policy positions, credibility, and track records.

The nature of our democracy can't help but deteriorate if the electoral process is obstructed by people who are in office mainly because they're able to raise more money or have a lot of their own. After all, we want to choose the person who can best *represent* our interests. We don't want someone who inherited a mountain of cash or whose friends all own Ferraris. We want credibility. And we might even welcome with open arms candidates who didn't self-promote or campaign for themselves. That would be wonderfully refreshing.

It's impossible to level the playing field and get a more representative government with laws that state or imply: "You can raise as much money as possible as long as you raise it in this country. You can then use those funds to advertise as much as you like. It doesn't matter if that advertising is partially or completely false. By the time we cull fact from fiction, it will be old news. You can then repay those who funded your campaign with government perks, despite the fact you should be working as best you can for all citizens."

Much of American democracy is mired in this problem. Candidates from less affluent ethnicities and socioeconomic groups struggle uphill to raise the funds to compete with incumbents. Elected representatives who are effectively incumbents-for-life prevent citizens from feeling a sense of ownership over their own country. This unfair funding advantage must be tackled if we are to have governments that represent and reflect all of society.

The US Supreme Court, whose members are nominated through a political process, ruled that being able to spend as much as you like on election campaigns is a matter of free speech. I get that my proposal to limit campaign spending interferes with how some Americans interpret the First Amendment. This right, though, is already limited in several common sense areas, such as fraud, child pornography, and terrorist threats, so let's not forget that it isn't absolute and unconditional. The US already has limits to free speech.

Despite the court's position, it's not surprising that ordinary Americans aren't agnostic about political campaign spending limits. In 2018, an overwhelming 88 percent of Americans wanted "limits on the amount of money individuals and groups can spend on campaigns."[9] That's an extraordinary majority—eight to one. To compare, of those Americans who have heard of Area 51, 74 percent think that alien craft are not held there.[10] However, I don't expect the US Congress to try to translate the people's voice into law, because almost every elected American elected official relies on the deeply unpopular unchecked fundraising to keep their job.

This harks back yet again to the protection that citizens unfortunately need from their democratic governments, a protection that our indirect and representative form of democracy needs. My argument here is: "Look, we recognize that the problem is that we citizens want to protect ourselves. Where's our board of directors? The corporations we've invested in have boards of directors to protect shareholders. Where's the government board of directors for taxpaying citizens? Who's protecting us from you, the executive, legislative, and judiciary branches?" It's an odd question which originates in the outsourcing of our government.

Instead of letting cash call the shots, spending and donation caps would encourage candidates to promote what works for citizens. This would encourage ordinary people to feel better connected with and participate more in their governments.

There's less incentive to participate in a democracy if you think that fat campaign contributions will drown out or compromise citizens' voices. Despite being a fierce "small-d" democrat, I can see a tragically strong case for not bothering to turn up to vote. In contrast, spending limits would reenergize our democracies.

Lowering campaign limits also means that we won't be fire hosed with ads. An astonishing US$6.8 billion was spent in the US 2016 congressional and presidential elections, and most went to advertising.[11] Trump and Clinton spent US$81 million on Facebook ads alone.[12] Facebook has got to love presidential elections, even if most of the content in the campaign advertising is false or exaggerated.[13] It may be that Facebook doesn't really care, as long as the Benjamins keep coming in.

The belief that an ordinary citizen can properly filter this noise or has the critical thinking skills to contend with such a barrage is untenable. Philip Tetlock, a University of Pennsylvania professor, cogently addressed this issue:

> "Usually, in most organizations, the people at the bottom are accountable to the people at the top, whereas in a democracy the people at the top are ultimately accountable to the people at the bottom. Of course, it's not that simple because the people at the top have a lot of resources—cognitive and financial—for manipulating the views of the people at the bottom. And the people at the bottom don't have nearly as many resources for coping with the influence tactics."[14]

If we were to cap election spending during a presidential election year at US$1 billion, which would still make it the most expensive election per capita in the world, and then share the US$5.8 billion savings with every homeless person in the country, each would get almost ten thousand dollars. In other words, we could almost eliminate homelessness in the most powerful country in the world for an entire year *and* improve our democracy. How can that be bad? I just can't see the vast majority of incumbent federal politicians agreeing to that. It would decimate their reelection prospects.

Alongside capping campaign spending, I'd also limit donations. If individual American citizens could donate no more than US$10,000 to all state and federal politicians, and all organizations were banned from any political donations, advertising, or funding whatsoever, we'd be a big step closer to a much more vibrant and representative democracy. The benefits would go some distance to restoring the social contract and invigorating the relationship between those who govern and those governed.

In New Zealand, the UK, and Canada, and indeed in most of Western Europe, there are already limits on national political campaign spending, in part to encourage a level playing field for those from poorer economic backgrounds. Even though Australia has lax political donation and spending rules, in the forty-eight hours before their national election, most political advertising must cease. There is, in any case, a growing sensitivity around and reaction to the impact of money on the integrity of Australian democracy.[15]

In Canada, federal campaign limits have been in place since 1974. In 2019, the most a citizen could donate to all federal politics was C$6,400. Canadian companies and organizations, including trade unions, simply cannot donate at the federal level. Canadian federal parliamentary candidates' campaigns generally spend between C$75,000 and C$115,000 in total. The most a candidate spent in the 2015 federal election was C$180,000, about US$140,000.[16]

In contrast, Beto O'Rourke's 2018 campaign for one of the two Texas Senate seats spent US$79 million—564 times that amount. And he lost. Another outlier in the Bloomberg mold. What does it say about our democracy that candidates feel that spending such sums is sensible, justified, or even sane? Please don't suggest that they do so out of an intense love for their country or state. He was so desperate to be elected that he and his backers funded the campaign with the equivalent of the debt of every single student in New York state.[17]

Granted, Canadian election outlays are still significant in a country where the average pretax income is below C$50,000. The rich and upper-middle class still have a huge advantage in becoming MPs. Poor earners, defined as those with an annual income of about C$22,133, have the deck stacked against them, not least because they're living hand to mouth—if even that.[18] And this doesn't even touch on the benefits, aside from campaign fundraising, of coming into politics from a position of economic strength.

But the situation is dramatically better in Canada than it is in the US. It's a whole lot easier to raise C$100,000 than to raise the US$10 million for a Senate seat, which explains why the two big Canadian political parties spent only C$84 million (US$61 million) in the entire 2015 federal election. That wasn't even one measly percent of what was spent in the 2016 US election, yet Canada's population is about 11 percent of the US's.[19] Despite what Americans like to believe, The Economist Intelligence Unit ranked the quality of America's democracy below that of Spain, Chile, and Mauritius. The US was practically level with Estonia.[20]

Can we cap donations in the US? Is such change even possible? Can powerful vested interests be taken on? The answer, I believe, however tentatively, is yes, given the current rate of social and technological change. It will admittedly be hard. However, sudden, far-reaching change is more possible now than it has ever been. Something that might have taken fifty years to happen a century ago can now take place in months or less. This accelerated rate of change is of course tied to the speed with which communications and other new technologies are being used and developed.

There will be three obvious sources of resistance: incumbent elected representatives; businesses in the advertising industry, including media platforms such as Facebook and Fox News; and organizations, such as the gun and hydrocarbon lobbies, whose agenda clashes with the general public's. These groups will lead the charge against donation limits, declaring any restriction undemocratic, tyrannical, or downright evil. That's a formidable alliance against the people. That I'm a Muslim will invoke at least a few lunatics to claim that I'm trying to implement Sharia law, whatever the heck that is.

None of these resistance groups exists to protect or enhance people power—thereby reducing the distance between citizens and their government—or democracy itself. Greater elected representative turnover and fewer political ads would at least allow us to breathe and curtail the lobbying industry. It would transport the citizen body one more step toward a genuine democracy. That's not a bad set of potential outcomes—for ordinary citizens at least.

SECONDMENTS

The Merriam-Webster dictionary, or at least the one that I use, defines "secondment" as "the detachment of a person (such as a military officer) from his or her regular organization for temporary assignment elsewhere." Secondments have become increasingly prevalent in the private sector, with personnel from one department temporarily assigned to another to learn more about the overall business.

My proposal is to employ secondments that temporarily place people from the private sector in the public sector and vice versa. By and large, secondments are not difficult to administer. As with splitting up government departments into competing units, the change may sound significant, but is actually not all that challenging to put into effect. At least in this instance, we already have private sector secondments. Public sector secondments would not require rewriting the constitution and would have profound cultural consequences.

This is another means of aligning our governments with the people, bringing private-sector practices and mindsets, including accountability, getting things done, and valuing time, into the public sector. The aim is to get people in government more attuned to the energy and pace of what's happening outside their cocoons and give the public sector an experience and sense of how other citizens work. Private-sector values and perspectives would be brought into government, enhancing the public sector's performance ethic. Seasoned private-sector employees going into the public sector would shake things up.

There are significant benefits to understanding what's on the other side of the fence. You develop new relationships and new perspectives. You then take that understanding back into your own organization, where it leads to ideas and conversations you would never have entertained before. Those who cross over and return become change agents. Even if the changes are small, such shifts often produce ripple effects.

While working for a bank, I was put on secondments and told, "You'll be spending three months in different departments so that you understand how they work." Was three months enough? I probably would have wanted more time, but the experiences were still valuable. I developed relationships I otherwise wouldn't have been introduced to. I got an understanding both of how different departments viewed my home department and of how the bank's parts worked with one another and saw the world in a different light. Trading desks, relying on gut instinct, had a different perspective on the world than that of research-based, corporate-finance teams.

Will the public sector be able to tolerate private-sector culture? Will private-sector employees struggle in an environment where their colleagues call in sick more than normal and can underperform without consequence? How will they respond when 95 percent of staff have checked out before 5:05 p.m. every day without fail? Or insist on their union-negotiated coffee break irrespective of any deadlines or work pressure? There would be clashes and fallout.

But, as a taxpayer, I'd rather have management deal with disruption than continue to overpay for poor performance. My thinking would be, "Okay, there's a possibility this won't go very far, but let's give it a try and see if we can improve the public sector. Let's help the public sector understand the people that they work for. Then let's see how we can manage the curve balls because anything as new as this is going to have unforeseen consequences. Let's see how we can learn from the process."

I'd suggest a few rules to start off with: twelve-month secondments from the public into the private sector, and shorter secondments, perhaps four months long, from the private to the public sector. The private sector is much bigger and can absorb more people. For instance, in Australia in June 2018, there were slightly fewer than two million public-sector employees, compared to more than ten million in the private sector.[21]

I'm inclined to suggest a few conditions to this process. Private-sector employees must have at least a decade of experience, or maybe more, before their secondment into the public sector. You want seasoned, courageous, and independent people able to ask why six sign-offs are needed when only one person understands what's being signed off on. You want experience and gravitas from the private sector at the heart of the public sector.

In the opposite direction, I'd limit secondments to those who've had less than five years of public sector experience. Their habit patterns will be less ingrained, and they should be more receptive to developing new perspectives. This "get them while they're young" approach would aim to instill the culture of accelerated performance more prevalent outside the public sector.

Uprooting employees into new, if temporary, situations is disruptive and needs to be—you guessed it—managed. There will be confidentiality issues, performance evaluations and their repercussions, and personnel and administrative costs. There might also be personal or organizational conflicts of interest. A secondment initiative would need administrative staff resources to be effective, and might be an appendage of the tax or national insurance department given the employment aspect of the project.

Could the private sector be subsidized for taking in or sending out talent? Might this be seen as a sort of national service, given that this initiative will benefit the country as a whole? Could civil servants be incentivized to take part? These are questions up for discussion. A small pilot project could help answer these and other questions and smooth out some wrinkles before the initiative is applied more broadly.

LOW-INCOME COMMUNITIES

The next proposal, for a particular type of secondment, deserves its own special mention. As we've noted, ministers and senior civil servants live in their own bubbles. This isn't a criticism. I'm not suggesting government's key decision-makers are selfish snobs. Most have worked hard, taken advantage of what life has presented them, perhaps had a bit of luck, and deserve to live well. I live in a cushioned bubble, too.

Because government's top tier is good at what they do, they deserve their exclusive standard of living—notwithstanding issues of privileged upbringing and family wealth. The public sector does have high performers; and a significant number, if they stick around, end up with responsibility and the economic and other benefits of a good career. Let's not resurrect Marx, Lenin, and their comrades from their tombs. We need to applaud the top tier for doing well.

However, we still need to recognize that those with influence in the public sector spend a significant proportion of their days, week after week, year after year, decade after decade, in the company of people who are anything but poor. It's an occupational hazard. Spending time with ivory-tower types, connoisseurs of fancy writing instruments, and experts on which business-class seats offer the most comfort, ministers and senior civil servants can lose sight of what's happening at the other end of the spectrum. That's where citizens who need the most help reside. Their lives easily become invisible to government's elite.

Our democracy should create mechanisms to remind, educate, and enable our most accomplished officials to connect with the vast majority of the low and lower-middle classes, the neediest and least heard. Ministers, secretaries of state, and civil service leaders need to be reminded that those they serve and represent aren't for the most part "their type," but people with no hope of getting the high-paying, prestigious jobs they enjoy. And that reminder can't be just a Post-it memo. It needs to be rooted.

I propose assigning senior civil servants and ministers to work full-time inside low-income communities for limited terms, perhaps for a couple of months, and possibly as a condition of or precursor to a senior promotion. This will meaningfully connect these government executives to precisely the social stratum they might easily ignore, forming a bridge that brings those most removed from the center of government power a few steps into its nucleus.

This proposal will also ground those who have otherwise spent an increasing chunk of their lives and careers behind desks in exclusive environments, especially as they continue to be promoted. We have a functional, not moral, objective here. This exercise will help officials focus on the reality of those who haven't done so well in life. And a positive, unintended yet quite likely consequence is that it might also make our officials better human beings.

Those in prominent government roles aren't stupid. Of course, they intellectually understand that the upper echelons of government are a niche in a much larger, more diverse society. In any Western democracy, there are far more people with low incomes than high ones. But let me resurface the difference between intellectual understanding and lived knowledge. My proposal is meant to distribute to decision makers lived knowledge about the part of society that tends to have the weakest political voice. Everybody in society, not just public-sector leaders and underprivileged citizens, will be better off for it.

Ministers and top-tier civil servants need to continually refocus on those who may not have gone to a university or had no opportunities or encouragement. They need to pay attention to communities underrepresented in government, and the economically poor are a good place to start. Often, these people have simply had bad luck—struggling to find and hold a job, dealing with extortionate debt collectors, living in an ugly tower blighted with nasty gangs. That bad luck may extend to being born in the wrong place to the wrong parents—which is something I'm grateful I never had to deal with.

While this proposal may not directly place individuals from lower-income groups into the influential tier of government, it will increase that tier's understanding of "a day in the life of" a more diverse population, with significant implications for representation. This proposal isn't about greater physical representation of the diverse citizen body in government. It's about the greater presence of those citizens. In doing so, we'll put the underrepresented closer to the top of government decision-makers' agendas.

After a couple of months outside their comfort zones, officials will be able to say, "You know what? I spent two months with a family that was barely able to make ends meet in a community where everybody was financially very poor. Narcotics were more available than organic milk. In fact, organic milk couldn't be found anywhere nearby. The local grocer in fact smirked when I asked for some. It's not an easy life. I had never understood how challenging it could be to deal with that, let alone try to escape it."

Imagine if, better still, every high-ranking civil servant and minister spent twenty-four hours on the streets, homeless. We'd certainly see a dramatic reduction in homelessness. No doubt about it. British MP Adam Holloway did exactly that and more.[22] He spent an entire week without a roof over his head in 2018 and learned that the homeless are not all the same, but as diverse as the society around them.

They include office workers, children, and those who have walked out of bad relationships, as well as drug addicts. As Holloway's understanding evolved and deepened, he found that a single solution to the "homeless problem" wouldn't work. While this may sound obvious to you, I'd always managed to group the homeless together, as a homogeneous single group, a position which clearly does little to foster potential solutions.

My personal experience of this type of "secondment" comes each year in the month of Ramadan, during which Muslims are required to fast from sunrise to sundown, taking no food or liquid, not even water. This annual experience viscerally brings home how difficult it is to get things done if you're hungry, thirsty, or sleep-deprived—normal conditions during Ramadan—the last because we typically stay up later and wake earlier solely to eat and drink.

I've learned from Ramadan something no book could possibly

have taught me—how hard it is to think about tomorrow, next week, or any future plans at all when you haven't had anything to eat or drink that day. Those living on the streets or who haven't had a meal for a day and a half experience life from a very different perspective than most of us. Unable to think clearly, they'll need help if they ever hope to pull themselves up by their bootstraps—even if that feels like a physical impossibility. Quality thinking on an empty stomach is not easy. Most elected politicians simply don't grasp any of this.

A government that respects the democratic social contract will be representative and accountable and won't be inefficient or wasteful. Our social contract is in pieces because our governments have broken all three of these basic tenets. Let's go on to discuss the third pillar of the social contract: accountability, which we think we have but really don't.

PART IV

ACCOUNTABILITY

CHAPTER 9

WHAT ACCOUNTABILITY?

Accountability is the most comprehensive of the democratic social contract's basic attributes. A people's government must be accountable to its citizens. It is government officials' responsibility to make government accountable to their constituents and the citizens' responsibility to hold those officials accountable. The problem is that neither party to the social contract takes this mutual responsibility seriously enough. Until this changes, we can talk all we want about holding government to account, but we won't get real accountability.

When I asked the deputy mayor of Markham why I should trust him and the municipal government he was part of, which had failed to build a park repeatedly promised over many years, I know I wasn't the only citizen offended when he replied, "Well, don't!" His lack of a sense of accountability was outrageously nonchalant. The social contract is broken because our democratic governments don't honor it or consider themselves accountable. They can commit or promise, fail to deliver, and then go to the next photo opportunity.

How can we make sense of what's happened? I believe there

are three pieces to the accountability puzzle: elections, the lack of consequences, and the lack of transparency.

PROMISES, PROMISES

Let's start with elections. How does our electoral process cultivate the absence of governmental accountability? This is somewhat counterintuitive because we're so used to thinking of our elections as accountability's bedrock. We think because we have the power to vote a representative in or out that we therefore have accountability. But the way the system is set up actually eats away at accountability. Oddly enough, those same elections unwittingly undermine it.

Electoral candidates make the promises you want to hear to get you to vote for them. Unlike in the private sector, track records aren't a necessary qualification. Instead, we allow candidates' facile talk and fluff to obscure what's important and what we should be focused on: How capable is this person at hearing and representing us? How good at getting things done on our behalf? And how would we know this?

We've already touched on the notion that those who get elected are good at getting elected. Politicians—orators—talk their way in. They fine-tune their promises to popular needs and cravings, edit their photos, and apply thick slabs of make-up before TV interviews. This ability is their core competency, whether the candidate has any underlying merit as an elected representative or not. Many politicians regularly lie and fabricate to get elected.

Some may remember Zac Goldsmith's intellectually deceitful electoral strategy in 2016 that tried to link London mayoral candidate Sadiq Khan to terrorists. Goldsmith, who inherited a fortune from his father, misjudged Londoners' appetite for Islamophobia. Boris Johnson and Donald Trump both have quite a history of falsehood. Billy McMahon, Australia's prime minister in the early 1970s, is another head of government who comes to mind in this space.

Back home, I've seen one Ontario politician tell a group of physicians that he'd ensure they get more funding from the provincial health system, only to turn around a couple of weeks later and remind an audience of fiscal hawks that Ontario's physicians are among the most highly compensated in the world, with out-of-control salaries. No other state or province anywhere, he told them, has as many physicians on million-dollar salaries as Ontario does. I thought that was an interesting fact.

If a candidate's campaign is spending US$79 million to win a Senate seat, for instance, they may be very tempted to say anything and everything it takes to get votes. Hundreds upon hundreds of claims, promises, and quasi-promises will be thrown around. US$79 million is a lot to lose, and, if you don't get elected, you do lose everything you and your donors have contributed. Even if you don't make such promises, somebody from your campaign team may well do so.

Our current version of democracy, the one we inherited but didn't design (important point warning), encourages candidates to say whatever they can to get elected. They need a return on their considerable electioneering effort and cash outlay. It's a case of political "win or die." I personally find this overall self-campaigning to be nauseating, to be honest, going around telling others why you're the best for the job. Anyhow, some of these promises and claims are part of the campaign's official marketing collateral. Journalists record others, publishing them in print or online. There are also pledges made in private meetings, in small gatherings, and on doorsteps, where few, if any, will report what was said.

At the end of the day, few people will know everything that's been promised. There's no official repository for these promises and assurances, which are barely scrutinized, because there's no one with enough independence and resources to take the task on. We have to remember that most elections aren't for the US presidency, with its truckload of fact-checkers. The vast majority of Western government elections are mundane affairs that fly well below the radar.

In any case, after two, four, five, or six years, a new election information (or disinformation) fire hose will blur our memories of what was or wasn't said back then. Far too often, political candidates have few qualms about disseminating truths, half-truths, and outright lies, all in the same sentence. Not every politician, but enough. They'll go on until they've delivered their message enough times to convince those who may have already been predisposed to believe it. Without a stable, definite memory of what's been promised, there can be no accountability in our democracies.

It's significant that most candidates are really in no position to promise anything other than, "We'll look into it" or "We'll try to fix it." Even the US president has to ask Congress for approval of the budget. Once elected, most representatives have only a small staff and office stipend. Again, don't treat the US president as typical of an elected representative. Unless the representative is amongst the select few with a major legislative role or ministerial appointment giving access to meaningful resources, they can do very little. This is why some people criticize representatives as little more than glorified selfie-snappers.[1]

Let's cut some slack here. Elected representatives can bring focus to, expedite, and intervene in government. They can lean on relationships and push a constituent's case within the system—because as we know, the system isn't going to respond as effectively to citizens. Let's not deny elected representatives the ability to do something within the legislature or even in engaging the executive. But most of them have no real authority over civil servants or to allocate any resources. And they only rarely change policy, at least policy with real consequences.

Elected officials' most meaningful power in the UK, Canada, Australia, and New Zealand is that MPs, not citizens, have a significant influence in deciding the prime minister, who calls the shots. The PM is the only person who commands meaningful resources, and he delegates that power at will. The party with the most MPs chooses a prime minister whenever they want, even outside a general election year. John Major became Britain's prime minister in 1990, outside an election cycle and with no citizen involvement, as Boris Johnson did in 2019. MPs elected Johnson despite more than 60 percent of Britons believing he was out of touch with ordinary people.[2]

In the US, elected representatives' influence is also limited. They don't choose their president, who is chosen by the electoral college process, which Americans inherited from the eighteenth century. It wasn't designed for 330 million people in the twenty-first century, but neither the legislature nor the executive is complaining. If American citizens did choose their presidents, Hillary Clinton would be in the White House today, and Al Gore would have been president after Bill Clinton. Instead, we got Donald Trump and George W. Bush. The first, the most divisive president since Nixon if not before, and the second with the lowest approval rating of any modern US president.

The chairs of the House and Senate's Budget Committees exert one of Congress's biggest influences on the federal government by overseeing and approving the president's budget. The citizen body, incidentally, didn't give those chair holders their job either. The vast majority of elected representatives, in contrast, have no such power. What they can do is severely curtailed. In fact, state governors have more power than members of Congress do, operating in many respects as the state's CEO.

PROMISES BROKEN WITHOUT CONSEQUENCE

The second piece to the accountability puzzle is a lack of penalties. Having made all sorts of campaign promises and assurances with almost no means to follow through, representatives aren't bound to their pledges. No one really remembers or is keeping track. As a result, there are few consequences to promising the universe—even a fantasy universe—yet delivering something with the look and feel of a disheveled and cracked Lego kit.

Clearly, many representatives feel a real obligation to deliver on commitments and promises. Many want to make "the world a better place," which I think is more effectively done outside of the public sector than in it. But the following through, the delivery is optional. We've already seen how little they can actually do to keep their word, having very few of the resources needed to honor commitments. They can vote in the legislature, but their party inevitably hijacks their votes on consequential issues. Our elected officials must, for the most part, get by on a very limited office budget and by asking colleagues for favors.

Since representatives are simply unable to follow through, the fundamental problem of broken promises and unfulfilled expectations undercuts the accountability on which our democratic social contract is built. They promise, or at the very least raise expectations, but can't deliver. That the public is resigned to this state of affairs makes the situation all the more disastrous. Things aren't so simple even for representatives with roles that afford them resources and an opportunity to deliver. Let's try a thought experiment to see what can happen.

Say a candidate makes fifty commitments and promises, including one to reduce taxes if elected. "I will work hard every single day to reduce your taxes!" he proclaims at all his campaign rallies (let's give him some latitude since he's only committed to *work hard*, not actually deliver, even if he's raised expectations). In fact, tax reduction is his overarching selling point, with a few other carrots interspersed. Again, to keep it real, let's imagine one of his staff, a Blue Jays fan, tries to convince a voter that the candidate actually believes that incomes should not be taxed. Our man is privately radical.

In any event, suppose our candidate wins, and his party has also done well, getting control of the government's purse strings. The representative throws a big celebration. You're not invited, in case you're wondering, because you didn't donate a few grand to his campaign. As we've seen, the democratic process, especially in the US, has in part become "pay to play." Again, I'm trying to keep this example as real and grounded as possible.

Our representative wants to deliver on his promises. But he walks into his office the next day and does very little, because he doesn't know what to do. He's not even up to speed on his job's basic rules and regulations. Being a rookie, his small office has one window. With a view of a brick wall. This makes him nervous because his wife and parents will also see the office for what it is—a glorified closet. He's also already gotten lost twice while looking for the legislature's restaurant at lunchtime, which has further unsettled his nerves.

A week or so later, somebody high up both in government and his party invites him to join the team that decides the country's fiscal affairs. This completely unexpected promotion gives him national impact and recognition, higher pay, a chauffeur, and an office with three big windows boasting great views. He realizes that if later he doesn't get reelected, which is a lesser possibility given his new profile and now enhanced campaign fundraising ability, he could easily move to a top private-sector finance job. It's a great career opportunity, which he shares with his wife, who tells him on the same day that she's expecting their first child.

There's a big but. The government fiscal team will raise, not reduce, taxes. The country's CEO wants to lower the budget deficit and cool the overheating economy. In fact, he's something of a closet socialist, marginally to the right of the likes of Michael Foot, Bernie Sanders, and Pierre Trudeau. But definitely to the left of Simon Bridges and Michael McCormack, Taxes will rise across the board. What to do? Though not all candidates make empty promises, some do, while most fall somewhere in between. Reality changes once they're elected.

Does our representative decline the job, and instead try to reduce taxes, without any authority or power to do so? Or does he turn away from that battle and get promoted, with all the associated national impact and trimmings? We'd like to think he would remain true to his commitment, but I'm not so sure he would, especially since taking the new job improves his current situation and long-term prospects. With his new prominence, he's less likely to suffer consequences for breaking his word. He may even be approached with a book contract for an autobiography. The family would be proud.

What about promises that elected officials could deliver on but choose not to? In 2015, Justin Trudeau promised, if elected, a federal budget deficit of C$10 billion. He won by a landslide and immediately forecast a deficit of C$29 billion. He also promised a balanced budget before the 2019 election, months before coronavirus hit our radar. Instead, there was a deficit of about C$20 billion. Nobody blinked an eye. In fact, eyes would have blinked if he *had* kept his promises.

I don't want to sound partisan, since Trudeau's rivals in the Conservative Party have treated their promises in similar fashion. Also, if we accept the findings of a few independent analysts, in his first term Trudeau fulfilled more than half of his two to three hundred 2015 election promises. He broke about a quarter, and the jury is still out on the rest.[3] Not a disaster by any means; certainly not a flagrant violation of his commitments and promises.

Still, Trudeau failed to deliver on a particularly important promise regarding the deficit. For some people, this is a big deal. I personally don't think small budget deficits are cause for concern, especially if they're used for national investment and during low interest rate environments, but there you go. Not delivering something you've committed to or raised expectations for if elected still raises two serious questions.

First, for those of us who voted for Trudeau, what recourse do we now have? Can we ask Trudeau, or any representative who breaks their pledges, to resign? Can we ask to vote again? Or perhaps some compensation? Second, if elected officials can commit and fail to deliver, why must we commit to our part of the bargain, let's say to commit to pay our taxes and then to actually follow through? How is it that our elected representatives can break their word without repercussions, but we can't? Is that fair?

Exactly the same could be asked of Markham's deputy mayor. Why were there no repercussions from his government's failure to honor their promise to build our park? In the earliest democracies, he might have been locked up for such a failure. That's radical, granted, but it's definitely one way to get politicians to deliver on their promises. I don't have evidence for this, but my gut instinct is that there'd be more support for this than Americans believing in alien craft at Area 51.

More realistically, shouldn't we be able to hold back the taxes that pay the deputy mayor's salary until he feels some consequences for his government's failure to act? Should he not be personally liable along with the mayor? Or perhaps we get a rebate for having to go without a park because his government couldn't tie its shoelaces? It's not very difficult to build a park. It's been done a few times. It doesn't need a controlled, high-tech, NASA-type lab. We can't hold our taxes back, however. If we even delay our tax payments for a single day, we'll be hit with a usurious penalty.

What can we do about these broken promises and unfulfilled expectations? Right now, basically nothing, I'm afraid, although we'll soon look at some possible solutions. By the time the next election comes around, we will be on the receiving end of a dense blast of information and disinformation that will obscure our faculties. Some of the failed commitments will be forgotten; others will be blamed on other parties. The politicians will get back to what they're demonstrably good at, electioneering and getting votes. Back to the same annoying cycle.

It's not just that election promises can be broken without consequence. Elected politicians can lie about tremendously important issues with astonishing immunity. Our leaders can lie to us, and we don't consider it to be a big deal. Citizens need to take responsibility for the integrity of our democracy. We need to step up. Take the case of Bush and Blair, a partnership that rolls deliciously off the tongue, much like Starsky and Hutch, Holmes and Watson, and Tom and Jerry. "The Adventures of Bush and Blair" or perhaps "The B Team"?

On March 19, 2003, an American-led coalition, which included a sizable UK and Australian presence, along with small numbers of soldiers from other countries, many of whom were bribed or had their arms twisted, invaded Iraq. The reason given was that a certain Mr. Saddam Hussein had failed to eliminate his country's weapons of mass destruction (WMD). To quote Blair in Parliament, "Our purpose is to disarm Iraq of weapons of mass destruction."[4] We won't touch upon several nearby countries already having weapons of mass destruction, which the US and UK developed.

While the US and UK really wanted a regime change, this wasn't the justification given to legislatures or the people. It would have made a mockery of international law to argue that we must invade a country because we want to change its leader. There were also marginal attempts to link Hussein to the events of 9/11, which were absurd, since he and Al Qaeda had long hated each other. That's like linking Harry Truman to North Korea's government when it invaded South Korea. These are lies because those selling them knew they were lies. And if for a moment they believed otherwise, they were simply stupid.

There was no proof that Iraq had these WMDs at the time, a point the UN made repeatedly, and no proof has ever emerged. We now know that Bush and Blair manipulated the information given to them and consciously lied. We know they made stuff up. US Secretary of Defense Colin Powell was made to look like a fool at the UN Security Council in what initially seemed the most humiliating moment of his life. In fact, he was just as guilty of telling lies on many occasions, like any seven-year-old on a school playground.[5]

Because of these lies and the invasion they led to, more than 4,600 American, British, and other coalition soldiers were killed, and more than 180,000 Iraqi civilians died violent deaths.[6] The invasion led to such starvation and sickness that *Lancet*, one of the world's leading medical journals, calculated that 654,965 Iraqi civilians, 2.5 percent of the entire population of Iraq died in 2003–2006 alone.[7]

I totally understand that life for Iraqis would not have been amazing under the dictatorship of Hussein, who incidentally was an American ally for longer than he was its foe. But let's get something clear—654,965 civilian deaths are more than three times the number of deaths, immediate and long-term, from the atomic bombs dropped on Hiroshima and Nagasaki. Estimates of the numbers who have died since the invasion of this former Western ally are now well in excess of a million civilians. Many millions mourn their loss. Could Saddam really have done any worse?

Bush and Blair didn't die in the war, nor did their family members. They're free men and haven't been arrested. They haven't been legally penalized in any way for their falsehoods or the resulting devastation to millions of completely innocent people.

And they've done very well from selling books and giving speeches. We've done our democracies a ruinous disservice by empowering politicians to make false statements without fear of consequence, to the point that their lies trigger events leading to the death of over a million people.

Less than a third of Americans believe that their elected politicians are honest.[8] Clearly, citizens are partly responsible for this, because, instead of prosecuting public officials for false statements, including those that led to the Iraq war, we kept calm and carried on, doing nothing. You don't need to be a rocket scientist to recognize that we lack even basic accountability if the B Team took us into a catastrophic war, based on a pack of lies, yet remain free men, free to hang out with the families of the fallen servicemen and servicewomen.

SEE YOU IN FOUR YEARS

Lack of transparency is the third and final problem leading to lack of accountability in the public sector. Elected representatives don't tell us what they're up to. There's no independent verification of what they're doing, how well they're doing it, or whether it makes a difference. To find out what officials have done after getting elected, we're at the mercy of their marketing campaigns, which claim: "I built that bridge. I reduced crime. I fixed our roads. It was all me." One local councilor here in Markham told a bunch of us that he'd built the new 122,000-square-foot community center. I thought he looked remarkably unfit given the quantum of bricks, steel, wood, and concrete he had put in place.

There's almost no visibility into what elected officials actually do during their tenures. It's not just that people are unaware of what their representatives do on a particular day or week. Rather, we get no real, independent, accurate information about what our representatives are doing or not doing during their entire two-, four-, five-, or six-year terms. And there is no real movement to change this either.

The economy may be going along very well, with low inflation, low unemployment, and high growth. A PM, president, or even a powerless representative can take as much credit as they want, even if they did nothing to achieve those results. On the other hand, if the economy tanked for reasons completely beyond their control, such as a war between other countries, they're not shy about blaming everyone else for the problem. Gordon Brown didn't precipitate the Great Recession of 2009 but he had to deal with it. How much of the country's performance really has anything to do with our appointed PM or president? We simply don't know.

The fate of former British Prime Minister Theresa May is a good example. She was, of course, yet another PM chosen by the ruling Conservative Party, rather than being elected by British citizens. Part of May's mandate was to implement Brexit, an incredibly challenging task. The opposition Labour Party consciously sat the process out, unwilling to compromise or contribute to the conversation. May's own Conservative Party was in a state of civil war.

May would have had to be a miracle worker to pull off a sensible Brexit. However, the general public didn't seem to appreciate that. They took one look at the result, or lack thereof, and said, "Okay, she's in charge, so she should be making it happen. And because Brexit is a mess, she's failed. She's terrible." A champion hurdler might try to jump to the moon and fail, but that doesn't mean they're a terrible hurdler.

A much more sensible and viable approach would have been to ask, "Okay, what happened today or this month? What did Theresa May do about Brexit? What conversations did she have? What did she try? How far did she get? Who helped and who stood in the way?" Such detailed assessments don't exist in government. Britons had absolutely no meaningful way of evaluating her performance. Instead, May's low popularity ratings, which didn't reflect the realities of what she was or wasn't doing, influenced her fellow Conservative MPs to encourage her to resign.

Even at a high level, politicians will lie about what they did or didn't do without meaningful consequences. On January 22, 2020, Donald Trump insisted with respect to coronavirus that, "We have it totally under control."[9] In fact, throughout February and into mid-March, Trump continued to insist that he had coronavirus under control.[10] Contrast that with reality. Trump's own intelligence and health agencies were telling him since January that thousands of Americans will die from the virus, and they warned him to rapidly step up preparations.[11] More Americans will die from this pandemic than died in fifty years of terrorism.[12]

By the time the penny dropped, Trump claimed, "I don't take responsibility at all," as he began to realize that the US was wholly unprepared for the largest social, economic, and political shock since the Second World War.[13] Instead, he tried to blame Barack Obama, who had been out of office for more than three years, the World Health Organization which had declared a global health emergency on January 30, 2020, and China.

The electorate is therefore faced with yet another conundrum. We can't reward our elected officials for their work, because without transparency, we have no idea whether they're doing their jobs or not. All we know is what they promise and claim. They put their best face forward—what they look like after four hours of preparing for a Saturday evening, rather than when they crawl out of bed on a Monday morning.

Civil servants will sometimes tell you, off the record, that a representative is beholden to special-interest groups, engages in nepotism, doesn't understand essential technicalities, or is simply an idiot who doesn't know what they're doing. More than one civil servant in my town of Markham has bragged to me how they were able to deliver a positive result by working around a representative.

In fact, I've had the privilege of being "represented" by one elected official who, I gradually learned, was something of a laughingstock in southern Ontario. One City of Markham official told me, "We get stuff done at meetings that he's not at. You can help yourselves and us by ensuring that he simply doesn't attend. He's really clueless." I thought that was rude and even arrogant. But after a few months, I realized it was spot on. The representative was good at winning elections but otherwise inept.

There's probably an inherent human bias against having your work examined. We might all want to avert scrutiny and inhibit others from checking whether we did the best we could. Nobody likes to be placed under examination unless of course, we think someone is going to praise us. While we're doing a job, we don't want other people staring at our each and every move, asking uncomfortable, probing questions. One of my friends was once a window cleaner. His worst jobs, he told me, were those where customers watched him while he worked. Close inspection generates anxiety and uneasiness.

Government officials, elected or unelected, are not evil people who constantly plan ways of obscuring their agendas and the public's right to know. But they don't easily embrace transparency in their activities either or operate in ways that might be better for the population at large, even if these create inconvenience or difficulty for them.

Some political leaders, such as John Major, Jimmy Carter, and Jacinda Ardern govern or have governed relatively transparently. But "relatively" is still far too opaque and covert for a viable social contract. Others, like Dick Cheney, who seemed to have had extraordinary power as a US vice president, didn't even try to be transparent. In this respect, as in most others, those at the top influence the behavior of those who report to them, and by extension a significant part of government as a whole.

Despite the human propensity to self-protect, if a business employed me, I'd still expect whoever was paying my salary to know what I was doing at work on a daily basis. In smaller businesses, which account for most private-sector employment, the owner-operator or entrepreneur must scrutinize what every employee is doing and what progress is being made. In fact, often the employer doesn't even have to ask, because they see or hear about everybody's work.

In larger businesses, as you know, corporate boards of directors are created to check on the company's CEO and other executives, making sure corporate funds aren't being used to build swimming pools for family members or pay for personal vacations on private jets. It's the directors' job to oversee what's happening on the shareholders' behalf, albeit at a very high level. Management, though, has targets against which they can be fired. And then shareholders (especially in listed companies) also have a tight set of reference points—earnings, dividends, and revenue growth—to help them keep tabs on management.

Being human, officials don't want citizens peering over their shoulders. Putting aside issues of confidentiality, that may be natural enough, but they weren't elected to avoid accountability. Unlike in the private sector, what we now have in government are expectations so skewed that everyone simply assumes officials aren't going to tell them anything. That's not people power. That's impotence. We pay government officials their salaries to do a job for us, and we need and deserve to know what they're doing.

THE CULTURE OF UNACCOUNTABILITY

Bringing these three strands together—empty election assurances and promises, the absence of consequences, and the lack of visibility into what government officials actually do or don't do on a daily basis—shows us the contours of government's accountability problem. You're probably able to see where I'm going when I say that elections don't mean that our government is accountable. Now let's make this a bit more real.

Imagine hiring somebody who makes a hundred promises, aspirations, and commitments in different interviews, some of which are recorded and others not. And these promises aren't just made to the interviewer, but practically everyone in your firm that the potential candidate gets a fleeting chance to talk to. Suppose you hire him and commit to a generous guaranteed compensation package over four years. His employment contract doesn't elucidate the scope of work or any deliverables. You also agree not to fire that employee during his four-year contract.

Once the contract is signed, you don't see or hear from him

except when he makes it into the papers or sends you an email every three months or so listing his accomplishments. But you notice your hire is ignoring at least some of his promises and commitments, not quite aware that he never had the resources to fulfill them in the first place. His office has a budget of $100,000, but he earlier committed to do things that cost several times that. Speaking of which, you don't fully recall his list of his promises during the interview process.

Four years later, he knocks on your door to renew his contract. Given the amount of time that has elapsed, you're even more blurry about most of his promises, but you do remember a couple that he has not kept. He counters your concerns with some intelligent-sounding explanations you can't validate, possibly because the topics being discussed are complex and technical, and they invoke government documents which you can't access. In any case, he produces a fat binder that parks the blame on somebody else. He then begins to connect with you, listens to your needs and wants, and leaves you feeling comfortable that he will look after your concerns.

How could an accountability process possibly take place under these circumstances? It simply can't. Likewise, we have our heads buried deep in the sand—which even ostriches don't do—if we think our democracy is meaningfully accountable. Our inability to hold our representatives responsible directly contributes to their nonperformance. If we can't even determine whether they're performing, we can't seek redress for nonperformance as we might in a normal dispute.

No wonder politicians campaign so hard to be elected. At times it feels as if they are always electioneering at some level. It's great to get perks, shake hands, receive and distribute medals, and benefit from a healthy compensation package for a few years, with no oversight or set deliverables. Not to mention the impact on their egos. In many elected representative jobs, you really could play with an Xbox all day, every day with no consequences. What or who would stop you?

If a group of citizens took it upon themselves to confront the government in the courts about its breach of the social contract, they wouldn't get far. The executive and legislative branches craft the very laws the courts administer and refine. It's pointless to seek judicial redress when the issue at stake is the law itself and how it ignores or at least insulates government failure. Our legal framework doesn't protect our social contract, which, rather than the infrequent act of voting, is the very soul of our democracy.

The result is a passive collusion between government, which wants to keep citizens at arm's length, and the governed, who accept this state of affairs. Taxpayers give no or very little pushback. At most, we mumble, "It's just the way things are," or "that's the system" and our cynicism deepens. We move on, numbed out, until things go off the rails, which is what seems to be happening now. To be honest, I'm kind of fed up with politicians telling me to play by the rules of the system—the one that nourishes them and doesn't place citizens in its center.

Let's not underestimate what "off the rails" looks like. In August 2011, spontaneous riots broke out first in London and then across other British cities. Five people were killed, sixteen were injured, more than UK£200 million in property was damaged, and more than 3,000 people were arrested. A comprehensive review of one of Britain's toughest weeks in decades pointed the blame at social injustice, deprivation, poor police relations in affected communities, and general opportunism.[14] Others pointed to the higher proportion of younger, underemployed people in these communities. What's interesting was the role of social media in congregating and dispersing rioters almost instantaneously. That connectivity infrastructure has, if anything, gotten stronger.

Taxpayers have no effective redress if they don't like or are even harmed by the way they're treated or the service they've received from faceless, public-sector employees. It's an uphill battle and time destroyer to try to get the public sector to acknowledge its mistakes, let alone compensate us for them. Unaccountable government systems and processes simply don't revolve around citizens, either as individuals or in the collective. This is not how the competitive private sector treats its customers.

I've heard a couple of pushbacks to this, only the first of which I partially accept. It's true that nobody waits four years to determine if unelected public-sector employees are actually turning up at work. Civil service managers routinely monitor their direct reports. This would seem to assure some accountability, but it's limited and circumscribed. The faceless 99.5 percent are seldom, if ever, accountable to us citizens. There's usually no public accountability framework in place, and, when there is, it's nonbinding.

The second pushback, the one harder to accept, is that most Western government agencies have complaint and appeals processes, ombudsmen, and tribunals, and therefore partial accountability. Yes, things are better than they were thirty years ago. Western governments, impelled in part by budget squeezes and the private sector's competitive drive, have made their civil services marginally more accountable.

However, these complaint processes are piecemeal, incremental, and differ in each department. This has meant that, unlike the private sector's reasonably consistent if uncodified practices, the public sector doesn't really have a process at all. It has hundreds of processes, depending on the agency and the nature of the complaint, each requiring its own expertise, and many demanding a great deal of time and paperwork.

Even our elected officials are often in no position to hold civil servants accountable. When I asked my local councilor what he could do about the Markham officials who had failed to deliver on our local park, he told me he could do nothing. My councilor is just one among many who appoint the City of Markham's chief administrative officer, whom Markham's civil servants report to. And it's up to him to decide if any action is to be taken. That being so, what redress mechanism is there for me as a citizen? There's simply nothing there.

It's important to remember that it's not just government's fault we're in this predicament. Through inertia and civic inactivity, far too many citizens allow governments to push the boundaries of what they can get away with. Government can't and won't be held accountable unless and until informed citizens demand that it is. It doesn't take much to understand that. Outsourcing government can be done passively, without the slightest clue. Or it can be done actively, sticking our hands into our democracy.

Those who stop to question realize that things aren't how they're meant to be. Citizens own the state, although government officials rarely bear this in mind. Our officials' overwhelming tendency is to look at themselves as the top of the hierarchy. We, as citizens, counterproductively encourage this. By attending their ceremonial speeches and giving them special privileges and awards, we put elected officials on a pedestal.

What can be done to put their feet to the fire?

CHAPTER 10

KEEPING TABS

We've seen how fundamental accountability is to the democratic social contract. We may have fooled ourselves into equating accountability with elections, but its real absence has rendered the social contract a mere chimera of what it can and ought to be. Western democracies now find themselves in the unacceptable situation where we have a democracy without "people power."

Some of my earlier proposals for reducing government waste and increasing representation also improve accountability. Each feeds into the others. Representation encourages accountability, and both raise performance levels. On the other hand, a government that represents only a segment of the population will be loath to make itself accountable to the citizen body. And by favoring the select few, its performance will be compromised.

The proposals I'm about to make are, again, all tactical interventions to improve the final leg in our democratic stool—accountability.

AUDIT AND COMMUNICATIONS UNIT

It makes little sense to expect government to reform itself and become more accountable. The habits and procedures that currently impede real accountability are ingrained and support the cozy environment our representatives and unelected officials operate in. Despite all the hot-air talk about democratic reform that we've seen from one president or prime minister after another, we seem to be enacting Samuel Beckett's *Waiting for Godot*. Little has changed.

My first suggestion to improve accountability, a government audit and communications unit, is familiar as an earlier suggestion for reducing government waste. There's a clear relationship between reducing waste and greater accountability. The audit and communications unit, proposed as one solution for inefficiency, would also hold government accountable at all levels. Presently, most government audit agencies hold government accountable only within a very narrow range of issues to an even narrower range of recipients. The breadth of both issues and recipients addressed needs a massive expansion.

Without repeating what's been said—after all, this isn't a business book—let's just remind ourselves of a couple key elements. Setting up a division to investigate and evaluate activity in all tiers of government, one with skills and experience beyond bookkeeping and accounting, will be an improvement in itself. If the unit has a powerful mandate and competent staff, the public sector will soon realize they could be called to account for any of their activities.

We don't want to replicate George Orwell's *1984* and its Big Brother surveillance. We do want the public sector to feel as if they're working in a small firm, with the owner-operator sitting a few desks away. I've said this before, but if you take money from everyone, including those in poverty, you need to feel some pressure to perform.

What measures could this unit deploy to make government accountable to citizens? The most obvious tactic is communication, reporting the successes and failures of public-sector departments, divisions, teams, and even individuals to both the taxpaying public and government itself. While this may sound tough, we're driving accountability through the system. Would I want to be on a bad performance list? No, but, in that case, I shouldn't have taken a job with an income guaranteed from taxes paid by everyone in the country. I am being held accountable.

As a key step in making government accountable, citizens have a right to know who wasted or misused their taxes. Tax is paid with the expectation that the toughest problems in society, including poverty, homelessness, and military combat, will be dealt with. The special nature of taxes demands, at least in my strong personal view, a high performance standard. Citizens are entitled to hold those who breach this trust to account. They deserve such consideration.

And then we can also think about penalties. Do we levy meaningful fines and penalties on elected and unelected government officials? Do we fire representatives who lie to us? Do we think about custodial sentences for elected representatives in extreme cases, such as lying or gross incompetence? I really think that we need a proper discussion about when and under what circumstances we as citizens should penalize those entrusted with governing us for not doing what they should be doing.

Let's not forget that this is the same state that issues penalties willy-nilly on us citizens for not fulfilling our part of the bargain. We get a ticket for parking illegally. We are sent to prison for serious fraud. Perjury in the UK can lead to a seven-year sentence. But when an elected representative doesn't do what they said they'll do, or perhaps makes up a bunch of stuff while live on TV in front of tens of millions of people, there's...nothing. That's completely unacceptable.

I'm not ten years old. I get that often it's hard to demonstrate that somebody has lied. Trump insisted on January 22, 2020, that the coronavirus impact was "totally under control."[1] Which is why, in Q2 2020, the US saw its worst economic (GDP) performance ever. Now, it's a hard stretch to suggest that things are "under control," and then have the worst quarterly economic contraction in the country's history.

And when you're lying 8.6 times per day, you can't possibly insist the lies are, in fact, all shades of gray.[2] There will be some blatant lies. When, in March 2019, Trump claimed that the Mueller report gave him "TOTAL exoneration," that was a clear lie.[3] "While this report does not conclude that the President committed a crime, it also does not exonerate him." Those are Mueller's words, not mine. There's a good reason why comedian Trevor Noah mocked the US president by saying, "No Trump speech would be complete without a blatant lie."[4]

Lying isn't the only thing that we want to put a stop to. And Trump isn't the only elected representative who needs to be held accountable.

PROTECTING PROMISES

The next accountability measure meets another desperate need, a duty at the heart of our democratic social contract. Its dereliction significantly contributes to our loss of confidence in elected politicians and ties in nicely to the previous issue. Politicians' failures to keep even vague, high-level campaign assurances and promises have contributed significantly to our becoming disillusioned with government. While many promises and commitments are kept, far too many are not. A significant proportion of constituents might be resigned to this state of affairs. That doesn't mean they're any less disillusioned, and this has an inevitably corrosive effect.

To keep elected officials accountable, we need to rigorously record and publicize the promises and commitments they make and the expectations they set. Without such records, those running for office find it all too easy to say something to one group of voters and the opposite to another group. Then, when elected, they break, dilute, or ignore some of the commitments that got them into office in the first place.

The independent, newly established unit administrating this oversight would demand that campaign promises be put in writing, then visibly publicized and circulated—and not just on the internet. The promises need to be treated with real reverence and adhered to. The pledges might, for instance, be put on billboards, in newspapers, and inside metro train platforms. The aim is to ensure that ordinary citizens understand what is and is not being promised in election campaigns and that, after elections, especially so, they are able to monitor progress or the lack thereof.

This would significantly reduce the number of promises and commitments candidates make, especially in the weeks just before election day. Contradictions would become obvious.

These pledges would then become part of a permanent record that could be referred to during an official's term of office. Did officials do what they said they would? With an empowered and well-resourced independent agency dedicated to this task, we would be able to find out.

Some privately funded websites already do this. However, the onus is on those websites to scavenge for what candidates may or may not have verbally committed to. I think that the state should bear this burden. Also, what we have now tends to focus almost exclusively on national leaders. The current spectrum doesn't cover lower profile politicians' promises, and we therefore miss and neglect many commitments, naturally including those made off the record.

Whatever agency we create for this would only accept as legitimate tangible promises made on the record. If candidates can't or won't make a commitment in something like a Book of Promises, available online, the electorate can seek it from their opponents. At the very least, citizens can now learn what one candidate is promising and another isn't and hold those elected accountable while in office.

If such a promise is not kept or is reneged on, that failure can also be widely communicated and publicized. Do we want to consider penalizing elected representatives for failing or breaking their commitments? Do we hold them personally responsible, with the possibility of garnishing their assets? This may sound harsh. But isn't it so much harsher that someone in poverty or even without shelter at night had to pay taxes to an official who didn't deliver? We sometimes forget who pays tax. It's something that we need to discuss.

We could also bar politicians from elected office after their terms are up. Or even throw them out of office for serious failures to meet their commitments. Yes, in extreme situations, I see no reason why the citizen body should outsource their democracy to somebody who reveals himself either a liar or inept and is then stuck with that person for several years. My business wouldn't tolerate it, other businesses won't, so why should we tolerate it for instances far more serious, the task of governing our country? Such public exposure would change the profile of those who stand for election in the first place.

Given the trust that citizens—even those living in poverty—extend in paying taxes on time, without choice, and the fact that so many critical aspects of our daily lives—from defense to transportation, from social security to water—rely on the use of those taxes, do we entertain asset seizures or criminal sanctions for elected representatives who break promises? Who fail really badly? Who blatantly lie to us? I think the citizen body should be able to strike back when it has fulfilled its part of the bargain, but its counterparty hasn't. We need a broader conversation in society on these issues, one which every politician would love to poke holes in.

Although it's clearly not possible to keep all promises due to factors beyond one's control, we might also require representatives to defend themselves when they fail to honor commitments, even for good reason. This is what accountability means, after all. We might introduce an independent review broadcast on YouTube—perhaps an interview where the politician is questioned, in front of, say, a nonpartisan jury or an expert panel. Maybe we'd realize an official wanted to keep a promise, but it turned out that would be impossible or unwise to do so. The coronavirus has blown a huge hole in almost every prime minister and president's fiscal plans.

Yes, I know that all this is tricky. My proposal raises concerns about protecting accountability from political processes—from preventing people going after government officials simply because they don't like their policies and personalities, as opposed to holding them accountable in much the same way that an employee is held to account. But there it is—if we can do this in our day jobs, if it can be done across the private sector between managers and direct reports, we can do it in the interface between citizens and government.

All this would go a long way to deterring politicians from making promises they can't or have no intention of keeping. It would make them think long and hard about what powers they'll actually have if elected, and what they can actually achieve. If they can commit to nothing except a catalog of "I will look into," "I will try my hardest," and "I will reconsider," let's record it in black and white, so we can compare them with candidates who genuinely believe they can offer more.

One consequence of raising this bar is that it would filter out an increasing number of elected representatives who have a wafer-slim track record and treat promises as marketing gimmicks. This may actually open up room for more thoughtful and serious contenders, such as a capable manager in a successful business who looks at the other candidates and sees a lot of hot air and empty promises. This manager decides he has something to contribute and makes promises he can actually keep. He announces his run, eager to publicize his commitments and welcoming the responsibility that comes with accountability.

If we are to make politics trustworthy—where getting the job done counts, and empty promises thrown about like confetti don't—we're going to have to protect and enforce commitments made during elections. We are going to have to introduce accountability and stop pretending that we already have it. It's because we don't have accountability that Banksy can portray our legislatures as being populated by chimpanzees—and then sell the piece for an incredible amount of money. Accountability is the very least we should demand of our democratic governments.

SHARING CALENDARS AND RESULTS

Do you know what your elected and unelected officials are doing on any given day or in any given week? Almost certainly not. This makes public-sector calendar-sharing vital. The public has a right to know what its representatives and civil servants are doing. How are they earning the tax dollars they're being paid? What did they accomplish for us?

Calendar-sharing began in the private sector, where it's natural for managers to monitor what their direct reports are doing, I don't know of any elected official who has suggested anything like calendar-sharing in the public realm—even at a time like the present, when police in various jurisdictions, such as New York City, ended up with such poor reputations that they started wearing small video cameras in the interest of transparency.

Of course, there's a good reason why no government official suggests calendar-sharing. Why on earth would an elected official want to let you know that he spent most of yesterday on the golf course? Why would a civil servant want to share that today was filled meaningless make-work meetings? Or a whole day with a couple of lobbyists who have great ties to a university that the representative's daughter is about to apply to? Government officials aren't incentivized to reveal the truth about their efficacy, performance, or work ethic.

Communications technology makes the implementation of this modest but potentially transformative proposal both possible and relatively simple. Most elected representatives already have websites. Most use calendar software. Those who don't could easily do so with less than a couple hours of outsourced help. In fact, if they don't use calendar software, that in itself should raise eyebrows.

One page of an official's website would then share their calendar, automatically updated whenever changes are made. Civil service departments could add calendar-sharing to already existing websites or build ones that would do the job. Sharing calendars is not difficult, although it's not quite as simple as turning on a light switch since we need to be mindful of privacy and national security issues.

Even taking these issues into account, why shouldn't I know what my representative actually delivered last week? Or what the civil servants in the local planning department did yesterday? We currently know nothing. We have no idea what any individual in government, elected or not, is up to. We have every right to know both what our representatives are doing and what they have achieved. Such transparency will go some way toward healing our faith in government and repairing the social contract.

For officials to share the results of a particular appointment adds a layer of complexity, but not an excessive one. An elected representative can ask an assistant to note on the calendar what, if anything, was accomplished during an appointment. Junior civil servants could log the data themselves. A notation on an 11 a.m. Wednesday slot might say, "Met treasury officials who pointed out the budget's fiscal implications for our department. Learned about treasury definitions for different cost categories."

Logging activity and accomplishment is a remarkably effective performance management technique, even without third-party oversight and analysis. It forces us to look at what we achieved, not just annually, but in every part of a day. I've been doing something like this for decades, reviewing at night what I accomplished during the day and reflecting on how I used my time. If I hadn't adopted this technique as early as I did, I'm sure I wouldn't have achieved even half the modicum that I have.

Sometimes, to be frank, I find that nothing tangible has been accomplished in a particular time slot except reconnecting with colleagues or collecting my thoughts. Intangible value, though, doesn't mean no value. On the other hand, a tangible accomplishment can later turn out to be pointless, because circumstances change. Ultimately, the question we should ask is if and how our officials have moved the ship of state forward.

Again, as in the vast majority of businesses, we're asking government officials to accept the same culture of oversight that small business operators exert over their staffs. Small- and medium-sized businesses account for at least 70 percent of all Canadian jobs.[5] This isn't Big Brother spying. It doesn't invade personal or home time. It's shining a spotlight on time at work, for which the public pays every government employee, elected or not. It's typical of oversight in small businesses. Sharper, tighter awareness of what officials did and have actually accomplished is the goal here, and it could even be made part of a more comprehensive individual performance review process.

REVIEW AND FEEDBACK

We've looked at the proposal of rewarding the top 5 percent of high performing government employees every year while cutting the weakest-performing 2 percent. I'd like to touch on this and the broader feedback cycle in terms of accountability because they also have a role in this context. As we've seen, quarterly reviews of all personnel are standard operating procedure in most larger private-sector enterprises. Similar review cycles can and should be set for elected and unelected public-sector officials.

A meaningful quarterly review of every civil servant would include feedback from supervisors, subordinates, and colleagues. I'd like consultants who are employed by a government for more than six months to be subject to the same review process because too many of them are de facto employees. In the private sector, this is known as a 360-degree review. It's a tried-and-true process that could be injected relatively easily into public-sector departments if it hasn't already been. The many iterations of this process in business have already worked through most potential problems.

If we are going to make government, especially the invisible 99.5 percent, accountable, the review process must have genuine consequences, such as promotions, bonuses, and terminations. Such consequences could be extended to penalties for those who manage projects that end up with significant delays and cost overruns. That's right. Let's discuss serious repercussions for the mismanagement of public funds and hold individuals personally accountable.

One mechanism to accomplish this would be citizen feedback. Many civil servants have little to no interaction with the general population, and in such cases public feedback would have limited applicability. It is appropriate, however, to incorporate public feedback on civil servants who do interact with citizens as a critical component of the review process, not just as a bit of irrelevant window dressing.

It might seem as challenging to require citizen feedback as it is to get those eligible to vote in elections to do so. But it can be done with today's technology. Imagine legislation that mandated that citizens give meaningful, consequential feedback on every official interaction with a government representative or agency. Citizens who didn't comply or who were clearly being unfair or inaccurate could perhaps be fined.

Suppose I phone the national tax agency. Let's say I wanted to pay less tax on importing twenty kilograms of British chocolate into Canada. It takes forty minutes to connect to a representative who answers my questions clearly and respectfully but advises me that the rules are that I can't do what I had hoped to do. The conversation ends. Or at least it does for the person I was talking with.

After the call, I am legally obligated to answer a couple of questions about what happened from the moment I dialed in until the representative connected with me. Then there are five questions about how the representative engaged with me—not in terms of policy content, but her communication, tone, and helpfulness. I complete the review. That takes me thirty seconds. Job done. I've done my bit in that instance to make government accountable.

My review is amalgamated with others and feeds into not only the representative's overall appraisal but that of whoever was responsible for what happened between my dialing in and connecting to the representative. This citizen review needs to carry serious weight because if it doesn't, it makes a mockery of government accountability. It's a waste of time and a burden that we don't need.

If I choose not to complete the review, because I am that sort of lazy, selfish, and short-sighted person, I get a $100 penalty in the mail. After the first jolt, I won't be likely to repeat that mistake for a while. Since, let's say, two percent of all reviews are independently audited, if mine is blatantly unfair or inaccurate, I get a $200 penalty in the mail. That's a serious punch to the gut.

We don't need to restrict such reviews to standard vanilla interactions. My interactions with Markham's park planning official over email could also oblige me to complete a review that asks me to include any supporting evidence. The details of such a review process can be worked on and would undoubtedly differ from jurisdiction to jurisdiction and issue to issue. Even the mode of interaction, such as email or an in-person meeting, might need to be accommodated.

That said, the underlying principle is clear. We must make the public sector accountable. We now have the technology to help do this and mend the social contract that is now broken, oddly enough in part because of the polarization that same technology has contributed to. What might be poison in a large dose can become a medicine in smaller doses or when applied differently. Medicine is a bit like that, in fact.

We've focused on specific interactions, but what about broader accountability? Each government has its goals. And each ministry or department has its own targets. We also have the conceptual and technological tools to identify units, teams, and individuals responsible for key deliverables. The Audit and Communications unit can again assist us in identifying both outstanding performers and laggards, which will help us, the citizen body, figure out precisely what's going on and hold the hidden unelected majority of our democracy to account.

What's the most important piece here? We need to have a mindset focused on effecting accountability. I firmly believe this is our responsibility as citizens.

CONCLUSION

Because we have the right to vote for our elected officials, we like to think that we live in a democracy. Also, without considering the issue too closely, we want to believe our democracies are a relatively efficient form of government that represents and is accountable to us, its citizens.

This simply isn't true. Western democracies are not particularly accountable to us, the people. They don't properly represent us either by mirroring the citizen population or in advocating primarily for their constituents. And they're far too wasteful when delivering the services they were created to provide and on which we, the citizen taxpayers, rely.

That we are able to vote in elections, in fact, masks the gulf between the democracy we think or hope we have and the government we actually do have. This gap is not at all a recent phenomenon, but it's become increasingly urgent to examine and overcome the shortcomings that have broken our social contract.

Much of our current political frustration comes from feeling disenfranchised. We pay a lot of attention to economic disenfranchisement while ignoring both its political causes and political symptoms. Unless we start examining and addressing this dilemma and the anxiety and irritation that accompany it, our politics will become even less effective and ever-more polarized. If the trend continues, our democracies will wind up as chapters in history books.

The neoliberal economic program put into place beginning in the 1980s benefited the wealthiest strata of society. This can serve as an example of the effects of the unrepresentative nature of our so-called democracies, as these policies have barely benefited the average person and arguably hurt the middle and working classes.

Frustrated citizens are increasingly projecting their economic anxieties onto politics. Growing nationalism idealizes a fictitious past and displaces resentment onto several buckets of minorities who don't fit in with idealized images of the "way things used to be." Political discussion and debate have become ever-more dangerously extreme. In fact, much of this discussion, especially on social media, has degenerated and polluted our society.

The problems we actually face in government, however, are attributable for the most part to human nature rather than to evil, callous conspiracies. Most people tend to think they're right and ignore other people's opinions. Our governments are wasteful, unrepresentative, and unaccountable largely because it's commonplace, indeed quite normal, to get lazy and to resent being told what to do.

The truth is that it wouldn't be all that difficult to improve the nature and quality of our democracies. We must actually engage with the issues before us and build the processes by which they can be addressed. Nothing will change until we prioritize mending the broken social contract. Much can be improved if we do.

It's only our lowered expectations that make taking these steps challenging. We've become so accustomed and resigned to government being unresponsive, unrepresentative, and inefficient that we throw up our hands and ask, "What can we do?"

The answer is, quite a lot.

The private sector has had to take steps to overcome some of the flaws that seem to be inherent in human nature, because businesses must, at the very least, be somewhat efficient and productive if they're to survive. We haven't yet taken such corrective steps in the public sector and find it difficult to see how because we currently lack the will to do what's necessary.

If we could get a man on the moon with a mainframe with less computing power than an iPhone, we can certainly begin introducing changes to make our governments genuinely democratic—more efficient, more accountable, and more representative of the public as a whole. We are not compelled to run the same systems and processes of two centuries back for our late-modern era.

This book has suggested several tactical measures capable of effecting such change. None would be particularly difficult to put in place, and all would have a disproportionately great and positive impact.

The initial step in this process is becoming aware of the problem—the gulf between the democracy we think we have and the pseudo-democracy we actually do have. Solutions can be generated only when a problem is recognized. We can then begin to consider how we can overcome the all-too-human tendencies that are causing our Western governments to operate undemocratically.

Above all, we need to reinsert citizens into the democratic process. There are a number of simple ways this can be done. The next time you go into a government office and don't receive the level of service you expect as a matter of course at a Starbucks, speak with the supervisor of the civil servant you've been dealing with. They work for you, among others. They are paid by you, among others.

On a broader level, you could begin advocating for one of the proposed tactical interventions in the democratic process, such as creation of an agency to look after the interests of the people our governments are supposedly meant to serve. Or you could come up with your own proposals to share and discuss with others.

Moving from individual to collective action will undoubtedly involve communications and other technologies that are currently contributing to the polarization of our political landscape. The rate of change is accelerating, and it's up to us to ensure that technology is leveraged to citizens' advantage and for the general good.

The solutions required will be practical rather than political. Bringing effective private-sector practices into the public sector does not at all necessitate or even imply the privatization of public services. Rather, it's a matter of looking around to see what might help make our governments more efficient, representative, and accountable.

I've said enough. Now, I want to dunk my Rich Tea biscuit into some tea.

ACKNOWLEDGMENTS

Many people have helped me personally, professionally, and in writing this book.

Some have sustained me. Others have enlightened me. Some have protected me. Others have encouraged me.

A few have been there for decades. A few have intervened for a few moments.

And while they may not all be physically present today, I really hope that they all know, from my personal interaction, of my gratitude to them.

Ultimately *they* are the privilege I was born into.

ABOUT THE AUTHOR

SAQIB IQBAL QURESHI has written for *The Financial Times*, *Entrepreneur Magazine*, and *The Independent*, and is a Fellow of the London School of Economics and Political Science, where he completed his undergraduate and PhD degrees. He is also the author of *Reconstructing Strategy: Dancing with the God of Objectivity*.

Qureshi leads a real estate firm, having previously worked at McKinsey & Co and HSBC Investment Bank. After decades of experiencing the dysfunctionality of various democracies up close, Saqib began conversations with government officials about problems and solutions, which he contrasted with his experience in the private sector. This became the basis for this book.

NOTES

INTRODUCTION

1   https://www.theglobeandmail.com/canada/toronto/
    article-six-years-to-build-a-bike-garage-really/

2   https://qz.com/1190595/the-typical-us-congress-member-is-12-times-richer-than-the-
    typical-american-household/

3   https://qz.com/1190595/the-typical-us-congress-member-is-12-times-richer-than-the-
    typical-american-household/

4   https://www.theguardian.com/society/2014/aug/28/closed-shop-deepy-elitist-britain

5   https://www.theglobeandmail.com/opinion/
    article-canadas-political-institutions-are-failing-the-next-parliament-must/

6   Charles Upton, *Dugin Against Dugin: A Traditionalist Critique of the Fourth Political
    Theory* (New York: Vintage, 2018)

7   https://www.cbc.ca/news/politics/
    canada-election-2015-niqab-debate-citizenship-turban-rcmp-1.3244817

8   https://www.inc.com/marcel-schwantes/warren-buffet-says-you-should-hire-people-
    based-on-these-3-traits-but-only-1-truly-matters.html

CHAPTER I

1   https://www.thestar.com/news/world/analysis/2019/01/25/trumps-first-year-was-the-
    most-dishonest-in-history-his-second-was-nearly-three-times-worse.html

2   https://www.cnn.com/2019/09/26/uk/rachel-johnson-calls-boris-johnson-reprehensible-
    scli-gbr/index.html

3   https://www.theguardian.com/politics/2019/sep/15/
david-cameron-slammed-for-horrendous-mistake-brexit-referendum

4   https://www.goodreads.com/
quotes/9870044-social-media-gives-legions-of-idiots-the-right-to-speak

5   https://www.epi.org/publication/income-inequality-in-the-us/

6   https://www.washingtonpost.com/news/wonk/wp/2017/12/06/the-richest-1-percent-now-
owns-more-of-the-countrys-wealth-than-at-any-time-in-the-past-50-years/

7   https://www.theatlantic.com/business/archive/2012/09/
us-income-inequality-its-worse-today-than-it-was-in-1774/262537/

8   https://www.epi.org/publication/charting-wage-stagnation/

9   https://www.epi.org/publication/charting-wage-stagnation/

10 https://www.commondreams.org/news/2019/06/14/eye-popping-analysis-shows-top-1-
gained-21-trillion-wealth-1989-while-bottom-half?utm_campaign=shareaholic&utm_
medium=referral&utm_source=facebook

11 Thomas Piketty, *Capital and Ideology* (Cambridge: Belknap Press, 2020)

12 https://www.equalitytrust.org.uk/how-has-inequality-changed; https://wid.world/
document/f-alvaredo-b-atkinson-s-morelli-2017-top-wealth-shares-uk-century-wid-
world-working-paper/

13 https://www.washingtonpost.com/news/wonk/wp/2017/12/06/the-richest-1-percent-now-
owns-more-of-the-countrys-wealth-than-at-any-time-in-the-past-50-years/

14 https://www.ft.com/content/6a7632a2-73a9-11ea-95fe-fcd274e920ca?shareType=nongift

15 https://www.equalitytrust.org.uk/scale-economic-inequality-uk; https://www.theguardian.
com/inequality/2018/sep/05/qa-how-unequal-is-britain-and-are-the-poor-getting-poorer

16 Naomi Klein, *The Shock Doctrine* (London: Picador, 2008).

17 https://www.inthepublicinterest.org/wp-content/uploads/InthePublicInterest_
InequalityReport_Sept2016.pdf

18 https://www.gartner.com/5_about/press_releases/pr11apr2003a.jsp

19 Joseph Stiglitz, *Globalization and Its Discontents* (New York: W.W. Norton, 2002)

20 https://fortune.com/2020/03/20/
senators-burr-loeffler-sold-stock-coronavirus-threat-briefings-in-january/

21 https://www.vanityfair.com/news/2020/04/
congress-coronavirus-richard-burr-stock-trades

22 Anand Giridharadas, *Winner Takes All: The Elite Charade of Changing the World* (New
York: Vintage, 2018)

23 https://www.ceicdata.com/en/indicator/new-zealand/
annual-household-income-per-capita

24 https://treasury.gov.au/sites/default/files/2019-03/p2017-t237966.pdf

25 https://business.financialpost.com/news/economy/
canadian-median-income-growth-sluggish-over-past-10-years-statscan-figures-show

26 Robert Reich, *Aftershock* (New York: Vintage, 2011)

27 https://www.ft.com/content/7eff769a-74dd-11ea-95fe-fcd274e920ca

28 https://www.newswire.ca/news-releases/breaking-canada-at-populism-trust-crisis-
tipping-point-613678663.html

29 https://energynow.ca/2019/06/trust-in-government-canadians-wary-of-politicians-and-
their-intentions-augus-reid-institute/

30 https://www.theglobeandmail.com/news/national/
canadians-particularly-trustful-of-their-democracy-poll-finds/article35495822/

31 https://www.environicsinstitute.org/docs/default-source/project-documents/
americasbarometer-2012/confidence-in-democracy-and-the-political-system.
pdf?sfvrsn=cb01off5_2

32 https://www150.statcan.gc.ca/n1/en/pub/89-652-x/89-652-x2015007-eng.
pdf?st=RiJMx89D

33 https://www.people-press.org/2019/04/11/public-trust-in-government-1958-2019/

34 https://www.people-press.org/2019/04/11/public-trust-in-government-1958-2019/

35 https://www.people-press.
org/2015/11/23/8-perceptions-of-the-publics-voice-in-government-and-politics/

36 https://www.people-press.
org/2015/11/23/8-perceptions-of-the-publics-voice-in-government-and-politics/

37 https://www.usatoday.com/story/money/personalfinance/2017/10/07/a-foolish-take-how-
much-does-the-average-american-pay-in-taxes/106237216/

38 https://www.theatlantic.com/ideas/archive/2020/03/
thing-determines-how-well-countries-respond-coronavirus/609025/

39 https://www.statista.com/statistics/977223/support-for-prime-minister-conte-in-italy/

40 https://www.theguardian.com/world/2020/mar/14/
only-36-of-britons-trust-boris-johnson-on-coronavirus-poll-finds

41 http://www.law.nyu.edu/sites/default/files/ECM_PRO_073503.pdf

42 https://www.hansardsociety.org.uk/publications/reports/audit-of-political-engagement-16

43 https://www.hansardsociety.org.uk/publications/reports/audit-of-political-engagement-16

44 https://www.hansardsociety.org.uk/publications/reports/audit-of-political-engagement-16

45 https://www.newstatesman.com/politics/uk/2019/05/end-trust-our-political-class

46 https://yougov.co.uk/topics/politics/articles-reports/2019/06/18/
most-conservative-members-would-see-party-destroye

47 https://www.bbc.com/news/uk-scotland-scotland-politics-52079106

48 https://www.dailymail.co.uk/news/article-8208049/Turkey-sends-planeloads-emergency-equipment-including-masks-protective-suits-Britain.html

49 https://www.ft.com/content/6416a20a-9805-11e9-8cfb-30c211dcd229; https://smallbusinessprices.co.uk/brexit-index/

50 https://www.independent.co.uk/news/business/news/brexit-cost-how-much-uk-economy-money-spent-a8854726.html

51 https://www.independent.co.uk/news/business/news/brexit-cost-how-much-uk-economy-money-spent-a8854726.html

52 https://www.theguardian.com/world/2020/apr/03/coronavirus-uk-business-activity-plunges-to-lowest-ebb-since-records-began; https://www.bbc.com/news/business-52158444

53 https://www.theguardian.com/world/2020/apr/09/german-army-donates-60-mobile-ventilators-uk-coronavirus-nhs

54 https://www.theguardian.com/world/2020/mar/30/uk-discussed-joint-eu-plan-to-buy-covid-19-medical-supplies-say-officials

55 https://www.theguardian.com/business/2016/nov/05/economic-woe-trump-style-movements-created-worldwide

CHAPTER 2

1 John Locke, "Two Treatises on Government" (CreateSpace Publishing, 2013)

2 https://www150.statcan.gc.ca/n1/pub/75-006-x/2018001/article/54982-eng.htm

3 https://news.gallup.com/poll/247823/men-less-concerned-2017-sexual-harassment.aspx

4 https://www.epa.gov/greenvehicles/greenhouse-gas-emissions-typical-passenger-vehicle

5 https://sbecouncil.org/about-us/facts-and-data/

6 https://www.theglobeandmail.com/business/commentary/article-canadian-small-businesses-are-facing-extinction-amid-lockdowns/

7 https://www.washingtonpost.com/news/post-politics/wp/2016/12/09/the-six-donors-trump-appointed-to-his-administration-gave-almost-12-million-with-their-families-to-his-campaign-and-the-party/

8 https://mississaugabudget2020.budgetallocator.com/#ba

9 https://www.politifact.com/global-news/statements/2016/nov/09/john-kerry/yep-most-people-clueless-us-foreign-aid-spending/

10 https://borgenproject.org/foreign-aid/

11 https://theconversation.com/new-research-shows-australians-have-wrong-idea-on-foreign-aid-spending-98772

CHAPTER 3

1   https://www.businessstudent.com/careers/20-most-popular-mba-jobs-ever/

2   https://www.ft.com/content/6e806580-d560-11e9-8d46-8def889b4137

3   https://www.mckinsey.com/industries/public-sector/our-insights/
     putting-people-at-the-heart-of-public-sector-transformations

4   https://www.theglobeandmail.com/politics/
     article-millions-of-canadians-cant-reach-federal-government-on-the-phone/

5   https://www.wsj.com/articles/
     wait-times-are-down-but-irs-still-faces-serious-challenges-1458898201

6   https://onlinelibrary.wiley.com/doi/abs/10.1111/puar.12441

7   https://www150.statcan.gc.ca/t1/tbl1/en/tv.action?pid=1410019601

8   https://www150.statcan.gc.ca/t1/tbl1/en/tv.action?pid=1410019101

9   http://www.etfo.ca/SupportingMembers/Employees/PDF%20Versions/Your%20Sick%20
     Leave%20Questions%20Explained.pdf

10   https://www.canadianbusiness.com/economy/an-epidemic-of-absenteeism/

11   https://www150.statcan.gc.ca/t1/tbl1/en/cv.action?pid=1410019001#timeframe

12   https://www.ctvnews.ca/canada/
     private-sector-workers-earn-less-work-more-report-1.2292650

13   https://www.thestar.com/news/gta/2016/06/30/york-region-police-officers-begin-work-
     to-rule-campaign.html

14   https://www.fraserinstitute.org/studies/
     comparing-government-and-private-sector-compensation-in-ontario-2018

15   https://www.fraserinstitute.org/studies/
     comparing-government-and-private-sector-compensation-in-ontario-2018

16   https://www.fraserinstitute.org/article/
     dirty-secret-behind-canadas-supposedly-successful-public-sector-pensions

17   https://www.theguardian.com/money/2018/jul/30/
     sick-days-taken-uk-workers-fall-lowest-rate-on-record

18   https://www.sciencedirect.com/science/article/pii/S1517758017300243

19   http://www.chamber.ca/media/blog/140917-a-path-forward-for-entrepreneurship-in-
     canada/140917_A_Path_Forward_for_Entrepreneurship_in_Canada.pdf

20   https://www.mckinsey.com/business-functions/organization/our-insights/
     attracting-and-retaining-the-right-talent

21   https://www.thecrimson.com/article/2018/1/16/mba-doubles-public-service/

22   https://www.cbc.ca/news/business/most-attractive-companies-1.5148413

23   https://info.lse.ac.uk/current-students/careers/what-graduates-do

24 https://www.theguardian.com/society/2018/sep/03/who-works-where-uk-public-sector

25 https://thehill.com/opinion/
education/443588-fewer-graduates-are-choosing-government-jobs

26 https://www.govexec.com/management/2014/03/
not-many-college-students-are-interested-federal-service/80692/

27 https://www.forbes.com/lists/best-employers-for-new-grads/#6c119f7f203a

28 https://thehill.com/opinion/
finance/431187-firing-bad-federal-government-workers-should-not-be-difficult

29 https://fortune.com/2016/07/19/goldman-sachs-layoffs-3/

30 https://freebeacon.com/issues/
workers-private-sector-3-times-likely-get-fired-govt-workers/

31 https://nationalpost.com/news/canada/
why-is-it-so-impossible-to-fire-a-government-employee

32 https://www.cbc.ca/news/politics/government-fired-misconduct-incompetence-1.4746602

33 https://nationalpost.com/news/canada/
why-is-it-so-impossible-to-fire-a-government-employee

34 https://www.nasa.gov/press-release/
record-number-of-americans-apply-to-beanastronaut-at-nasa

35 https://nationalpost.com/news/canada/
why-is-it-so-impossible-to-fire-a-government-employee

36 https://www.cbc.ca/news/canada/toronto/
toronto-ontario-police-suspended-with-pay-1.3424010

37 https://www.theglobeandmail.com/opinion/why-bad-teachers-dont-get-fired-in-ontario/
article4249405/

38 https://www.ctvnews.ca/canada/teacher-suspended-students-lived-in-fear-of-going-to-
school-diagnosed-with-ptsd-1.4464763

39 https://www.fraserinstitute.org/studies/
comparing-government-and-private-sector-compensation-in-ontario-2018

40 https://en.wikipedia.org/wiki/Nudge_theory

CHAPTER 4

1 Ray Kurzweil, *The Singularity is Near: When Humans Transcend Biology* (New York: Penguin, 2006).

2 Anthony Gidden, *The Consequences of Modernity* (Palo Alto: Stanford University Press, 1991).

3 https://www.bbc.com/news/world-us-canada-51231047

4   https://www.people-press.org/2019/04/11/public-trust-in-government-1958-2019/

5   https://www.cbc.ca/news/politics/fake-news-facebook-twitter-poll-1.5169916

6   https://www.middleeastmonitor.com/20200331-three-muslim-doctors-become-first-
    medics-in-uk-to-die-from-coronavirus/

7   https://cep.lse.ac.uk/pubs/download/brexit05.pdf

8   https://cep.lse.ac.uk/pubs/download/brexit05.pdf

9   https://www.theguardian.com/society/2014/jan/26/
    nhs-foreign-nationals-immigration-health-service

10 https://theconversation.com/
    nhs-reliance-on-eu-staff-in-numbers-full-scale-of-brexit-risk-revealed-105326

11 https://www.ethnicity-facts-figures.service.gov.uk/workforce-and-business/
    workforce-diversity/nhs-workforce/latest#by-ethnicity-and-type-of-role

12 https://lordashcroftpolls.com/2016/06/how-the-united-kingdom-voted-and-why/

13 https://www.politico.com/magazine/story/2016/09/
    donald-trump-pat-buchanan-republican-america-first-nativist-214221

14 https://www.theatlantic.com/politics/archive/2019/01/
    trump-embraces-white-supremacy/579745/

15 https://www.businessinsider.com/
    over-half-americans-think-trump-emboldens-white-supremacy-2019-8

16 https://www.axios.com/immigrant-work-coronavirus-
    nurses-health-care-744f5229-6381-4ac2-9f53-ef0a78e0489e.
    html?utm_source=newsletter&utm_medium=email&utm_campaign=newsletter_
    axiosam&stream=top

17 https://www.huffingtonpost.ca/entry/twitter-white-nationalist-problem_n_5cec4d28e4b0
    0e036573311d

18 https://www.rmg.co.uk/discover/behind-the-scenes/
    blog/18th-century-sailing-times-between-english-channel-and-coast-america

19 https://www.trackalytics.com/twitter/profile/realdonaldtrump/

20 https://qz.com/1503024/2018-was-the-year-the-white-house-press-briefing-died/

21 https://expandedramblings.com/index.php/email-statistics/

22 https://www.statista.com/statistics/456500/daily-number-of-e-mails-worldwide/

CHAPTER 5

1   https://www.newsroom.co.nz/2018/04/23/106009/details-of-plagued-it-project-revealed

2   https://www.theglobeandmail.com/business/
    article-toronto-home-buyers-pay-significantly-higher-taxes-development/

3   http://www.thefiscaltimes.com/Articles/2013/07/24/
    The-Government-Is-Wasting-More-Money-than-You-Think

4   https://www.usatoday.com/story/news/politics/2014/04/08/
    billions-spent-on-duplicate-federal-programs/7435221/

5   https://www.ourpursuit.com/report-identifies-billions-in-federal-program-duplication/

6   https://www.taxpolicycenter.org/sites/default/files/publication/154096/reconsidering_
    americans_overestimates_of_government_waste_and_foreign_aid_0.pdf

7   https://www.theguardian.com/business/2009/aug/23/public-sector-inefficiency-costs

8   https://www2.deloitte.com/content/dam/Deloitte/au/Documents/Economics/deloitte-
    au-the-procurement-balancing-act-170215.pdf

9   http://www.scoop.co.nz/stories/PO1809/S00184/evidence-of-huge-government-waste.
    htm

10 https://www.fraserinstitute.org/sites/default/files/PublicSectorEfficiency.pdf

11 https://www.theglobeandmail.com/news/politics/
    ontario-liberals-gas-plants-scandal-everything-you-need-to-know/article23668386/

12 https://www.canada.ca/en/department-national-defence/corporate/reports-publications/
    transition-materials/defence-101/2020/03/defence-101/defence-budget.html

13 https://www150.statcan.gc.ca/n1/daily-quotidien/190226/dq190226b-eng.htm

14 https://www.downsizinggovernment.org/government-cost-overruns

15 https://www.themanufacturer.com/articles/
    us-super-carrier-gerald-r-ford-begins-sea-trials/;

16 https://fas.org/sgp/crs/weapons/RS20643.pdf

17 https://fas.org/sgp/crs/weapons/RS20643.pdf; https://www.cnet.com/pictures/13-billion-
    and-counting-this-is-the-biggest-most-expensive-warship-in-history/21/

18 https://www.businessinsider.com/ford-class-carrier-not-ready-2016-7

19 https://www.downsizinggovernment.org/government-cost-overruns

20 https://www.washingtonpost.com/investigations/pentagon-buries-evidence-of-125-
    billion-in-bureaucratic-waste/2016/12/05/e0668c76-9af6-11e6-a0ed-ab0774c1eaa5_story.
    html?noredirect=on

21 https://www.blogto.com/city/2019/06/toronto-average-commute-time-2019/

22 https://www.businessleader.co.uk/
    how-long-is-the-daily-work-commute-for-the-average-londoner/44325/

23 https://www.cp24.com/news/
    toronto-has-worst-commute-in-north-america-sixth-worst-in-world-study-1.3983200

24 https://www.telegraph.co.uk/
    news/2017/10/23/20-minute-increase-commute-time-bad-taking-pay-cut-study-finds/

25   https://www.thestar.com/news/gta/2019/04/04/key-subway-project-has-been-delayed-years-and-has-gone-way-over-budget.html

26   https://toronto.citynews.ca/2016/01/15/
     ttc-woes-toronto-york-spadina-subway-extension-550-million-budget/

27   https://scarboroughtransitaction.ca/2018/07/14/
     the-dark-underside-of-the-toronto-york-spadina-subway-extension/

28   https://www.cbc.ca/news/canada/toronto/ontario-auditor-general-findings-1.4933334

29   https://www.theglobeandmail.com/news/politics/
     metrolinx-in-ontario-a-gs-sights-for-cost-overruns/article6240825/

30   https://www.theglobeandmail.com/news/toronto/
     union-pearson-express-looks-unlikely-to-break-even/article35483928/

31   https://www.webcitation.org/63aPozqEG?url=http://news.gc.ca/web/article-eng.
     do?crtr.sjrD=&mthd=advSrch&crtr.mnthndVl=&nid=79449&crtr.dptrD=&crtr.
     tprD=&crtr.lcrD=&crtr.yrStrtVl=&crtr.kw=weston&crtr.dyStrtVl=&crtr.audrD=&crtr.
     mnthStrtVl=&crtr.yrndVl=&crtr.dyndVl=

32   https://globalnews.ca/news/3097773/
     poor-oversight-of-ontario-road-and-transit-contracts-cause-for-concern-auditor-general/

33   https://www.cbc.ca/news/canada/toronto/it-is-scandalous-224m-spent-on-transit-projects-but-several-now-in-limbo-report-reveals-1.5083405

34   https://www.theglobeandmail.com/business/commentary/
     article-restructuring-looms-at-canadas-new-infrastructure-bank/

35   https://www.caninfra.ca/insights-6

36   Washington *Post* 2013; https://www.washingtonpost.com/local/1-million-bus-stop-opens-in-arlington/2013/03/24/49e5c47e-917c-11e2-9abd-e4c5c9dc5e90_story.html?utm_term=.
     dee4f7e135b1

37   https://www.seattletimes.com/seattle-news/transportation/
     soaring-land-and-construction-costs-push-light-rail-line-to-federal-way-over-2-5-billion/

38   https://sacramento.cbslocal.com/2020/02/12/
     california-high-speed-rail-cost-raises-1-billion/

39   https://pedestrianobservations.com/2019/03/03/
     why-american-costs-are-so-high-work-in-progress/

40   BBC, https://www.bbc.com/news/uk-scotland-north-east-orkney-shetland-47258237

41   https://www.ft.com/content/27ab2f5c-a976-11e9-984c-fac8325aaa04

42   https://www.ft.com/content/e9d35b76-c894-11e9-af46-b09e8bfe60c0

43   https://dailycaller.com/2016/10/19/
     irs-spent-12-million-of-taxpayer-money-on-email-system-find-out-after-it-doesnt-work/

44   http://www.thefiscaltimes.com/Articles/2013/11/26/
     Another-Failed-Gov-t-Tech-Project-Cost-11-Billion

45 https://www.themandarin.com.au/61749-auditor-blasts-ict-project-budget-blowouts/

46 https://www.nzherald.co.nz/nz/news/article.cfm?c_id=1&objectid=11369088

47 https://www.nzherald.co.nz/nz/news/article.cfm?c_id=1&objectid=11369088

48 https://www.taxpayersalliance.com/cost_overruns_of_major_government_projects

49 Stanley L. Engerman and Kenneth L. Sokoloff, "Digging the Dirt at Public Expense: Governance in the Building of the Erie Canal and Other Public Works," National Bureau of Economic Research Working Paper 10965, December 2004, p. 29.

50 https://theconversation.com/a-privatised-monopoly-is-still-a-monopoly-and-consumers-pay-the-price-28384

CHAPTER 6

1   http://ftp.iza.org/dp10719.pdf

2   https://www.bls.gov/news.release/union2.nro.htm; https://www150.statcan.gc.ca/t1/tbl1/en/tv.action?pid=1410013201

3   https://www.wgtn.ac.nz/__data/assets/pdf_file/0004/1816429/new-zealand-union-membership-survey-report-2016.pdf

4   https://www.theguardian.com/commentisfree/2016/aug/08/secret-life-trade-union-employee-work-benefits-workers-rights

5   https://www.anao.gov.au/work/annual-report/anao-annual-report-2018-19

6   https://www.vox.com/2018/9/24/17896034/murder-crime-clearance-fbi-report

CHAPTER 7

1   https://www.rollcall.com/news/hawkings/congress-richer-ever-mostly-top

2   https://www.bostonglobe.com/ideas/2014/01/12/america-white-collar-congress/nsFNlQ7LAZgJpdmzQji8oO/story.html

3   https://www.cnbc.com/2019/05/14/the-net-worth-of-the-average-american-family.html

4   https://www.pewresearch.org/fact-tank/2019/10/01/the-number-of-people-in-the-average-u-s-household-is-going-up-for-the-first-time-in-over-160-years/

5   https://poverty.ucdavis.edu/faq/what-are-poverty-thresholds-today

6   https://www.usnews.com/news/blogs/washington-whispers/2013/07/31/paul-ryans-poverty-hearing-included-no-one-living-in-poverty

7   https://www.oecd.org/unitedstates/Tackling-high-inequalities.pdf

8   https://poverty.ucdavis.edu/faq/what-current-poverty-rate-united-states

9   https://www.economist.com/graphic-detail/2020/01/20/higher-minimum-wages-are-linked-to-lower-suicide-rates

10 https://www.nytimes.com/2020/03/13/us/coronavirus-deaths-estimate.html; https://www.
    nytimes.com/2020/03/16/us/coronavirus-fatality-rate-white-house.html

11 https://www.congress.gov/amendment/116th-congress/senate-amendment/1559/
    actions?r=2&s=a

12 http://www.cwp-csp.ca/poverty/just-the-facts/

13 https://www.usnews.com/news/blogs/washington-whispers/2013/07/31/
    paul-ryans-poverty-hearing-included-no-one-living-in-poverty

14 https://www.theguardian.com/news/datablog/2014/aug/28/
    elitism-in-britain-breakdown-by-profession

15 https://www.opendemocracy.net/en/opendemocracyuk/
    these-figures-show-how-out-of-touch-uk-politicians-are-from-everyone-else/

16 https://www.cnn.com/2018/11/22/uk/homelessness-britain-rise-gbr-intl-scli/index.html

17 https://www.bbc.com/news/uk-england-derbyshire-48713049

18 https://www.theguardian.com/commentisfree/2019/jul/02/
    mark-field-homeless-people-mp-charity-victoria

19 https://www.thelondoneconomic.com/news/14-mps-turn-up-to-discuss-un-report-on-14-
    million-people-living-in-poverty/08/01/

20 https://www.bbc.com/news/uk-42421583

21 https://www.independent.co.uk/voices/grenfell-tower-fire-inquiry-government-failure-
    broken-promises-sprinklers-social-housing-a7946086.html

22 https://www.theguardian.com/society/2017/may/16/poverty-election-vote-apathy

23 https://www.theguardian.com/inequality/2017/sep/24/
    revealed-britains-most-powerful-elite-is-97-white

24 https://researchbriefings.parliament.uk/ResearchBriefing/Summary/SN01156

25 https://www.independent.co.uk/news/uk/politics/black-and-asian-civil-servants-facing-
    discrimination-by-old-boys-network-10140037.html

26 https://www.globalgovernmentforum.com/
    uk-civil-service-going-backwards-on-diversity-survey-finds/

27 https://www.newstatesman.com/politics/staggers/2016/06/
    our-personal-prejudices-are-blinding-us-rise-far-right-terrorism

28 https://www.commondreams.org/news/2019/04/10/
    just-trump-media-outlets-rarely-label-far-right-attacks-terrorism-study

29 https://www.theguardian.com/us-news/2018/jul/20/
    muslim-terror-attacks-press-coverage-study

30 https://www.unodc.org/unodc/index.html

31 https://www.aljazeera.com/indepth/features/2016/06/australia-parliament-
    white-160628081201615.html

32 https://thespinoff.co.nz/atea/16-05-2019/
    the-public-sector-is-white-to-its-core-heres-why-thats-a-problem/

33 https://www.ey.com/Publication/vwLUAssets/EY_-_Worldwide_Women_Public_Sector_
    Leaders_Index_2014/$FILE/EY_Worldwide_Index_of_Women_22Oct14.pdf

34 https://www.theguardian.com/us-news/2019/may/14/
    abortion-bill-alabama-passes-ban-six-weeks-us-no-exemptions-vote-latest

35 https://www.bloomberg.com/politics/graphics/2016-presidential-campaign-fundraising/

36 https://www.theguardian.com/politics/2019/sep/15/
    david-cameron-slammed-for-horrendous-mistake-brexit-referendum

37 https://yougov.co.uk/topics/politics/articles-reports/2019/07/23/
    everything-we-know-about-what-public-think-boris-j

38 https://thehill.com/homenews/administration/425879-watchdog-group-trump-had-over-
    1400-conflicts-of-interest-in-first-two

39 https://www.reuters.com/article/us-usa-trump-emoluments-exclusive/
    exclusive-foreign-government-leases-at-trump-world-tower-stir-more-emoluments-
    concerns-idUSKCN1S80PP

40 https://www.people-press.org/2015/11/23/1-trust-in-government-1958-2015/

41 https://www.theglobeandmail.com/opinion/
    article-canadas-political-institutions-are-failing-the-next-parliament-must/

42 https://www.vox.com/first-person/2017/6/29/15886936/
    political-lobbying-lobbyist-big-money-politics

43 Nicky Hager, *Dirty Politics: How Attack Politics is Poisoning New Zealand's Political
    Environment* (Nelson NZ: Craig Potton Publishing, 2014).

44 https://www.opensecrets.org/lobby/

45 https://www.statista.com/statistics/257364/top-lobbying-industries-in-the-us/

46 https://www.foodnavigator.com/Article/2016/09/13/
    How-the-sugar-lobby-paid-scientists-to-point-the-finger-at-fat-JAMA#

47 https://www.marketwatch.com/story/
    lawmakers-who-take-the-most-money-from-the-gun-rights-lobby-2017-10-03

48 https://leftfootforward.org/2019/03/
    report-uk-firms-are-the-biggest-spenders-in-global-climate-change-lobbying/

49 https://www.smh.com.au/politics/federal/coal-industry-campaign-dwarfs-political-
    spending-by-green-groups-20180201-p4yz6i.html

50 https://www.ft.com/content/9a688caa-8eb1-485b-8bbe-d090d82648be

51 https://fas.org/sgp/crs/misc/R41545.pdf

52 https://fas.org/sgp/crs/misc/R41545.pdf

53 https://fas.org/sgp/crs/misc/R41545.pdf

54   https://fas.org/sgp/crs/misc/R41545.pdf

55   https://fas.org/sgp/crs/misc/R44762.pdf

56   https://www.opensecrets.org/lobby/

57   https://www.cnbc.com/2018/04/26/here-is-why-incumbents-in-congress-are-hard-to-beat.html

58   https://globalnews.ca/news/5664518/29-former-mps-federal-election/

59   https://smithinstitutethinktank.files.wordpress.com/2015/05/who-governs-britain.pdf

60   https://www.kingsfund.org.uk/publications/health-care-workforce-england

61   https://www.theguardian.com/business/2017/jan/16/private-medical-insurance-sales-surge-health-nhs

62   https://www.bls.gov/news.release/tenure.nro.htm

63   https://www.ons.gov.uk/employmentandlabourmarket/peopleinwork/earningsandworkinghours/articles/ispayhigherinthepublicorprivatesector/2017-11-16

64   https://www.canada.ca/en/treasury-board-secretariat/services/innovation/human-resources-statistics/demographic-snapshot-federal-public-service-2016.html

65   https://phys.org/news/2019-04-white-majority.html

66   https://www.businessinsider.com/steve-jobs-describing-the-moment-he-decided-to-do-the-ipad-2013-5

67   https://www.cnbc.com/2018/10/30/apple-says-the-ipad-is-outselling-every-laptop-on-the-market.html

68   https://fitsmallbusiness.com/entrepreneurship-statistics/

69   https://hbr.org/2014/03/government-entrepreneur-is-not-an-oxymoron

CHAPTER 8

1   https://www.theguardian.com/science/2018/may/16/living-in-an-age-of-anger-50-year-rage-cycle

2   https://www.npr.org/sections/health-shots/2017/10/24/559116373/poll-most-americans-think-their-own-group-faces-discrimination

3   https://www.sciencenews.org/article/coronavirus-why-african-americans-vulnerable-covid-19-health-race

4   https://www.bbc.com/news/uk-52255863

5   https://www.brookings.edu/blog/fixgov/2018/01/18/five-reasons-to-oppose-congressional-term-limits/

6   https://www.opensecrets.org/elections-overview/did-money-win

7 https://www.npr.org/2020/02/21/808163144/
   bloomberg-has-already-spent-450-million-on-ads-since-launching-his-campaign

8 https://www.cnn.com/2020/03/20/politics/bloomberg-fec-filing/index.html

9 https://www.pewresearch.org/fact-tank/2018/05/08/most-americans-want-to-limit-
   campaign-spending-say-big-donors-have-greater-political-influence/

10 https://www.ipsos.com/en-us/news-polls/
    americans-believe-crashed-ufo-spacecrafts-held-at-area-51

11 https://www.cbsnews.com/news/election-2016s-price-tag-6-8-billion/

12 https://www.vox.com/2017/11/1/16593066/
    trump-clinton-facebook-advertising-money-election-president-russia

13 https://www.politifact.com/truth-o-meter/article/2016/
    nov/03/10-most-aired-political-ads-fact-checked/

14 https://www.theatlantic.com/science/archive/2017/01/
    government-accountability-psychology/512888/

15 http://theconversation.com/after-clive-palmers-60-million-campaign-limits-on-political-
    advertising-are-more-important-than-ever-117099

16 https://www.cbc.ca/news/politics/federal-election-finances-campaign-spending-1.3519357

17 https://www.forbes.com/sites/zackfriedman/2019/02/25/
    student-loan-debt-statistics-2019/#240a9dff133f

18 https://globalnews.ca/news/4302151/san-francisco-low-income-housing-canada/

19 https://www.theglobeandmail.com/news/politics/
    liberals-outspent-conservatives-by-12-million-in-2015-election/article30524115/

20 https://www.eiu.com/topic/democracy-index

21 https://www.abs.gov.au/ausstats/abs@@.nsf/mf/6248.0.55.002; https://www.aph.gov.au/
    About_Parliament/Parliamentary_Departments/Parliamentary_Library/pubs/rp/rp1819/
    SmallBusinessSector

22 https://www.telegraph.co.uk/men/thinking-man/
    rough-sleeper-learned-spent-week-streets/

CHAPTER 9

1 https://www.dailymail.co.uk/news/article-6731453/RICHARD-LITTLEJOHN-wishes-
   self-obsessed-MPs-stop-trend-chamber-selfies.html

2 https://www.economist.com/graphic-detail/2019/07/23/
   boris-johnsons-approval-ratings-are-surprisingly-high

3 https://trudeaumetre.polimeter.org

4 https://publications.parliament.uk/pa/cm200102/cmhansrd/vo020924/debtext/20924-05.
   htm

5 https://theintercept.com/2018/02/06/lie-after-lie-what-colin-powell-knew-about-iraq-fifteen-years-ago-and-what-he-told-the-un/

6 https://www.iraqbodycount.org/database/

7 https://en.wikipedia.org/wiki/Lancet_surveys_of_Iraq_War_casualties

8 https://www.people-press.org/2019/04/11/public-trust-in-government-1958-2019/

9 https://www.rollingstone.com/politics/politics-news/
   trump-coronavirus-timeline-dismissed-969381/

10 https://www.cnn.com/2020/03/16/politics/coronavirus-us-president-donald-trump-fauci-politics/index.html

11 https://www.cnn.com/2020/03/20/politics/us-intelligence-reports-trump-coronavirus/
   index.html

12 https://www.cnn.com/2013/04/18/us/u-s-terrorist-attacks-fast-facts/index.html

13 https://www.politico.com/news/2020/03/13/trump-coronavirus-testing-128971

14 https://www.theguardian.com/uk/2012/jul/01/introducing-phase-two-reading-riots

CHAPTER 10

1 https://www.theguardian.com/world/2020/mar/18/coronavirus-donald-trump-timeline

2 https://www.thestar.com/news/world/analysis/2019/01/25/trumps-first-year-was-the-most-dishonest-in-history-his-second-was-nearly-three-times-worse.html

3 https://www.nbcnews.com/politics/donald-trump/
   president-donald-trump-s-10-biggest-false-claims-2019-one-n1101151

4 https://www.theguardian.com/culture/2020/feb/05/
   trevor-noah-trump-state-of-the-union-daily-show-recap

5 https://www.theglobeandmail.com/business/commentary/
   article-canadian-small-businesses-are-facing-extinction-amid-lockdowns/